THE CONCEPT OF DISCRIMINATION IN INTERNATIONAL LAW

E. W. VIERDAG

THE CONCEPT OF DISCRIMINATION IN INTERNATIONAL LAW

WITH SPECIAL REFERENCE TO HUMAN RIGHTS

MARTINUS NIJHOFF / THE HAGUE / 1973

ISBN 90 247 1525 3

PRINTED IN THE NETHERLANDS

PREFACE

This book was written as a dissertation for the Doctorate of Laws, University of Amsterdam.

I am most grateful, first of all, to Professor A. J. P. Tammes, who acted as *Promotor*. Throughout my working at this study he managed to afford at the same time guidance, inspiration, and complete freedom. I have also benefited much from the suggestions and advice of Dr. Th. C. van Boven of the Dutch Ministry of Foreign Affairs, Member of the U.N. Commission on Human Rights, who was a very helpful *Coreferent*.

In earlier stages of the work, the critical remarks by Mr. S. A. Kuipers, Dr. H. Meijers and Miss J. M. van Wouw were of great importance to me. So was the experience of participating in the program of graduate studies of the Columbia University School of Law, in 1968–1969. I owe gratitude to the Amsterdam Law Faculty for having offered this opportunity to me.

I am indebted to Miss Sinja Alma for her transforming a chaotic manuscript into a neat typescript in a most capable and patient manner; to Miss E. D. J. Jongens for her assistance in sorting out the United Nations documentation; and to Howard S. Gold (Gersonovitch), who was so kind as to correct the faults in my English. Since I went on tinkering with the text I am to blame for all linguistic errors in it.

The research for this study was concluded in October, 1972.

E. W. Vierdag

"Dans l'état de nature les hommes naissent bien dans l'égalité, mais ils n'y sauroient rester. La société la leur fait perdre, et ils ne redeviennent égaux que par les lois."

MONTESQUIEU
De l'esprit des lois, VIII, III

LIST OF ABBREVIATIONS

A/...	Document of the General Assembly of the United Nations
A/C.3/...	Document of the Third (Social, Humanitarian and Cultural) Committee of the General Assembly
Add.	Addendum
A.J.I.L.	American Journal of International Law
E/...	Document of the Economic and Social Council of the United Nations
E/CN.4/...	Document of the Commission on Human Rights of the United Nations
E/CN.4/AC.1/...	Document of the Drafting Committee on the International Bill of Human Rights
E/CN.4/AC.2/...	Document of the Working Group on the Declaration of Human Rights
E/CN.4/Sub.2/...	Document of the Sub-Commission on Prevention of Discrimination and Protection of Minorities
ECOSOC	Economic and Social Council of the United Nations
G.A.	General Assembly of the United Nations
GATT	General Agreement on Tariffs and Trade
I.C.J.	International Court of Justice
I.L.O.	International Labour Organization
I.M.C.O.	Inter-Governmental Maritime Consultative Organization
L.	Limited distribution
O.R.	Official Records
P.C.I.J.	Permanent Court of International Justice
Res.	Resolution

Rev.	Revision
R.I.A.A.	Reports of International Arbitral Awards
SR.	Summary Records
ST./SOA	Document of the Secretariat of the United Nations, Bureau of Social Affairs
ST./TAO	Document of the Secretariat of the United Nations, Office of Technical Co-operation
U.N.	United Nations Organization
UNCIO	Documents of the United Nations Conference on International Organization
UNCTAD	United Nations Conference on Trade and Development
U.N.E.S.C.O.	United Nations Educational, Scientific and Cultural Organization
U.N.T.S.	United Nations Treaty Series
US	Reports of the Supreme Court of the United States

TABLE OF CONTENTS

I. INTRODUCTION

The Scope of the Study

Numerous international multilateral conventions concluded both before and after the Second World War contain provisions which prohibit "discrimination." Non-discrimination clauses figure in nearly all instruments concerning the international protection of human rights concluded after the Second World War, such as the Universal Declaration on Human Rights (1948), the European Convention on Human Rights and Fundamental Freedoms (1950), the Covenant on Economic, Social and Cultural Rights, and the Covenant on Civil and Political Rights (1966), not to mention documents that are exclusively aimed against some specific type of discrimination, such as the I.L.O. Discrimination (Employment and Occupation) Convention, 1958, the UNESCO Convention against Discrimination in Education, adopted in 1960, and the Convention on the Elimination of all Forms of Racial Discrimination, adopted by the General Assembly of the United Nations in 1965. But such clauses figure also in conventions in other fields of international law. Examples include instruments regulating economic relations such as the General Agreement on Tariffs and Trade (1947) as well as the Treaties establishing the European Economic Communities (1951, 1957); further the Conventions on Diplomatic and on Consular Relations (1961 and 1963; articles 47 and 72 respectively), the Treaty on Principles Governing the Activities of States in the Exploration and Use of Outer Space Including the Moon and Other Celestial Bodies (1967; article 1 (2)), the Convention on the Territorial Sea and the Contiguous Zone (1958; articles 16 (3) and 18 (2)), the Treaty on the Non-Proliferation of Nuclear Weapons (1969; articles 4 and 5), and many more.

In each of these instruments the concept of discrimination has been employed. Yet there is no consensus with respect to the exact meaning of "discrimination" in international law; and it is not quite clear against what inequalities the notion is intended to be aimed. In the course of just one meeting of the Third (social, humanitarian and cultural) Committee of the General Assembly of the United Nations, discussing the draft of article 26, the non-discrimination clause of the Covenant on Civil and Political Rights, widely diverging views on these questions were offered: it was asserted that "avoidance of discrimination is essential for effective equality before the law"; that "there are three basic principles: equality before the law, the right to equal protection of the law, and equality before the courts"; that the insertion of the words "without any discrimination" applies "less to the principle of equality before the law than to equal protection of the law"; that "the principle of equal protection of the law is perhaps implicit in the principle of equality before the law"; that "the guarantee of equality of all before the law entailed protection of everyone against the discriminatory application of that principle," and so on.[1]

Originally, discrimination is a municipal legal concept. From municipal legal systems it was adopted in international law, which in turn employs the concept in rules that it imposes on municipal legal systems. In the present study the analysis of the concept has to be limited to its international legal aspects. National laws, or national discriminatory practices, public or private, historic or contemporary, offer materials that may occasionally be used as examples to illustrate the reasoning, but they are not described or analysed as such. Sociology, economics, psychology and social psychology are disciplines that deal with questions concerning discrimination no less than law does; yet no attempt has been made to analyse these aspects as well. For example, we do not describe the policies of "apartheid," nor shall we examine concepts such as "class" or "social stratification," or try to trace the nature of "social prejudice."

In international law discrimination may occur in a great many fields of the law, such as treatment of aliens, transports, trade, labour, shipping, establishment, investments, taxes, and so on.[2] Our analysis will be focused mainly on the international protection of human rights, because we think that this field offers the most suitable materials.

[1] A/C.3/SR.1098.

[2] In some of these fields, such as e.g. the treatment of aliens, the non-discrimination principle may also function independently of conventional obligations, as a principle of general international law.

Illustrative examples can also be found in other parts of international law, however, and reference to them is made wherever that seems useful.

Discrimination is an evasive concept, and it plays a rôle at several levels: legislation, administration, adjudication, private relationships. For the purposes of legal analysis it is therefore necessary to make a relatively long preliminary inquiry into the two elements on which, in our opinion, the concept of discrimination is based: the equality and inequality element (Chapter II) and especially the treatment element (Chapter III).

The "Idea" of the Study

It is submitted at the outset that two meanings of "equality" can be distinguished, namely "formal" and "material" equality. The first notion simply implies equal treatment, the second implies economic, social and cultural equality. Consequently, it would seem that there are two functions for the non-discrimination principle to perform: each of these functions aimed against violations of each of the two notions of equality. Violations of the latter, the material equality, however, may consist of equal treatment, namely in cases where, because of a prevailing situation of social and economic inequality, the attainment of material equality would call for unequal treatment.

The "formal" conception of the non-discrimination principle is by no means always supplemented by the 'material" conception. In the United Nations bodies that occupy themselves with the protection of human rights, the formal conception of non-discrimination is the one generally adhered to. Compare for example article 26 of the Covenant on Civil and Political Rights.[3] Originally, the prohibition of "formal" discrimination, enunciated in the first sentence, was supplemented by the material notion contained in the next. But through the insertion of the much contested words "In this respect" at the beginning of the second sentence, this sentence has admittedly been reduced to a mere elaboration of the notion of formal equality. (See further on this paragraph 54).

According to the traditional reasoning a non-discrimination clause

[3] "All persons are equal before the law and are entitled without any discrimination to the equal protection of the law. In this respect, the law shall prohibit any discrimination and guarantee to all persons equal and effective protection against discrimination on any ground such as race, colour, sex, language, religion, political or other opinion, national or social origin, property, birth or other status."

must protect against discriminatory *action*, chiefly at the administrative and judicial levels, thus guaranteeing "equality before the law." As such it is regarded as an essential part of any system of rules for the protection of human rights. The non-discrimination principle does not relate, in this view, to the group of human rights that supplements the classic set of freedom rights, namely economic, social and cultural rights. To comply with these rights requires, in the traditional view, not state abstention (as is the case with the freedom rights) but state action. The non-discrimination principle prohibits only a certain action; therefore it does not relate to such inaction, not even if this inaction would violate social rights and lead to a discriminatory situation at that.

In our opinion, no clear line of separation can be drawn between state action and state abstention, and on the basis of this criterion between a group of civil rights and a group of social rights. Equality and inequality occur simultaneously and are necessarily closely related to one another. If the prohibition of discrimination is an attempt to realise justice, then it cannot be sufficient to prohibit discrimination only in the form of unequal treatment; the prohibition should then cover discrimination in the form of equal treatment as well, e.g. resulting from abstention, and should call for state action.

In international law, such a material interpretation of the non-discriminatie concept brings it very close to the protection of national, linguistic and religious minorities. This closely related legal institution is usually regarded as being characterized by its requirement of special rules to the benefit of the minorities. This requirement seems to imply state action, which would make the protection of minorities resemble the granting of social rights.

But again, it appears that no clear obligation to active state interference can be deduced from the instruments on the protection of minorities. Thus the difference between non-discrimination as we think it should be understood, and protection of minorities is only a relative one. Both require both equal and unequal treatment; the difference being merely a matter of emphasis.[4] Our view that compliance with the non-discrimination principle, after its being confronted with such international legal institutions as social rights and protection of minorities, may also involve state action, is therefore much less bold and excessive than it might seem to be at first sight.

[4] See on this especially the distinctions made below, at p. 157.

Only very few rules providing for the protection of minorities can be found in international law of today. The non-discrimination clauses should be utilized optimally so as to afford a similar protection. Finally, since in many cases questions concerning "racial," "linguistic," or "religious" minorities are in fact no less questions of an economic and social nature, it is appropriate to speculate about the potentialities of an international non-discrimination principle that also relates to the treatment of economic and social "minorities."

But although the principle, in the material interpretation that we think it should be given, implies also unequal compensatory treatment wherever the notion of material equality indicates the need of state intervention, there is as yet no international rule that requires such action. According to the available texts, "special measures of protection" *may* be, but *must* not be granted where a need of compensation is held to exist.

The Plan of the Study

Part One is mainly theoretical; Part Two is devoted to a discussion of materials of a more legal, positivistic nature.

"Equality" and "inequality" on the one hand, and "treatment" on the other hand are considered to be the two elements on which the concept of discrimination is based. In the second Chapter some aspects of the former notions are discussed, chiefly in a legal context, though in a rather abstract way. The notions become socially relevant through their being attached to some form of "treatment," which is analysed in the third Chapter.

On the basis of the combination of these elements, the concept of discrimination is developed in Chapter IV. Discrimination is described as a type of treatment characterized by the partial or total absence of a "sufficient connection" between factual equalities and inequalities, and the nature of the rights and duties involved.

The (lack of a) sufficient connection – a rather vague element – can be clarified considerably by the enumeration, in a rule of positive law, of a number of human characteristics on the basis of which no such sufficient connection can be made: race, language, religion, and so on. Chapter V is chiefly devoted to a discussion of the main "forbidden grounds for differentiation" in present day international law.

Since it appears that the granting of "special measures of protection" can nevertheless be allowed even on the basis of forbidden grounds, the grounds do not render a sufficient connection necessarily impossible, in an absolute way, but they must be related to the type of treatment. The same is the case in the protection of minorities; this fact finally leads to a comparison between non-discrimination and protection of minorities, in Chapter VI.

PART ONE

II. EQUALITY AND INEQUALITY

1. Introduction

"Discrimination" has a "treatment" element and an "equality" (or "inequality") element. We shall first deal with the equality element; the "treatment" element will be discussed in the next Chapter.

The conceptual relationships between "discrimination" on the one hand and "equality" and "inequality" on the other hand are so close, that an inquiry into the former necessarily entails consideration of the latter. And consideration of the equality principle immediately leads to the perennial problem of justice,[1] because "equality" plays a dominant role in the thinking on justice. We can state what justice is in terms of equality by saying – as has been said so many times before – that justice requires equal treatment of equals. This is the classic formula in its most simple form, from which it follows,[2] as a second part, that justice likewise requires unequal treatment of unequals. This addition implies the notion of proportionality, which underlies the principle of *suum cuique tribuere*. The formulations may differ one from another, but basically they all amount to something like: "Equal treatment of equals and unequal treatment of unequals in proportion to the inequality." It can safely be asserted that no theory of justice of a principally different nature has ever been able to detract from its influence permanently or to a considerable extent. This is not only true in what

[1] That is: "formal" justice, as contrasted with the broader notion of "material" justice, which does not only refer to the mode of distribution of burdens or favours, but rather also to the character of the "just act" as such. "Material" justice thus relates for example to the "just king" who e.g. will punish the guilty and release the innocent. In the following we rely to some extent on our note "Non-Discrimination and Justice" in *Archiv für Rechts- und Sozialphilosophie*, Vol. LVII (1971), p. 187 ff.

[2] In our opinion it cannot be regarded as compliance with a rule that stipulates equal treatment of equals when equal treatment is granted to unequals, no more than when equals are granted unequal treatment.

could be called the "Western" (European) ideology;[3] it needs hardly be argued that in societies with an ideology based on a Marxist social philosophy "equality" has an even more crucial function. And the ideal of justice as the equality of all human beings has no less appeal in what is sometimes referred to as the "third world."[4] It is quite remarkable that the idea of equality as an important element, or even as the essential element of justice, could not only remain unchanged and nearly unchallenged for more than twenty centuries, but that it seems even more influential now than it ever was.

To explain the remarkable general and widespread acceptance of this idea we must emphasize the both ambiguous and formal nature of the formula.

By insisting upon the ambiguity of the formula we want to stress the fact that the requirement of equal treatment is always supplemented by that of unequal treatment if the unequalness of the case is recognized. This dual character of equality is already explicit in its Aristotelian fashion. A learned student of Aristotle's concept of justice[5] expressed this duality in a clear and pregnant way:

"Das, warum es letzten Endes geht ist die Unterscheidung einer Gleichheit in Ansehung oder ohne Ansehung der Person, also symbolisch gesprochen einer iustitia ohne oder mit der Binde vor den Augen. Und das ist der Grund, weshalb sich die Gleichheit aufspaltet, und zwar in einfache Gleichheit – ἰσοτης – und verhältnismässige Gleichheit – ἀναλογια –; Gleichheit bedeutet einmal: jedem das Gleiche, einmal: jedem das Seine."[6]

We use the word "formal" here in order to indicate that obviously equality in itself cannot determine the nature of the treatment in question. It seems to us that it is precisely because of this dual charac-- ter and formality that the principle of equality is still alive, and that it was able to survive twenty centuries of political philosophy.

[3] See for references to the immense literature: J. Stone, *Human Law and Human Justice* (London 1965) p. 325 ff.; *Nomos IX, Equality* (New York 1967); Morris Ginsberg, *On Justice in Society*, (London 1965); G. del Vecchio, *Die Gerechtigkeit* (Basel, 1950); H. Nef, *Gleichheit und Gerechtigkeit* (Zürich 1941); R. Briner, *Zur Funktion der Gleichheit in der menschlichen Gerechtigkeit* (Wädenswil, 1948). Also H. Kelsen, *Reine Rechtslehre* (2nd ed., Wien 1960), p. 357 ff., especially p. 390 ff.

[4] Compare for example the recent "Lusaka Manifesto", proclaimed at the Fifth Summit Conference of East and Central African States, held in Lusaka, Zambia, in April 1969, in the second paragraph of which it is said that "by this Manifesto we wish to make clear, beyond all shadow of doubt, our acceptance of the belief that all men are equal, and have equal rights to human dignity and respect, regardless of colour, race, religion of sex." Text in *Objective: Justice*, Vol. I, no. 1 (U.N. Office of Public Information, New York 1969, p. 20 ff.).

[5] See the *Nicomachean Ethics*, Book Five, Ch. 2–8.

[6] Max Salomon, *Der Begriff der Gerechtigkeit bei Aristoteles* (Leiden 1937), p. 26.

2. *Equality and Inequality*

It needs hardly be argued in this connection that we, unlike such philosophers as Plato, Aristotle and Rousseau, do not "know" whether men are equal or not. We do not even know in general what is equal and what not. All we really do know is that equality is a matter of more or less abstraction.

Equality in the sense of complete equality is identity: one and the same thing.[7] Absolute equality can only be said to exist between abstract notions ("A = A") such as in mathematics. Plurality of objects, therefore, entails some inequality because two objects which are completely equal one to another (for example: two copies of the same book) still must differ necessarily as to their respective places. Hence equality implies non-identity, and consequently equality can only be relative equality: equality in some aspects, inequality in other aspects. And "relative equality" shows immediately that "equality" is an abstraction of more or fewer differences. Inequality as to place appears to be only the very minimum of otherwise innumerable inequalities between objects in the concrete world. And more obviously than to anything else, it seems, do these considerations apply to human beings. It depends on whether one wants to stress the attributes which are different, or whether one wants to stress those in common. Both activities, to distinguish and to generalize, are essential to knowledge and inherent in the functioning of the human mind.

The dialectical relationship between "unity" and "diversity," between "generality" and "individuality" poses a problem with metaphysical implications.[8] Kant discusses this problem in a section of the "*Kritik der Reinen Vernunft*."[9] He makes a distinction between two types of reasoning ("Denkungsarte"), one based upon the principle of homogeneity, and one based upon the principle of specification. And he points out that to employ the former principle rather than the latter is not dictated by the nature of the object studied, but merely expresses the diverse interests of reason:

[7] See for the following in general Nef, *op.cit.*, Part I (pp. 3–51).

[8] For a survey of the various approaches to the problem in Western metaphysics, see for example H. Heimsoeth, *Die Sechs Grossen Themen der Abendländischen Metaphysik und der Ausgang des Mittelalters* (1922, 4th ed., Stuttgart 1958), Chapters I and V.

[9] *Kritik der Reinen Vernunft*, ed. by R. Schmidt (Leipzig 1926); "Von den regulativen Gebrauch der Ideen der reinen Vernunft", pp. 604–624.

"Auf solche Weise vermag bei diesem Vernünftler mehr das Interesse der Mannigfaltigkeit (nach dem Princip der Specifikation), bei jenem aber das Interesse der Einheit (nach dem Prinzip der Aggregation). Ein jeder derselben glaubt sein Urteil aus der Einsicht des Objekts zu haben, und gründet es doch lediglich auf der gröszeren oder kleineren Anhänglichkeit an einen von beiden Grundsätzen, deren keine auf objektiven Gründen beruht, sondern nur auf dem Vernunftinteresse...."[10]

The judgment whether aspects of equality or aspects of inequality prevail is a value judgment, a matter of choice, of will. This logical state of affairs cannot be changed through claims to the effect that some cases are "essentially" equal, or that certain differences are "really substantial," "pertinent," etc.,[11] however important such judgments may be morally or politically.

It is interesting to note that a similar view results from a psychological analysis of the formation of concepts through generalisation and classification.[12]

3. Legal Equalities and Inequalities

Seen from this perspective the law consists of a system of abstractions and differentiations, expressing common value judgments made by a community which has set up and maintains a social order. Therefore, we now find a rule that ignores inequalities and under which "all" are to be treated alike, now a rule that acknowledges inequalities and accordingly establishes differential treatment.[13] There are no inherent logical or legal limits to the capacity of human judgment – such as the judgment underlying the creation of rules of law – to ignore, to re-

[10] At p. 623; compare also Nef who likewise speaks of "das Interesse des Subjekts." *Op.cit.*, p. 26.

[11] This important thesis, upon which our whole argumentation is based, seems somehow rather difficult to accept. For example, in *Men and Nations* (Princeton 1962), Louis J. Halle refers to the Kantian passage quoted in the text above, and observes: "It is pointless to ask whether the world as seen through a microscope or the world as seen through a telescope is the world as it really is. The experience of the earthworm and the experience of the eagle are, equally, experiences of reality. There is a distinction, however, in terms of meaningful experience. If the ultimate reality ... is a single order that comprehends all being, then the larger view will be more revealing of it than the smaller. Because the order of the universe is found in the association of its particles, all the great visions that have advanced human understanding have been those of minds that, to use Kant's language, were influenced more by the interest of unity ... The nobler and more meaningful view, in international relations, is that which reduces the differences between men and nations" (pp. 124–125). It seems to us that Halle thus has missed the point that Kant so emphatically makes; but of course, by the same token the opposite of what Halle asserts would not do justice to Kant's view either.

[12] See L. S. Vygotsky, *Thought and Language*, (Moskow 1934). We refer to the English edition (Cambridge, Mass., 1962), pp. 76–77.

[13] In the following we shall use "unequal treatment," "differential treatment," "differentiation" and "classification" as synonyms.

cognize or to introduce inequalities on whatever grounds. We acknowledge here yet another consequence of the separation of the fields of "is" and of "ought to be." It follows from this logical principle that, for example, the often mentioned fact that we are all human beings does not necessarily imply that we all ought to be granted equal treatment, and that for example the fact all human beings are born different as to character and intelligence need not necessarily lead to unequal treatment.[14]

Apart from factual, "natural" differences on which the law may base unequal treatment (e.g. kinship, age, invalidity, sex, unemployment, illiteracy, and so on) there are also differences established by the law itself on which unequal treatment may be based (e.g. bankrupcy, delinquency, membership of parliament, alienage, birth out of wedlock, diplomatic status etc.). The unequal treatment corresponds in such a case to a distinction that is itself of a legal nature. But notwithstanding the fact that human inequalities can be of a factual and of a legal nature, whenever the law introduces a distinction or takes a factual inequality into account, the resulting inequality is a legal one. Just as the law can connect legal consequences to certain events, facts or actions (birth, agreement, possession, death), it can also connect legal consequences to certain "facts" that distinguish one human being from another, such as insanity, age, illiteracy, sex, and so on. The law can do so, but need not do so. These legal consequences may affect the whole legal status of a person (such as insanity, on account of which the law may deprive a person of his complete legal capacity), or affect only certain rights (such as age: the infant may not vote, for instance, but at a certain age he can contract a marriage). The law can also refrain from connecting legal consequences to facts or actions that constitute differences between people. For example, it can ignore poverty or illiteracy in granting the right to vote.

We conclude that it is positive law which creates legal equality or inequality, and therefore it is the law which decides in the dilemma whether aspects of equality or aspects of inequality shall prevail.

[14] See on this "naturalistic fallacy" e.g. A. Podlech, *Gehalt und Funktionen des allgemeinen verfassungsrechtlichen Gleichheitssatzes* (Berlin, 1971), p. 37–38. Compare also Kelsen's reaction to article 1 of the Universal Declaration of Human Rights ("All human beings are born free and equal in dignity and rights"): ". . . from the point of view of a bill of rights, it is not the question how human beings are born, but how human beings shall be treated by the law, regardless how they actually are born, and regardless of the great differences which actually exist between them." *The Law of the United Nations*, London 1951, p. 41.

4. The Role of Equality

Traditionally, most approaches to justice start out from equality and are aimed, in one way or another, to come out at equality. Equality of treatment is the first and most simple model. It is based upon both a moral and a legal principle. The moral one might be called the "*presumptio egalitatis*"[15] which appears to correspond to a strong instinct of appropriateness. Equality of treatment has the most direct appeal because it constitutes "justice *seen* to be done"; it has the widest appeal because to appreciate a differentiation in the treatment requires insight in the nature of the case; and insight is generally reserved to only a few. Compare the classic example of the man behind the office window or the counter who treats all waiting in the queue on a "first come first serve" basis, thereby roughly equalizing the time each has to wait.[16] He will have to justify why he would make an exception for a particular person, and let him wait a shorter or longer time than another. Deviations from the equal treatment rule require rationalisation and justification on the part of those who deviate. The principle results from, or is at least reinforced by the rhetoric of numerous declarations, in national constitutions and international documents, to the effect that "all are equal before the law" and "all are born equal in dignity and rights."

The legal factor which fosters equality is the fact that a norm in its simplest formulation (e.g. "Thou shalt not kill") is applicable to *all* who are subjected to the legal system of which the norm is a part on account of its general character which results from the simplicity of the formulation.[17] Such rules in a legal system will tend to have an equalizing effect. To restrict the number of addressees of the rule requires the addition of an exceptive clause to it, which complicates the form of the rule. The simpler the rule, the more abstract it is; and equality is a matter of abstraction. To restrict the number of adressees of a rule is to introduce an inequality into the law. (The hangman, the policeman and the soldier may kill under certain circumstances).

"Equal treatment," it must be added, may often, rather than the outcome of a careful evaluation, be the result of an attitude of inaction,

[15] Stressed by Briner, *op.cit.*, p. 32 f.

[16] See Nef, *op.cit.*, p. 64, and also H. Henkel, *Einführung in die Rechtsphilosophie* (München and Berlin 1964), p. 362–363.

[17] Compare H. Kelsen, *Reine Rechtslehre* (2nd. ed. Wien 1960), p. 393.

of passivity, for instance on the part of governmental authorities. It may very well result from unwillingness to differentiate, from inability to do so because of lack of insight in prevailing social conditions, or from favouring administrative convenience.

5. Ambiguities of "Equality"

In the dialectics of unity and diversity, of equality and inequality where differences are now considered to be relevant, now considered not to be relevant, the process of law creation takes place.[18] Equality is the generally accepted starting-point, but we would argue that it should not be more than that. It seems a paradox that, no less than equality, also inequality based on classification and differentiation constitutes the very essence of the legal system. To understand or eliminate this paradox we must investigate what the term "equality" stands for in the law. Hence a distinction must be made between on the one hand "equal treatment," and on the other hand what can provisionally be called "equal social conditions" (resulting in many cases from unequal treatment). These two "forms" of equality are sometimes both referred to as "equality" or "equal treatment" which may be a source of confusion.

With regard to the classic formulation of justice as set out above the following possibilities come up, among which we must distinguish:

(i) if equal treatment is accorded to equals the result is equal social conditions;
(ii) if equal treatment is accorded to unequals the result is unequal social conditions;
(iii) likewise if unequal treatment is accorded to equals the result is unequal social conditions;
(iv) if unequal treatment is accorded to unequals, then, depending on the factual unequalness and the character of the treatment:
    (a) the inequality as to the social conditions has increased, has become wider, or
    (b) the inequality as to the social conditions is compensated, a certain levelling has come about.

[18] One author (R. M. Unger, "Isonomy and Justice" in *Archiv für Rechts- und Sozialphilosophie*, Vol. LVI, 1970, p. 183) puts what seems to be a key question in this way: "How is it possible for generality and differentiation to coexist within the legal system?" We would say that the problem is not how they can coexist, but rather that they necessarily doc oexist. Therefore the question should be: in what cases must the former and in what cases must the latter prevail?

Thus the distinction is between the *nature* of the treatment and the *result* of the treatment, the connecting factor between these being the nature of the subjects treated.

It must be emphasized now that we presume that the "quest for equality" in the United Nations' endeavours toward a comprehensive system of rules for the protection of human rights, is a quest for justice in the relations between the Member States and individuals, be these individuals their own nationals or not; and that we presume that this quest for equality implies both equality as "equal treatment of equals" (i) and equality as "unequal treatment of unequals" (iv, b). The latter, though unequal treatment in itself, is in many cases required in order to reach what the Permanent Court of International Justice called "equality in fact,"[19] and what we referred to as "equality in social and economic conditions." We also presume that the concept of "discrimination" in international law is meant to designate an impingement upon both forms of equality.

It could be somewhat misleading to conceal the vital element of unequal treatment behind terms like "proportional equality," "material isonomy"[20] "equality in fact" and similar expressions.[21] Social conditions of equality in the material sense is what is aimed at, but the legal technique may in many cases be unequal treatment. True, this means favourable unequal treatment of the weak, the deprived, the illiterate and so on. But at the same time it nearly always implies unfavourable unequal treatment of those who do not fall within a specially protected category.

This second part of the formula of justice is often referred to as "*suum cuique tribuere*," to grant to everybody his due. Obviously this phrase does not tell us who belong under the concept of "everybody" and who do not. Nor does the phrase indicate the character of that which is due. And least of all could it determine at how much everybody's due must be assessed. But at any rate it contains a clear obligation to investigate the nature of these problems actively.

Both forms of equality (equality as to treatment and equality as to final result) function simultaneously, since it cannot be imagined that

[19] In judgments concerning questions of minority protection; see for a general survey: H. Lauterpacht, *The Development of International Law by the International Court* (London 1958), Chapter 17: "The Effectiveness of Equality Clauses" (p. 257 ff.).

[20] R. M. Unger, *op.cit.*, p. 183.

[21] In the Anglo-American terminology of law (also of international law) sometimes the expression "equity" is used to designate this "equality." It is then regarded as an exception to the strict rule of equal treatment.

subjects of treatment are all totally different or totally alike. Thus it appears that the dual character of the notion of justice corresponds with this duality in the concrete world. The coexistence of equality and inequality entails the simultaneous functioning of both forms of equality, if justice is to be done.

The forms of equality we are discussing must not be understood as bringing among human beings "real" equality, or "complete" equality, and not as legal "fictions" of equality either. They consist in the enjoyment of equal rights, the performance of equal duties. Hence such equal legal position occurs each time in the exercise of one specific right or duty, and equality as to one right or duty is coupled with inequality as to other rights or duties.

Whether equality or inequality prevails is a matter of value judgment, a matter of choice, we said. Yet we qualified classification and differentiation (both resulting in unequal treatment) as the very essence of the legal system. We do so because at the technical level the degree of refinement and development of a system of law can be measured by the system's capacity to meet the ever increasing complexities of life, and thus to acknowledge the uniqueness of each human being. Since equality is an abstraction from inequalities, equal treatment abstracts from the inequalities among those subjected to it. The necessity for the law to deal with the ever increasing complexities of social life is in part the result of the transition from the nineteenth century "night-watch State" – as Lassalle dubbed it – to the State that must take into account, and react to, the multiple and diverse social needs of the people. The "abstract" citizen of the nineteenth century has, in the twentieth century, become the concrete human being who asks that his particular social needs are taken care of. From a legal point of view this process can be characterized as a transition from a predominantly "individualistic law" to a "social law."[22] It is the transition from legal equality to economic, social and cultural equality. Thus, in more and more fields the State has to take up and perform the role of the great divider, the distributor and re-distributor of the total of available material and cultural wellbeing.[23] This distributing and redistributing is typically the activity to which the classic formula of justice applies.

[22] See for example the essays which Radbruch devoted to this theme: "Der Mensch im Recht", "Klassenrecht und Rechtsidee" and "Vom individualistischen zum sozialen Recht", collected in: *Der Mensch im Recht* (2nd ed., Göttingen 1961) p. 9–49.

[23] H. Schambeck, *Grundrechte und Sozialordnung, Gedanken zur Europäischen Sozialcharta* (Berlin 1969), p. 89; see also R. H. Tawney, *Equality* (5th ed., London 1964), Ch. IV.

6. *"Formal" and "Material" Equality; Equality "before" the Law*

We have come across the distinction between "formal" and "material" justice. "Formal" referred to a certain mode of division, while whatever is divided is left undetermined. "Material" referred to the nature of a certain act itself. Next we have come to a distinction between "formal" and "material" equality: thus are the terms by which sometimes are characterized the two forms of equality that we discussed in the previous paragraph as "equal treatment" and "equal social conditions" respectively. However, the terms "formal equality" and "material equality" are also used to designate the two types of legal equality that we must shortly discuss now: "equality before the law," and "equality in the law," respectively.

The equality principle functions at two levels that can to some degree be distinguished: at the level of law creation, and at the level of law application. No clear-cut line can be drawn between the two: to create law implies the application of the rules which govern the procedure of law creation; to apply law implies to create law for a particular situation. There is a continuum of increased concretisation, and no clear separation. Yet it is possible to distinguish between the typical forms of the two, each of them at one end of the continuum. When problems of international law are involved it is very often even necessary to do so, because international law operates with a concept of the State that presupposes typical "state-functions" and distinguishes between them: legislation, administration, adjudication, irrespective of whether there is a separate organ for the performance of each of these functions.

At the law application level the equality principle is usually called "equality *before* the law." This form of the equality principle has been aptly described as follows:

> "The guarantee of this equality means only that the law-applying organs are permitted to consider only those differences which the statutes to be applied by them expressly recognize. Thereby nothing else is stipulated but the general principle of the lawfulness of the application of the law, imminent in all law. . . ."[24]

This does not mean that the administrative and judicial levels would never be confronted with the dilemma how to satisfy the requirements of justice (presenting itself as a dilemma between equal and unequal

[24] H. Kelsen, *Pure Theory of Law* (M. Knight's translation, Berkeley 1967), p. 146.

treatment). The choice of one among several alternatives, none of of which can be proved to be quite indefensible is the essence of legislation. Since the administration or the judiciary, or both, have to "finish" this task which the legislature must necessarily leave half done, it appears, as said, that the difference between law creation and law application is only one of degree of concretisation.[25] Does the case at hand fit under rule A or B, given the fact that it contains elements relevant to both rules? Does the case belong in this category of cases or is it so different that it belongs in another line of precedents? Or is it such that it cannot be brought under either? Cases, as much as anything else in the world, tend to be equal yet different. However this may be, the decision must always be found within the framework of the legal system, and may not violate clear standards that are incorporated in the system.

Equality before the law can be considered as a predominantly legal and technical principle. It involves the application of rules of law to those to whom the rules in question are addressed. This requires a correct operation of the syllogism through which facts and actions are brought under the applicable rules. It requires nothing but the application of the law to whom it is applicable according to its own terms.

7. *Equality "in" the Law*

In contrast, the principle of equality in the law appears to be a preeminently political principle. Based on a clearly egalitarian ideology it involves the value-judgment as to which cases must be considered as equal, and which cases as unequal. It involves the notion *suum cuique tribuere*, the notion also that equality of treatment must prevail, but only as long as there are no relevant inequalities to be taken into account. Equality "before" the law does not at all relate to the legal differentiations as such; it only requires equal treatment within a classification, within *any* classification that may be made, whatever its character may be.[26] Equality "in" the law, however, has directly to do with the character of the legal differentiations themselves. It does not purport to limit the number of classifications, or to abolish them; on the contrary, it supposes that there are differentiations, that there is

[25] H. Henkel, *op.cit.*, Ch. 32 ("Typus und Individualität im Recht").

[26] Compare on this the statements by the Polish delegate in the debate on draft article 26 of the Covenant on Civil and Political Rights in the Third Committee of the General Assembly, 13 November, 1961, (A/C.3/SR 1101, §§ 15–21) reproduced in part below, p. 124 f.

unequal treatment as a technique inherent in legislation. But the principle of equality in the law requires that this technique should follow certain rules, should comply with certain standards such as, for instance, the international non-discrimination principle.[27]

The two notions of equality which we called "material" (equality in the law, and equality as to "social conditions") are of course closely related to each other. While at the law application level equality before the law (formal equality) is essential to the preservation of either equal or unequal treatment as has been established by legislation to that effect, it cannot by itself create equality in the law, and thus equality of "social conditions." This equality of social conditions can only be brought about at the law creation level, through equality in the law. And equality in the law results – dependent on the factual situation, in particular the nature of the subjects treated – from either generality or differentiation in legislation, i.e., equal or unequal legislative treatment.

[27] In this connection the situation in German Constitutional Law may be mentioned as an illustrative example. Originally, article 109 (1) of the Weimar Constitution laid down only the equality of all Germans "before" the law. Soon after the adoption of this Constitution a controversy started as to whether not only the administrative and judicial branches were bound by this provision, but also the legislature. One of the most influential authors on this problem was Gerhard Leibholz who published "*Die Gleichheit vor dem Gesetz*" in 1925 (second enlarged edition, München and Berlin, 1959). The title of this monograph ("vor") merely reflects the wording of article 109 (1) of the Constitution; the author in fact strongly advocated – as did some other writers – the broad interpretation of the equality clause, asserting that it should also apply to the legislature, and that the judiciary should review legislation in the light of it. The judiciary tended to follow this interpretation, be it reluctantly and with much restraint. After the Second World War there has been no controversy on this point because the Bonner Grundgesetz adopted the broad interpretation by providing in article 1 (3) that "The following basic rights shall be binding as directly valid law on legislation, administration and judiciary." Among the "basic rights" that follow is the equality clause of article 3 quoted below, p. 83. The standard to be applied in review of legislation that was expounded by Leibholz and applied by the Constitutional Court in a great number of cases is the prohibition of arbitrariness ("Willkürverbot").

III. THE FIELD OF APPLICATION

A. DELIMINATION OF THE FIELD

8. *"Treatment"*

So far we have discussed equality and inequality in an entirely abstract way. We did not ask who were "treated," and compared to whom they were "treated" equally or unequally. We did not specify whether we discussed international or national law, whether the "treatment" was national or international, and what rights were involved.

These aspects of the problem will be dealt with now on the basis of the notion "treatment." We have employed this term already many times in the previous pages. It is an expression that occurs very frequently in legal terminology, in both national and international law. It plays an important role in discussions on justice, on human rights, on discrimination, and similar matters of a social, political or legal nature. Yet the concept "treatment" has (as far as we know) never been defined or analysed; at least not for legal purposes.

We shall understand discrimination in this study as a specific type of treatment. Not so much only as "bad" or "harsh" treatment, or treatment described with similar adjectives,[1] but rather as either "equal" or "unequal" treatment. It is useful to try to analyse this notion in order to gain a greater degree of clarity, because our definition of discrimination will be based on it.

But that is not the only reason why we pay attention to this notion. The other reason is that with the help of "treatment" we can determine the field of application of discrimination, because international rules

[1] Compare article 5 of the Universal Declaration: "No one shall be subjected to torture or to cruel, inhuman or degrading treatment or punishment." Similarly article 7 of the Covenant on Civil and Political Rights.

concerning non-discrimination must be directed against a specific kind of treatment. Accordingly we can list different types of treatment and thus find the fields where such non-discrimination rules can be operative. However, not the whole field of application of the notion treatment will also be the field of application of the notion discrimination. The fact that discrimination implies equal or unequal treatment necessarily limits the range of treatment that can be relevant: for our purposes it must be possible and meaningful to describe the treatment in terms of equal and unequal treatment. A certain degree of generalization, of similarity and comparability must exist among the objects treated, so as to make it possible and meaningful to speak of classes, of categories.[2] From this it follows that treatment of particular, isolated, individualized cases cannot be regarded as an interesting instance of treatment for a study of discrimination.

9. *"Distinction," "Limitation," "Restriction," etc.*

It is not superfluous to stress that discrimination is a form of treatment, in order to arrive at a sound conceptualization. A possible source of ambiguity that must be mentioned here is a term such as "distinction." Very often "distinction" is used in French versions of texts, the English version of which employs "discrimination." An example is article 14 of the European Convention on Human Rights.[3] "Distinction" is also used in some cases in English texts: in the Charter of the United Nations we do not find the word "discrimination," but only "distinction." Article 55(c) speaks of "universal respect for, and observance of human rights and fundamental freedoms for all without distinction as to race, sex, language or religion." Likewise, in the Study "Main Types and Causes of Discrimination" a description of discrimination is given which starts with the words: "Discriminatory practices are those detrimental distinctions..." etc.[4] The ambiguity we mentioned is also perceptible in the definition of discrimination

[2] This is meant in a "pre-legal" sense; in a legal sense a "category" is of course a group that is constituted through the identical treatment of its members (as to a certain right or duty). Compare on "classes" and "classification" also A. Podlech, *op.cit.*, p. 65–77.

[3] "The enjoyment of the rights and freedoms set forth in this Convention shall be secured without discrimination on any ground such as sex, race, colour, language, religion, political or other opinion, national or social origin, association with a national minority, property, birth or other status"; French: "La jouissance des droits ... doit être assurée sans distinction aucune..." In Dutch generally "onderscheid" is used, which raises the same problem.

[4] E/CN. 4/Sub. 2/40/Rev.1 (1949), § 87

given in the "Dictionnaire de la terminologie du Droit international,"[5] which reads as follows:

"Discrimination: Traitement differentiel. Distinction consistant à refuser à certains des droits ou avantages reconnus ou accordés à d'autres."

It is certainly correct to say that discrimination is – among other things – differential treatment. But it is difficult to appreciate how a mere distinction can "consist" of a denial of rights or privileges. The terminology of these examples could lead to the view that discrimination in fact only amounts to a distinction. But "distinction" is an abstract notion that in itself need not necessarily have social consequences. In so far as action has thinking as its origin, differential treatment will be based on a decision to distinguish that was made initially. But this decision cannot be identical to the social action that the denial of rights or the imposition of duties must be in order to have direct social consequences for the victims of the discrimination.

The word "distinction" in the Charter may at first sight seem to be used without connection to any forms of action. But in the Charter-clauses concerned the distinctions are related to "respect" for human rights (articles 1(3) and 76), and to the "realization" of human rights (article 13(1) b) as well as to "respect and realization" (article 55 (c)). Likewise in other, more recent documents, the non-discrimination principle is always connected to some expression designating the social action *via* which it must be realized. For example, in article 2(2) of the International Covenant on Economic, Social and Cultural Rights the rights are "exercised" without discrimination. Article 24(1) of the Covenant on Civil and Political Rights[6] grants non-discriminatory "measures of protection"; article 2(1) of this Covenant lays down that each State party .... undertakes to "respect and ensure" ... the rights recognized. Article 4 of this Covenant forbids "emergency measures" which would involve discrimination. Finally, article 14 of the European Convention on Human Rights says that the "enjoyment" of the rights shall be "secured" without discrimination.

[5] Paris 1960, p. 217.

[6] Art. 24 (1) of the Covenant on Civil and Political Rights; "Every child shall have, without any discrimination as to race, colour, sex, language, religion, national or social origin, property or birth, the right to such measures of protection as are required by his status as a minor on the part of his family, society and the state." Compare also Art. 10 (3) of the Covenant on Economic, Social and Cultural Rights which partly runs as follows: "Special measures of protection and assistance should be taken on behalf of all children and young persons without any discrimination for reasons of parentage or other conditions."

Not only "distinction" is a possible source of confusion[7]; the legal terminology with which we have to deal also contains such concepts as "limitation," "exception," "restriction," "exclusion," "preference," "privilege," "prerogative" and so on.[8] "Equality," "inequality," "distinction" and similar abstract notions are of an accessory character only, and need to be attached to social action in order to come to social relevance and legal existence. Both "social relevance" and "legal existence" are aspects of the concept "treatment."

10. Categories of Treatment

"Treatment" plays an important role in many fields of the law. In international law, for example, aliens are "treated," goods and exports are "treated" and likewise there is the treatment of ships and planes, territories and diplomatic missions, individuals and minorities, corporations and other juristic persons, prisoners of war and wounded and sick in the field and at sea, enemy property, and many more.

These persons and "objects" are usually treated by States, through state-organs. And either indirectly via persons and "objects," or directly, States "treat" other States as well.[9]

In the following we are interested in international treatment. Thus, when we make an inventory of international forms of treatment, we shall limit ourselves to those forms where either the author of the treatment is addressed by a rule of international law concerning the treatment in question, or where the subject treated is protected by a rule of international law concerning the treatment in question, or where both is the case. If we regard States, international organizations and individuals as the subjects of international law who are either authors or subjects of treatment, we can, at least theoretically, distinguish between nine forms of international treatment. We shall use the following categories also as a means to indicate the limitations imposed by our final interest: equal and unequal treatment.

[7] See for example the discussion in the Commission on Human Rights on an unsuccessful Australian amendment to replace "discrimination", in the draft article 7 of the Universal Declaration, by "distinction." E/CN.4/SR.53, p. 5–10.

[8] See below, p. 68.

[9] See e.g. also Wilhelm Wengler, "The Significance of the Principle of Equality in the Conflict of Laws", on *inter alia* the equal treatment by Courts of substantive law of different States in private international law cases. (*Law and Contemporary Problems*, Vol. 28, 1963, p. 822 ff).

Taking into account the active side and the passive side of treatment, we come to the following enumeration:

(a) Treatment of a State by a State;
(b) Treatment of an international organization by a State;
(c) Treatment of an individual by a State;
(d) Treatment of a State by an international organization;
(e) Treatment of an international organization by an international organization;
(f) Treatment of an individual by an international organization;
(g) Treatment of a State by an individual;
(h) Treatment of an international organization by an individual;
(i) Treatment of an individual by an individual.[10]

We must comment now already on the relevance of these forms for the purposes of a study of discrimination, in order to deliminate our field of investigation. This means basically that we shall have to eliminate from our investigations most of these forms of treatment. To that end we must anticipate our discussion of the definition of discrimination and describe discrimination provisionally as

"wrongly equal or unequal treatment."

Thus discrimination occurs, for example, through equal treatment of cases that must be considered as essentially unequal, or through unequal treatment of cases that must be considered as essentially equal. It goes without saying that for the qualification of a particular unequal treatment as "wrong" it must be possible to point at relevant elements of equality in the objects treated that should have lead to equal treatment.[11] It appears that it is chiefly this lack of "relevant elements of equality" that compels us to the elimination of most of the forms of treatment that figure in the list.

[10] The treatment of *minorities* by the State is understood to be covered by the treatment of individuals; so it is not listed as a separate form. This is not meant as an answer to the unanswerable question whether the rights that constituted the protection of a minority were rights of the minority as a whole or of the individuals who formed the minority. The typical "minority" rights were rights of individuals, since the minority as such has no legal personality and consequently could not exercise rights; the individual's "minority" rights, however, were rights he could only enjoy as a member of, and together with the other members of the minority.

[11] This qualification can in its turn only be made on the basis of the specific right, the specific regulation in which the inequality is introduced. This essential element in the concept of discrimination will be dealt with later; see below, p. 61.

11. Equality of States; Reciprocity

Treatment of a State by a State involves the principles of the legal "equality of States" in international law.

We submit at the outset that the classic international legal principle of "equality of States" cannot be regarded as a relevant principle for the purposes of a study of discrimination. We do not intend to say that "discrimination of States" can never occur, but only that it is not a fruitful concept for a study of discrimination. We agree with Hoffmann's observation that "the international order regulates a small number of subjects. Consequently, its law is a law of differentiation, which vacillates from the Charybdis of universality at the cost of vagueness to the Scylla of precision at the cost of heterogeneity."[12] Short of explicit treaty obligations the particularized character of the relations of States *vis à vis* other States in international law precludes in most cases the occurrance of treatment of a number of States as one homogeneous class. At this level in international law it is therefore hardly, if ever, possible to point at situations where there is such class treatment, so that it could be claimed that one state or some States were treated differentially in a "wrong" way, and thus were discriminated against. The individualization of the legal relations of States and their policies in international law frustrates the emergence of situations of comparability such as are ordinary under rules of municipal law. The conclusion that we draw from this opinion was clearly expressed by the Court of Justice of the European Communities:

> "... the view that any comparison between several (entities) must take into account all conditions which affect them would lead to the result that every (entity) would be comparable only with itself. The notion of "comparable circumstances," and, hence, that of "discrimination" becomes devoid of meaning."[13]

And even if such a situation occurred, then it would, at this *eo ipso* pre-eminently political level, be rather futile to hold a differentiation

[12] Stanley Hoffmann, "International Systems and International Law," in K. Knorr and S. Verba, eds., *The International Systems* (Princeton 1961), p. 206.

[13] *Barbara Erzbergbau and others v. the High Authority of the E.C.S.C.* (Joint Cases 3–18, 25 and 26/58, Judgment of 10th of May, 1960). The case concerned a decision by the High Authority that the rebates on transport tariffs which the German Government granted to mining companies in certain areas of Germany violated non-discrimination provisions of the E.C.S.C. Treaty (Art. 4, Art. 70) Text taken from *The Court of Justice of the European Communities*, Vol. II, *Judgments and Documents*, translated and edited by D. G. Valentine (London 1965), p. 325 ff, at p. 337.

"wrong." For example, article 23 of the Charter denies to 128 members out of a whole class of 133 members the possibility to ever become a permanent member of the Security Council. Yet article 2(1) of the Charter stipulates that "The Organization is based on the principle of the sovereign equality of its members." If in the Charter itself article 2(1) and article 23 can coexist peacefully, to what standard could the 128 members appeal in order to claim that article 23 of the Charter is discriminatory?[14]

The principle of "equality of States" leaves an enormous discretion to the States in their mutual relations. It suffices to mention the fact that States can maintain especially cordial relations with one State, while it cannot be said that they incur international responsibility for doing an "unfriendly act" to another State at the same time. Whether equal or unequal treatment is granted –

"Some political motive, some service rendered, some traditional bond of friendship, some reciprocal treatment in the past or in the present may furnish the ground for discrimination."[15]

Short of special treaty obligations to grant equal treatment (be it to "all nations" or to two or more States within the context of a special conventional regime, such as a most-favoured-nation clause), "Equality of States" is relevant not to more or less concrete "treatment"-situations, but only as a general principle from which no other, or more rules can be derived than can be derived from the legal qualification of states as subjects of international law, and that States are only equal in this abstract sense, namely *qua* subjects of law.[16] But the principle relates only in a very loose way to a notion of justice in terms of equal (or unequal) *treatment*. Quite recently it was given a most authoritative interpretation, since it figures among the "Principles of International

[14] See on this problem also H. Weinschel, "The Doctrine of the Equality of States and its Recent Modifications," in *A.J.I.L.*, Vol. 45 (1951), p. 427/8, 438; and B. Boutros-Ghali, "Le principe d'égalité des Etats et les organisations internationales," in *Receuil des Cours*, Vol. 100 (1960, II), p. 34–36.

[15] British-American Claims Arbitral Tribunal in the case concerning the *Eastern Extension, Australasia and China Telegraph Company Ltd.*, 9 November 1923. *Annual Digest of International Law Cases* 1923–1924, Case no. 225, at p. 418. Also in *Reports of International Arbitral Awards*, Vol. VI, p. 117. It is obvious that the Tribunal employs the expression "discrimination" here as meaning no more than "unequal treatment." We disagree with the use of "discrimination" in this sense, but this does not detract from the accuracy of the Tribunal's observation.

[16] Compare J. L. Brierly, *The Law of Nations* (6th ed., Oxford 1963), p. 130–133. It is remarkable that it is the doctrine of the legal equality of states that induced this otherwise so equanimous author to use quite strong language: "... the doctrine of equality is worse than merely redundant, for it may become seriously misleading..." etc. (p. 132).

law concerning Friendly Relations and Co-operation among States" as embodied in a solemn Declaration adopted by the General Assembly of the United Nations.[17]

In this Declaration it appears in the following fashion:

The principle of sovereign equality of States

All States enjoy sovereign equality. They have equal rights and duties and are equal members of the international community notwithstanding differences of an economic, social, political or other nature.

In particular, sovereign equality includes the following elements:

a) States are juridically equal.
b) Each State enjoys the rights inherent in full sovereignty.
c) Each State has the duty to respect the personality of other States.
d) The territorial integrity and political independence of the State are inviolable.
e) Each State has the right freely to choose and develop its political, social, economic and cultural systems.
f) Each State has the duty to comply fully and in good faith with its international obligations and to live in peace with other States.

Where it is said that States "have equal rights and duties" the interpretation is obviously wrong; for the rest, we submit, it confirms our view as stated above (though it introduces some heretofore independent elements (in paragraphs d and f), that are only indirectly connected with "Equality of States.")

We would argue that at this level of relations between States the notion of equal treatment is transformed into, or that its function is taken over by the no less fundamental principle of *reciprocity*. This notion designates that a State in its bilateral relationships – mostly contractual relationships – or in legal situations based upon such relationships, "... grants or promises to another State, to its officials, or nationals, or trade, etc., treatment that is equal or equivalent to the treatment this latter state ensures or promises to the former."[18] Reciprocity implies no less than equality a certain degree of similarity of positions, of proportionality between partners, but reciprocity functions typically within the context of particular, concrete legal relations.[19]

[17] Adopted 24 October 1970, on the occasion of the 25th Anniversary of the Organization. Resolution A/2625 (XXV).

[18] "Réciprocité: Situation qui se présente quand un Etat assure ou promet à un autre Etat, à ses agents, à ses nationaux, à son commerce, etc., un traitement égal ou equivalent à celui que ce dernier Etat lui assure ou promet": *Dictionnaire de la Terminologie du Droit International*, p. 504. See generally M. Virally, "Le principe de réciprocité dans le droit international contemporain", in *Receuil des Cours*, Vol. 122 (1967, III), p. 1–101; also W. Schaumann, "Gegenseitigkeit", in *Wörterbuch des Völkerrechts*, Vol. I, p. 630 ff.

[19] What is known as the problem of "unequal treaties" (see e.g. Ingrid Detter, "The Problem of Unequal Treaties," in *International and Comparative Law Quarterly*, Vol. 15, (1966), p. 1069 ff.) is in our opinion not so much a matter of treaties violating the equality-

A good illustration of how the possible functioning of the non-discrimination principle between States is substituted by notions of reciprocity is offered in Article 47 of the Convention on Diplomatic Relations (Vienna, 1961).[20] The field of diplomatic relations is especially interesting since it is a field where States relate to one another typically as sovereign and equal entities, while at the same time diplomatic contacts are of a rather concrete nature. It is one of the very few examples of not too abstract a nature where all States can nevertheless assert themselves on an essentially equal basis.

Article 47 runs as follows:

> "1. In the application of the provisions of the present Convention, the receiving State shall not discriminate as between States.
> 2. However, discrimination shall not be regarded as taking place:
> (a) Where the receiving State applies any of the provisions of the present Convention restrictively because of a restrictive application of that provision to its mission in the sending State;
> (b) Where by custom or agreement States extend to each other more favourable treatment than is required by the provisions of the present Convention."

Thus, while section one of this provision purports to forbid discrimination, section two indicates the assumption that unfavourable unequal treatment will all the same occur. And it implies that unfavourable unequal treatment of a sending State by a receiving State loses its discriminatory character through the mere reciprocity of the restrictive treatment. Likewise, when a receiving State grants more favourable treatment to a given sending State than to a third sending State, the latter cannot complain that it is discriminated against if only the receiving State can show that it enjoys the same more favourable treatment on the part of the former sending State. In its Commentary on the draft of this article the International Law Commission referred to "cases in which, although an inequality of treatment is implied, no discrimination occurs, inasmuch as the treatment in question is justified by the rule of reciprocity which is very generally applicable in the matter of diplomatic relations."[21]

In order to be assured of equal treatment (e.g. in trade, or shipping) States traditionally had to take recourse to treaty regulation, especially

principle, but rather of treaties which are not or not sufficiently in accordance with the reciprocity principle.

[20] Article 72 of the Convention on Consular Relations (Vienna 1963), the text of which is in *U.N.T.S.*, Vol. 569, p. 261 ff. The text of the Convention on Diplomatic Relations is in *U.N.T.S.*, Vol. 500, p. 95 ff.

[21] *Yearbook of the International Law Commission 1958*, Vol. II, p. 105.

to most-favoured-nation clauses, through which they could profit from the effects of reciprocity between the treaty partner and a third State.[22]

But also among States the classic international "law of individuality" may gradually be supplemented by an international "social" law. To illustrate this view we point at the difference between GATT – based for a large part on reciprocity between supposedly equal partners [23] – and UNCTAD, aiming at preferential treatment of economically weak States.[24] Likewise the Secretariat of UNCTAD observes – with characteristic terminology –:

> "The traditional most favoured nation principle is designed to establish equality of treatment ... (The principle) ... does not take account of the fact that there are in the world unequalities in economic structure and levels of development; to treat equally countries that are economically unequal constitutes equality from a formal point of view but amounts actually to unequality of treatment." [25]

Hence the necessity of granting trade-preferences in favour of developing countries.[26] But as yet no clear legal "classes" of States have come up in general international law, not even in these economic and social fields.[27]

[22] And even this equality through most-favoured-nation treatment is again endangered by the reciprocity principle, namely when the most favoured nation treatment is conditional, directly or indirectly, as in GATT, where "a veiled form of the element of reciprocity" is brought in (Kurshid Hyder (Hasan), *Equality of Treatment and Trade Discrimination in International Law*, The Hague 1968, p. 60). This results from the requirement, implicit in Article II, that tariff negotiations must have been succesfully concluded. This requirement, as Mrs. Hyder observes, "is not in accord with the unconditional most favoured nation clause. Reciprocity is substantive bilateralism – and bilateralism is the antithesis of equality of treatment. Equality of treatment is not the exchange of satisfactory concessions between two nations." (*ibidem*).

[23] Compare G. Schwarzenberger, "Equality and Discrimination in International Economic Law," *Yearbook of World Affairs* 1971 (London 1971), p. 165: "Economic equality is purely formal. Even if granted on a reciprocal basis, it neither presupposes nor necessarily leads to substantive equality between contracting partners. In this, the concept corresponds closely to freedom of contract under the municipal law of any *laissez-faire* society." See also K. Hyder (Hasan), *op.cit.*, p. 187.

[24] Hyder, *op.cit.*, p. 193: "Rules of reciprocity in trade negotiations should thus be changed because of the economic inequality between countries." See generally pp. 187–199.

[25] UNCTAD, *Proceedings of the Second Session* (New Delhi 1968), Vol. III, p. 10.

[26] Compare on this problem in general e.g. Gunnar Myrdal, *The Challenge of World Poverty* (New York 1970), Ch. 9.

[27] Apart from a rather isolated instance such as article 2 (3) of the Covenant on Economic, Social and Cultural Rights: "Developing countries, with due regard to human rights and their national economy, may determine to what extent they would guarantee the economic rights recognized in the present Covenant to non-nationals."

12. "Equality of International Organizations"

If the arguments why we discarded treatment of States by States are valid then they must also be valid for the two other forms of treatment of States (d and g). And then they must be even more valid for the three forms of treatment of an international organization (b, e and h). As we indicated before, if it is to be meaningful to talk of discrimination, it must be possible to show that among the many aspects of similarity and diversity in the entities treated, the "wrong" aspects of the latter were chosen as against aspects of the former (for the decision on the inequality of treatment in a given right). To show this a minimum of relevant aspects of similarity is required. And also a certain number (at least two) of relatively similar, comparable objects for treatment is necessary in order to be able to speak of equal or unequal treatment in a meaningful way. The problem with international organizations in this respect is not that there are so few of them, but rather that there are so few similarities between them. The organizations that the Charter of the United Nations in article 57 calls the "*specialized* agencies" are not the only ones that are "specialized": they all are.[28] International organizations are created to be different, designed each to accomplish a particular task. To that end each one has its own special structure, powers, range of membership, and so on.

13. Treatment of Individuals by International Organizations

Thus only the three forms of treatment of individuals are left as potentially fruitful fields of investigation.

We shall first discuss very shortly the treatment of individuals by international organizations. The growing importance of organizations of States in international relations poses questions as to whether the organizations will have to comply with international standards concerning the treatment of individuals. Though in this study we only deal with international law of the peace we may mention here the problem of the obligation of United Nation Forces to respect the laws of war, especially the Red Cross Conventions of 1949.[29] Or as another example, the question whether the European Economic Communities are bound

[28] Compare Ch. Chaumont, "La signification du principe de specialité des organisations internationales," in *Mélanges Henri Rolin* (Paris 1964), p. 58.
[29] Compare for example Finn Seyersted, *United Nations Forces* (Leyden 1966), Ch. V.

to respect the European Convention on Human Rights and Fundamental Freedoms (Rome 1950).

These problems transcend the scope of our study; but we do mention here the treatment of the individuals that have the closest relations with the organizations: the international civil servants. In this respect U.N. Staff Regulation 4.3 – to single out one global example – is of interest to us. In pursuance to Article 8 of the Charter it lays down that

"In accordance with the principles of the Charter selection of staff members shall be made without distinction as to race, sex or religion ..."[30]

As an example relating to a regional organization we mention article 27(2) of the "Statut des Fonctionnaires" of the European Communities, which runs as follows:

"Les functionnaires sont choisis sans distinction de race, de croyance ou de sexe."

And section 3 of the same provision states also that

"Aucun emploi doit être réservé aux ressortissants d'un Etat déterminé."[31]

This amounts to a prohibition of discrimination based on nationality, in accordance with article 7(1) of the E.E.C.-treaty, which stipulates that

"Within the field of application of this Treaty, and without prejudice to any special provisions contained therein, any discrimination on the ground of nationality shall be prohibited."

A general rule prohibiting "discrimination," in the treatment of individuals, adressed to an international organization, can be important if the organization has, in any way, authority over individuals besides its own personnel. Therefore it is by no means irrelevant to ask whether, and if so, to what extent, a highly developed organization such as the European Economic Community which in some fields performs state-like functions, can be considered to be bound to the European Convention on Human Rights,[32] and especially to article 14 of that Convention (quoted above, p. 20. The Court of Justice of the European

[30] Text in *International Organization and Integration* (Deventer and Leyden 1968), p. 104 ff.

[31] *Règlement* no. 31 (EEC), and 11 (Euratom); Text in *Journal officiel* 1962, p. 1385 ff.

[32] Compare e.g. G. Ziegler, *Das Grundrechtsproblem in den Europäischen Gemeinschaften* (Tübingen 1970), and Pierre Pescatore, "Fundamental Rights and Freedoms in the System of the European Communities," in *American Journal of Comparative Law*, Vol. 18 (1970), p. 343 ff.

Communities acknowledged the problem in a short passage in its preliminary ruling in the *Stauder* case[33] by observing:

"Thus interpreted, the decision in question does not contain any element that might jeopardise the fundamental rights of the individual contained in the general principles of the law of the Community of which the Court must ensure the observance."[34]

14. Treatment of an Individual by an Individual

We described international treatment as treatment the author of which is addressed by a rule of international law, or the subject of which is protected by such a rule, or both.

A discussion of the treatment of individuals by individuals not acting in an official capacity would raise the following problem: to what extent are private individuals – authors of the treatment – addressed by rules of international law? Consequently, to discuss the "private" form of treatment would lead to the examination of concrete questions concerning the relations between national and international law, in particular concerning the possible "self-executing" character of international human rights conventions, of the non-discrimination clauses in these conventions, and the possible legal effects of these rules on "private" legal relations.[35] Because it would again transcend the scope of our study to go into these problems, we must discard this form of treatment too. We can do so the more easily since most human rights documents are predominantly directed at legislatures, and are not intended to be "self-executing." The majority of the provisions of for example the recent Covenants on Economic, Social and Cultural Rights, and on Civil and Political Rights are addressed to the States Parties, and do not concern private but public action.

This leaves us with one final form of treatment (c), the treatment of the individual by the State. This is the form of treatment that involves at the passive side the principal subject of protection in the field of the international protection of human rights, and at the active side the principal subject of international law and the prime actor in international relations.

[33] *Stauder v. City of Ulm*, Case 29/69. *Common Market Law Reports 1970*, p. 112 ff.

[34] At p. 119. See also Case 11/70, *Internationale Handelsgesellschaft v. Einfuhr und Vorratsstelle für Getreide und Futtermittel*, *Common Market Law Reports 1972*, p. 255 ff, at 283.

[35] For example, article 5, section f of the Convention on the Elimination of All Forms of Racial Discrimination stipulates non-discrimination with respect to "the right of access to any place or service intended for use by the general public, such as transport, hotels, restaurants, cafés, theatres and parks."

B. TREATMENT OF THE INDIVIDUAL BY THE STATE

15. *Treatment as Social Action*

Treatment itself can be regarded as a form of "social action," which is the most general concept of all. "Social action" is, in Max Webers well-known definition, "ein solches Handeln ... welches seinem von dem oder den Handelnden gemeinten Sinn nach auf das Verhalten *anderer* bezogen wird und daran in seinem Ablauf orientiert ist."[36]

For the purpose of legal analysis we can – with some simplifications[37] – describe "treatment" within the context of a given national legal order as comprising the following forms of social action:

(i) action which is aimed at the creation, modification or nullification of rights or duties of an undetermined number of subjects of law by the organs of a legal system to which they are subjected (the organ to be considered will generally be a legislature);

(ii) action which is aimed at ascertaining or modifying particular rights or duties of a subject of law, or at ascertaining or modifying the conditions under which a subject of law enjoys rights and performs duties (administrative and judicial organs);

(iii) action not falling under (i) or (ii) as far as it is the contents of a rule of law, that is, as far as the action can be considered in terms of law-compliance or law-violation, *viz.* either allowed – with or without conditions – or forbidden, or prescribed (individuals).

It is clear that the elaboration of the concept of "social action" into the legal concept of "treatment" reduces the contents of "social action" considerably. Originally so broadly conceived as to comprise all action related to the conduct of others, from the legal point of view it amounts to a matter of granting or denying rights and imposing duties, while all action that remains entirely internal is excluded.[38]

It makes sense to regard treatment as a form of social action, and to refer to Weber's definition of that concept. In section 91 of the Judgment of the International Court of Justice in the *Continental Shelf*

[36] M. Weber, *Wirtschaft und Gesellschaft,* (Köln and Berlin, 1964; 1st ed. Tübingen, 1921), Vol. I, p. 3. (Italics in original).

[37] For example, we dot not consider legislation that is not enforced (see § 19), no administrative and judicial treatment that is patently illegal, or rather: so illegal as not even to be based on a rule of law at all. Likewise instances of treatment are left aside that are not directly based on a specific rule, but can be regarded as the exercise of free discretionary judgment by the administration or the judiciary.

[38] Weber included also "inneres Handeln" in his definition; *op.cit.*, p. 16 f.

Cases we come across a curious type of "treatment," namely "treatment by nature." The Court observes:

"... in the present case there are three States whose North Sea coastlines are in fact comparable and which, therefore, have been given broadly equal treatment by nature, except that the configuration of one of the coastlines would, if the equidistance method is used, deny to one of these States treatment equal or comparable to that given the other two ... [39]

This expressive terminology should not obscure the fact that the equal treatment is given through the application of the same rule to all parties concerned; this particular case involved the application of the equidistance rule of article 6 of the Continental Shelf Convention. It is of course not "nature" itself, or more specifically the "configuration of the coastlines," that constitutes treatment and that can deny equal treatment to a State.

"Social action" is the broadest term; "treatment" is the *species* in relation to this notion; it is generally used – in a legal context – as the shorthand expression that designates the social action consisting of the granting or denying of rights, or the imposition of duties, as defined above. We shall follow this practice and employ treatment as a legal shorthand expression (also in "equal treatment" and "unequal treatment"). Thus, when we define discrimination in its turn as a particular type, a *species*, of treatment, this likewise implies the granting of rights or the imposition of duties.

16. Other Expressions; Status

"Treatment" is sometimes replaced by other terms that are closely related to it, such as "status," "position" or rather "legal position," and in some cases "protection." In French e.g. also "condition," such as in "la condition des étrangers." In German legal language a few more, and more precise terms are employed. Apart from "Behandlung," "Rechtstellung" (Status), and "Gleichbehandlung," one may find – for example in the law of aliens – also such expressions as "Berechtigung," "Gleichberechtigung," "Gleichstellung," "Schlechterstellung," "Besserstellung," [40] and more general, "Sonderstellung."

Some of the terms mentioned here refer to the point of view of the

[39] Denmark and the Netherlands v. The Federal Republic of Germany; International Court of Justice, *Reports* 1969, p. 1 ff, at p. 50.

[40] See e.g. the terminology in D. Schindler, *Die Gleichberechtigung von Individuen als Problem des Völkerrechts* (Zürich 1957).

"active side" (treatment, protection); some refer to the "passive side" where the rights that result from it are enjoyed (status, legal position, Berechtigung). Especially the German terms containing the element of "Recht" demonstrate the legal character of the type of social action that we call treatment. Traditionally the concept of "status" clearly also has legal overtones. It originates from Roman law where the *status* determined the legal capacity of individuals (which varied among the several categories of persons: status libertatis, status civitatis, status familiae). More than half a century ago the notion served as the basis of a still important analysis of the various types of legal relationships between the individual and the State.[41] In international law "status" also generally designates the total of rights and duties of individuals (e.g. "the status of aliens", "diplomatic status"), or the whole of rules conditioning an international legal régime ("the international status") of a particular territory, a canal, a zone, and so on. As such it usually amounts to the total of rights and duties of the States that are parties to the instrument – sometimes called "status-treaty"[42] – that created the status.[43]

It can be said that to some extent these related expressions are used to point at a specific aspect of the general notion of treatment; a term such as "protection" refers for example clearly to what we called the "passive" side of treatment.

17. Treatment through Inaction

We divided treatment within a given legal order into three forms: legislative, administrative and judicial treatment. Quite a different „form" of treatment must now be mentioned: treatment seemingly not in the form of social action, but rather in the form of inaction.[44] It may seem senseless to distinguish between action and inaction: inaction is

[41] Georg Jellinek, *System der Subjektiven Öffentlichen Rechte* (1892, 3rd. ed. Tübingen 1919), p. 81–83, 86 ff. Jellinek speaks in this connection of the "Zugehörigkeit zum Staate," the "Relation von Staat und Einzelpersönlichkeit," and of the "Stellung des Individuums im Staate" within the framework of his theory of the four different forms of "Status", the passive, the negative, the positive, and the active form, constituting the "öffentliche Rechtstellung" of the individual in the State. See on this further below, § 33.

[42] See e.g. G. Dahm, *Völkerrecht*, Vol. I, (Stuttgart 1958), p. 24.

[43] It is somewhat inappropriate therefore that in the usual terminology of international law one usually refers to the status "of" rivers, territories, permanently neutralized zones, and so on, as if it were these objects that had rights and duties. (See on this W. Wengler, *Völkerrecht*, (Berlin, Göttingen, Heidelberg, 1964), Vol. II, p. 1305–1306).

[44] Kipp speaks of treatment that may have "eine positieven oder negatieven Inhalt..." H. Kipp, "Das Verbot der Diskriminierung im modernen Friedensvölkerrecht," in *Archiv des Völkerrechts*, Vol. IX (1961–62), p. 148.

also action, and inaction fits as much in the definition of "social action" as action does, which becomes obvious when the term "conduct" is employed. Weber included also inaction: "Soziales Handeln ... einschliesslich des Unterlassens und Duldens ..."[45] However, from a legal point of view there is nothing paradoxical in the distinction: there are legal rules which are of such a nature that they can be violated only through omission,[46] as much as there are legal rules that are applicable to human activity only, not to abstinence from activity. Compliance with rules that are violated through omission requires of course positive action on the part of the addressees. Rules of this character (also international rules) may very well be addressed to the State and its organs.[47] In accordance with this it can be contended that "treatment" in our formula of justice can also consist of inaction, of a failure to act.[48] For example, "equal treatment of unequals" can thus be described as a failure to act, namely, as a failure to differentiate with regard to a particular treatment.[49]

18. "Objects" of Treatment

Some of the authors who deal mostly with trade, shipping, taxation and so on – at least who do not put the emphasis on human rights – speak also of the treatment of "objects."[50] This term may stand for imports, investments, ships, goods and the like, rather than for individuals or states. We adhere to the view that legal relations can only be established between subjects of law such as individuals and States. As to "objects," legal relations exist between subjects of law "regarding"

[45] Max Weber, *op.cit.*, p. 16.

[46] The best-known examples of such rules can of course be found in criminal law.

[47] The legal consequences of inactivity on the part of organs of an international organization can be found in article 175 of the E.E.C. Treaty, which reads in part: "Should the Council or the Commission in infringement of this Treaty fail to act, the Member States and the other Institutions of the Community may bring the matter before the Court ... Such proceedings shall only be entertained if the institution concerned has first been called upon to take action..."

[48] Thus the European Court of Human Rights observed with regard to the effect of article 14 of the European Convention on Human Rights (reproduced above, p. 20): "No distinctions should be made ... (as to) whether the respect due to the right concerned implies positive action or mere abstention." Judgment of 23rd July 1968 in the case "*Relating to certain aspects of the laws on the use of languages in education in Belgium*," paragraph 9 *in fine*. (Strasbourg, 1968, at p. 34). See also Briner, *op. cit.*, p. 64–65; and A. J. P. Tammes: "Het gerechtigheidsbegrip sluit in beginsel niet uit het handelen van meer speciaal rechtspersonen, noch sluit het uit, naar goede juridische opvatting, het handelen dat gelegen is in dulden." (*De Gerechtigheid in de Internationale Verhoudingen*, Zwolle 1954, p. 32).

[49] See further below, paragraph 32.

[50] E.g. G. Jaenicke, *Der Begriff des Diskriminierung im modernen Völkerrecht* (Berlin 1940), p. 20; see also Kipp, *op. cit.*, p. 141.

objects, not "with" objects. Since treatment eventually amounts to a legal relationship, there is no treatment of objects, no social action regarding objects, no rights or duties of objects (in the sense of goods etc.; we may in a different sense speak of individuals as the objects of treatment). Kipp mentions "objects or states of affairs" (Objekte oder Sachverhalte) – not quite a clear terminology. He explains it by observing that objects of unequal treatment can be first of all persons, be it natural or juristic persons, be it persons under international law. The expression "state of affairs" is meant to designate the more complex character of what is unequally treated. And he then goes on to say that it appears that also behind states of affairs, wares and similar things it is a person that is the object of the discrimination.[51]

Thus, when it is said that the customs authority of a State "treats" certain imported goods unequally by imposing heavier duties on these goods than on similar goods (*ceteris paribus*) in violation of a most-favoured-nation clause, the discrimination does not concern the goods in question, but the individuals or the State who have rights with respect to the goods. The exporters expected to be under the protection of the most-favoured-nation clause, or, at the diplomatic level, their State was entitled to require equal treatment to the benefit of its traders. Whether in a given case (e.g. the case of the violation of a most-favoured-nation clause) the natural or juristic person is injured or the State itself may seem difficult to say. We touch here upon a well-known problem in the law of aliens and diplomatic protection of individuals. In an earlier period of international law the Permanent Court of International Justice stated that

> "By taking up the case of one of its subjects and by resorting to diplomatic action or international judicial proceedings on his behalf a State is in reality asserting its own rights – its rights to ensure, in the person of its subjects, respect for the rules of international law. The question, therefore, whether the ... dispute arises from an injury to a private interest, which in point of fact is the case in many international disputes, is irrelevant from this standpoint. Once a State has taken up a case on behalf of one of its subjects before an international tribunal, in the eyes of the latter the State is the sole claimant."[52]

But apparently this holding concerns only the procedure *via* which rights are vindicated. This procedure is merely a legal technique, a construction which must be used as long as individuals have inter-

[51] Kipp, *ibidem*.

[52] *Mavrommatis Palestine Concessions* (*Jurisdiction*), P.C.I.J. *Series* A, No. 2 (1924), p. 12. Also International Court of Justice, *Nottebohm case* (*Second Phase*), I.C.J. *Reports* 1955, p. 24.

nationally recognized rights but no *ius standi* before international tribunals to assert these rights.[53] This construction has lost much of its meaning as far as the field of human rights is concerned. International protection of human rights is pre-eminently the field where through international commitments of States rights have been granted to the individuals themselves rather than to individuals as nationals of States and as mere beneficiaries of their treaty relations. Human rights are surely due to stateless persons and refugees no less than to nationals of States; no less to aliens than to citizens. It is the field where the individual has been accorded rights, the excersice of which can in some cases[54] even be maintained and protected against interference by his own State. That is why we can indeed speak here of the international treatment of individuals, rather than of the treatment of a State in the person of its subjects.

19. Categories of Individuals

Since we focus on the field of human rights it is useful to survey the different categories in which these "individuals" can be divided from the point of view of international law. We shall also indicate which type of international non-discrimination clause is (actually or potentially) applicable to the category concerned.

(1) *Aliens*

Rules on the treatment of aliens are to be found in the general international law of aliens, and in a great number of separate treaties. The richest and most direct sources are the treaties which traditionally are called treaties of "Friendship, Commerce and Navigation." Noteworthy are also treaties on establishment, double taxation, trade agreements with most-favoured-nation clauses (e.g. as to imports, duties) and so on. Treaties on the protection of foreign investments and consular conventions can be mentioned as well. Two types of non-discrimination rules in the law of aliens can be distinguished; the first functioning as between aliens of different nationalities; the second functioning as between aliens and nationals.[55]

[53] See on this D. P. O'Connell, *International Law* (2nd ed., London 1970), Vol. I, p. 108–109, Vol. II, p. 1029–1031.

[54] Such as under the European Convention on Human Rights and Fundamental Freedoms.

[55] See Schindler, *op.cit.*, Part I and Part II.

(2) *Refugees and Stateless Persons*

Two fairly recent multilateral conventions must be mentioned under this heading: the Convention on the Status of Refugees,[56] and the Convention on the Status of Stateless Persons.[57] These conventions are closely related; the second is intended to supplement the first. They contain a common article 3 which runs as follows:

"The Contacting Parties shall apply the provisions of this Convention to refugees (stateless persons) without discrimination as to race, religion or country of origin." [58]

(3) *Nationals*

The international non-discrimination clauses applicable to nationals (be it in a direct, be it in an indirect way) are contained in the international instruments on the protection of human rights. These are the only legal texts which penetrate into the State and intervene between the State and its nationals.

Under this same heading must also be listed the treaties and declarations concerning the protection of

(3*a*) *national, linguistic and religious minorities,*

at least as far as minorities proper are concerned, which means: minorities consisting of nationals of the State in question. The rules protecting alien members of a minority must by the same token be found in the law of aliens.[59]

Though we only deal with the law of the peace, we add here nevertheless as a fourth category:

(4) "*Persons taking no active part in the hostilities, including members of the armed forces who have laid down their arms and those placed* hors de combat *by sickness, wounds, detention or any other cause...*" [60] This category may comprise individuals from all of the previous categories. According to the same Article 3(1) of the Red Cross Conventions the persons in this category

"shall in all circumstances be treated humanely, without any adverse distinction founded on race, colour, religion, faith, sex, birth or wealth, or any similar criteria."

[56] Geneva, 25 July 1951. Text in *U.N.T.S.*, Vol. 189, p. 150.

[57] New York, 28 September 1954. Text in *U.N.T.S.*, Vol. 360, p. 130.

[58] Apart from this, article I (2) of the Refugee Convention defines a refugee in such a way that he can be described as a (potential) victim of discrimination, namely on the basis of race, religion, nationality, membership of a particular social group, or political opinion.

[59] See H. Wintgens, *Der Völkerrechtliche Schutz der Nationalen, Sprachlichen und Religiösen Minderheiten* (Stuttgart 1930), p. 57.

[60] Art. 3 (1) of the four Red Cross Conventions (Geneva, 1949).

(5) Another category which possibly comprises persons from all other categories, and may make these superfluous – as to certain rights in certain circumstances – has been introduced by human rights conventions, with formulations such as:

"Everyone within (...) the jurisdiction (of a contracting Party) ...,"[61] and "Individuals within the territory (of the State Party) and subject to its jurisdiction" ... [62]

The emergence of an international law of human rights has expended the field of application of the international non-discrimination principle considerably: traditionally limited to aliens (and minorities) it now applies to nationals as well.

20. Genocide as Treatment

A meaningful delimination of the "treatment-element" (and so of the concept of discrimination itself) finally leads to one more restriction, this one not as to objects or subjects of treatment, but with respect to the nature of the treatment. We exclude from it genocide and similar actions. Such acts could be called "treatment," and actually *have* been called "treatment," or rather, "special treatment" ("Sonderbehandlung"). But we do not find it useful to regard such actions as genocide and mass expulsion as types of "discrimination" that should be discussed within the context of the present study. Though the international crime of genocide has characteristics which bring it formally under our notion of discrimination,[63] it goes without saying that in the material sense it is far beyond it. The quantitative difference is such that it turns into a qualitative one.

Schwarzenberger[64] noted "the involuntary, grim humour" which inspired the author of the United Nations Study on "*The Legal Validity of the Undertakings concerning Minorities*," in which it is said:

"Obviously, wherever minority populations have disappeared from a territory either as a result of annihilation – which was unfortunately the case for the

[61] Article 1, European Convention on Human Rights.

[62] Article 2, Covenant on Civil and Political Rights.

[63] Article II of the Convention on Genocide (adopted by the General Assembly of the United Nations on 9 December 1948): "Genocide is any of the following acts committed with intent to destroy, in whole or in part, a national, ethnical, racial or religious group, as such: (a) killing members of the group; (b) ... etc." See on the relationship between genocide and d scrimination in particular *Contribution of the Convention on the Prevention and Punishment of the Crime of Genocide to the Prevention of Discrimination and the Protection of Minorities* (E/CN.4/Sub. 2/80).

[64] *Power Politics*, (Second Edition, London 1951), p. 647.

Jews – or compulsory transfer to the territory of another state – as was the case for the bulk of the German minorities in Poland, Czechoslovakia and Hungary – or because they had fled without hope of returning, their protection is no longer necessary." [65]

21. Types of Treatment: Executive, Judicial, Legislative

Within the context of a national legal order we distinguished on the one hand "administrative" and "judicial" treatment, and on the other hand "legislative" treatment. By adopting this classic division we did not intend to assert that it constitutes an accurate description of the functioning of the State. But the division is helpful because it is employed in international conventions concerning the treatment of individuals. We distinguished between these forms of treatment but they are of course closely connected. Administrative and judicial treatment imply in fact double treatment, because in general they are both based on legislation; thus they take place simultaneously with legislative treatment.

"Administrative" and "judicial" treatment are forms that bring us back to the distinction between equality "before" the law and equality "in" the law which was made earlier – in § 6 – and discussed there, though in a rather theoretical and abstract way. Both the treatment by the administration and by the judicial authorities are related to "equality before the law." In contrast, what is distinguished as "legislative treatment" relates to "equality in the law." Both forms of legal equality are safeguarded, so to speak, by the principle of non-discrimination.

Executive action and the administration of justice are in municipal law subordinated to legislation, at least in international law they are supposed to be. Also in cases where there is a kind of "common law" developed primarily by a judiciary, from the international law point of view the law is what the legislative organ leaves of e.g. a judge-made common law, or what it creates as law. At least the judiciary is not considered to be the organ which ultimately decides: its holdings can always be changed by a higher, political organ. Executive and judicial action are primarily regulated by national law; whether they can be directly bound by rules of international law depends on the municipal legal (constitutional) system. International law leaves it entirely to the

[65] UN Doc. E/CN.4/367 (7 April 1950). Submitted to the Commission on Human Rights in the name of the Secretary-General. At p. 33.

different constitutional systems whether, and if so, how international rules shall be admitted in, or transformed into national law; whether by acts of legislation or transformation, or without such acts. If the executive or the judiciary has a certain discretionary freedom, e.g. let to it through delegation by a statute in a given field of state action, in general no more discretion can be delegated than the delegating organ itself possesses. It is possible that an executive organ to which a task is delegated (e.g. a Minister) finds it necessary to introduce a novel distinction, but in doing so he certainly cannot go against an international (or constitutional) standard, such as a non-discrimination rule. A State cannot avoid compliance with its international legal obligations by internal delegation to lower state-organs. It goes without saying that, likewise, in case the discretionary freedom is original, e.g. falling within a traditional field of executive governmental activity (not delegated by a particular statute), the executive organ may not shape a policy that is incompatible with an international obligation of the State.

We said that the international quest for equality is "chiefly" aimed at the law-creating process: but of course, the non-discrimination clauses in most international human rights conventions also concern law application. For example, article 26 of the International Covenant on Civil and Political rights stipulates at the beginning of its opening sentence that "All persons are equal before the law," and are "entitled equal protection of the law." If such standards are violated (for example: an administrative agency denies a certain licence to someone on account of his race, or social origin, or a similar factor not recognized in the applicable rule of law) then this will be called "discrimination" (no less than we would call "discrimination" the passing of a statute that did recognize such grounds for unequal treatment). In the debates on the draft of the first part of article 26 in the third Committee of the General Assembly a delegate spoke in this connection of "discrimination before the law," a wholly adequate expression that somehow sounds quite innovative.[66] However, it seems to us to be preferable to deal with the rules themselves rather than with the administrative or judicial authorities violating the rules.

[66] A/C.3/SR. 1099, § 3. The delegate was *Père* Dr. L. J. C. Beaufort of the Netherlands.

22. *"Legislative" Treatment*

The ultimate aim of the international protection of human rights is the realisation of justice within national legal orders. In the final analysis, what is at stake is a "just" distribution, in a given society, of the available cultural and material well-being among the members of the society. This distribution is established – from a legal point of view – through legislation, through the law-creating process. The international standard of non-discrimination applies pre-eminently to this law-creating activity in the national legal order.[67]

The question might be asked how legislation, how the creation of rules of law, or rather, in our context, the granting or denying of rights to individuals, or the imposition of duties to individuals can amount to "social action" as defined above. (Of course, not all legislation constitutes also legislative treatment of individuals, that is, affects directly the legal position of individuals. Legislation may regulate an indefinite number of issues and need not in all cases concern the direct legal interests of individuals). In a wider sense this question touches on the general problem how a rule relates to action.[68] We must leave this problem aside and presume that legislation – the creation of abstract and general rules – amounts to social action, treatment, because we base ourselves on the assumption that each rule so enacted will eventually be enforced *vis à vis* the individuals to whom the rules are addressed. It is on the basis of this same assumption that a State can incur international responsibility under international law for acts of mere legislation.

[67] "Eine Gerechtigkeitsnorm schreibt ein Bestimmtes Verhalten von Menschen gegenüber Menschen vor. Dieses Verhalten kann in der Setzung von Normen bestehen." Kelsen, *Reine Rechtslehre*, p. 360.

[68] Kelsen deals indirectly with the nature of the relationship between moral or legal rules and human action where he discusses the notion "violation of the law." He observes: "The existence or validity of a norm commanding a certain behavior is not broken by the opposite behavior – in a way that a chain might be broken that fetters a man. The chain of law fetters even the man who "breaks" the law; the law is not "violated," as a human being can be violated (that is, injured in his existence) by an enforcement action directed against him." (*Pure Theory of Law*, Knight translation, p. 113; in the original at p. 118–119). Elsewhere he calls "violation of the law" a "figure of speech" (*Principles of International Law*, 2nd. ed., 1966, p. 6). It goes without saying that the problem represents an aspect of the dichotomy between norm ("Sollen") and action ("Sein"), and hence the possibility and the nature of the relationship between norm and action. Alf Ross and Kelsen have had an exchange of views on the possibility of such relations, given the place of this dichotomy in Kelsen's theory of law, to which we can only refer for the sake of brevity. See Ross, *Towards a Realistic Jurisprudence* (Copenhagen, 1946), p. 39 ff., and Kelsen, *Reine Rechtslehre*, p. 6, 16. See on this also J. F. Glastra van Loon, *Norm en Handeling* (Haarlem 1957), p. 219–235.

Illustrative in this connection is the controversy between England and the United States concerning the Panama Canal Tolls, which occurred in 1912 and 1913. In the Panama Canal Act, passed by the United States Congress in 1912, provisions were laid down which exempted certain shipping activities by American citizens from the payment of tolls. The British government immediately claimed that the exemption violated article 3 of the Hay-Pauncefote Treaty (1901), section (1) of which runs as follows:

"The Canal shall be free and open to the vessels of commerce and of war of all nations observing these Rules, on terms of entire equality, so that there shall be no discrimination against any such nation, or its citizens or subjects, in respect of the conditions or charges of traffic, or otherwise. Such conditions shall be just and equitable." [69]

The United States replied that they did not intend to react to the British contentions until the effects of the Act would actually be that British vessels were subjected to "inequality of treatment, or to unjust and inequitable tolls, in conflict with the terms of the Hay-Pauncefote Treaty." But Great Britain maintained its position by stating that

"... international law or usage does not support the doctrine that the passing of a statute in contravention to a treaty right affords no ground of complaint for the infraction of that right, and that a nation that holds that its treaty rights have been so infringed or brought into question by a denial that they exist must, before protesting and seeking a means of determining the point at issue, wait until some further action violating those rights in a conclusive instance has been taken, which, in the present instance would, according to your (the U.S.) argument seem to mean until tolls have been actually levied upon British vessels from which vessels owned by citizens of the United States have been e-empted." [70]

The disputed legislation was repealed in 1914 at the urgent request of President Wilson. Illustrative is also the Judgment of the Permanent Court of International Justice in the case of the *Phosphates in Morocco*.[71] In this case the Court held that it had no jurisdiction because the French activities about which Italy complained had occurred before and not subsequent to the ratification by France of its acceptance of the compulsory jurisdiction of the Court. The Italian complaint concerned acts of legislation by France; this legislation was enforced well into the period for which the French submission was valid. But the

[69] Text in M. Fleischmann, *Völkerrechtsquellen*, (Halle a.S., 1905), p. 321–322.
[70] *British Digest of International Law*, Vol. 2b, (London 1967), p. 321–338, at p. 336.
[71] Preliminary Objections, P.C.I.J. *Series* A/B, No. 74 (1938), p. 25–26.

Court regarded as decisive the time of the enactment of the disputed legislation.

Although it thus appears to be possible and justified in international law to focus on legislative treatment, as we do, it is indeed true that legislation only amounts to treatment to the extent that the rules actually are or will be enforced by judicial and administrative organs, that is, through judicial and administrative treatment: rights must be enjoyed, duties must be performed. But then, a similar remark must be made as to the judicial and administrative rulings: these too must in their turn be enforced in order to qualify as treatment. Thus the chain eventually ends with physical force, treatment in its most concrete and factual form: aliens expelled, persons thrown in jail, fines executed, goods confiscated, and so on. All forms of treatment suppose the threat or the possibility of physical force. It is the last phase of the legal process, the final form of treatment from which the other forms, such as legislation, ultimately derive their social relevance.

23. Unequal treatment

Equal and unequal (legislative) treatment of individuals functions as the basis for our considerations of discrimination. From a legal point of view we regard treatment as the granting or denying of a right or a number of rights to a person, or the imposition of a duty or a number of duties on a person. Accordingly, unequal treatment can be defined as

(i) the denial of a right to some that is accorded to others;
(ii) the diminution of a right for some while it is fully accorded to others;
(iii) the imposition of a duty to some that is not imposed on others; or
(iv) the imposition of a duty to some that is not imposed as heavily on others.

It is clear that each form of unequal treatment requires a comparison and consequently a standard of comparison. To that end it is necessary to ascertain who are the "some" and who are the "others" in a given case, that is, which categories are to be compared with each other as to their respective legal positions.[72] This may arise various questions. For

[72] Compare the *Oscar Chinn* case (United Kingdom v. Belgium, Permanent Court of International Justice, *Series* A/B, no. 63, 1934). The British Government compared the position of Mr. Chinn to the position of the Belgian "Unatra" Company, which was under State supervision, the Belgian government owning more than half of the shares. The Court observed, however, that Mr. Chinn's position had to be compared to the other private companies engaged in transportation activities on the Congo river basin, of whatever nation-

example, is the treatment of a specific group of aliens to be compared with the treatment of a (justly or unjustly) privileged, or humiliated[73] group of citizens of the State in which they reside? Can the treatment of a specific group of aliens be compared with the legal position of the most favoured aliens in that State? Questions like these are discussed in the Advisory Opinion of the Permanent Court in the case concerning the *Treatment of Polish nationals and other persons of Polish origin and speech in the Danzig territory*,[74] which case can be referred to as an illustrative example. Article 104 (5) of the Peace Treaty of Versailles reads as follows:

> "The Principal Allied and Associated Powers undertake to negotiate a treaty between the Polish Government and the Free City of Danzig... with the following objects:
> (5) to provide against any discrimination within the Free City to the detriment of citizens of Poland and other persons of Polish origin or speech."

The population of Danzig was predominantly German, and the separation of the City from Germany in order to secure free access to the sea for Poland was not approved of by the German population. A guarantee against discrimination had to be and was indeed inserted in the Convention concluded between Poland and Danzig in Paris on 9 November 1920[75] in pursuance to article 104 of the Treaty of Versailles, because "some apprehension might be entertained lest the Polish people in Danzig would be exposed to discriminatory measures on the part of the

ality: "... the position of the British national Oscar Chinn was not, as such, either better or worse than that of the other concerns not under State supervision; these included, according to the evidence produced, Belgian concerns and a French concern." (p. 87). The claim that Mr. Chinn was discriminated against was accordingly dismissed. (It must be asked, however, whether a measure that discriminates against aliens in violation of a Treaty obligation loses this discriminatory character merely because it also applies to some nationals of the offending State. Compare the Dissenting Opinion of Judge Altamira, *loc. cit.*, p. 102).

[73] American diplomatic protests against the treatment of American Jews (e.g. in Russia and Rumania at the turn of the century and in Germany and Italy in the 1930's) were rejected with the argument that American Jews were treated in the same way as Jewish nationals. G. H. Hackworth, *Digest of International Law* (Washington. D.C., 1942) Vol. III, p. 640 ff; Schindler, *op. cit.*, p. 99 f.

[74] P.C.I.J. *Series* A/B, no. 44 (1932).

[75] Article 33 (1) of this Convention reads as follows: "The Free City of Danzig undertakes to apply to racial, religious and linguistic minorities provisions similar to those which are applied by Poland on Polish territory in execution of Chapter I of the Treaty concluded at Versailles on June 28th, 1919, between Poland and the Principal Allied and Associated Powers, to provide, in particular, against any discrimination, in legislation, or in the conduct of the administration, to the detriment of nationals of Poland and other persons of Polish origin or speech, in accordance with Article 104, paragraph 5, of the Treaty of Versailles." The Court was asked to give an interpretation of both article 104 (5) and article 33, but we can confine ourselves to its comments on article 104 (5); the Opinion itself is somewhat ambiguous, as are the texts it sought to clarify. Compare J. H. W. Verzijl, *The Jurisprudence of the World Court*, Vol. I (Leyden 1965) p. 275–279.

Free City for no other reason than that they were Poles" as the Court put it.[76] There were three different population groups in the Danzig territory that were relevant to this particular case: a) citizens of Danzig of German origin and speech; b) citizens of Danzig of Polish origin and speech; and c) citizens of Poland who were presupposedly of Polish origin and speech. Danzig and Poland could not come to an agreement as to the intended meaning of the relevant provisions. It was *in confesso* among both parties in the dispute that the phrase "persons of Polish origin or speech" included Danzig citizens as well as citizens of other States, and thus the Court took it to cover "all persons of Polish origin and speech, regardless of their nationality."[77]

Poland brought forward two contentions: it claimed not only that Polish citizens and all persons of Polish origin and speech were entitled to equal treatment as compared to Danzig citizens of German origin (what is called "national treatment," with an express exception with regard to the rights to vote and to be elected), but it also claimed that these persons were further entitled, under the prohibition of discrimination, to enjoy equal treatment as compared with Danzig citizens of Polish origin ("minority treatment") involving the use of the mother-tongue in education, internal administration and the administration of justice in accordance with Chapter I of the Treaty between Poland and the Principal Allied and Associated Powers, to which article 33(1) referred. As the Court remarked: "Here the comparison is not with Danzig citizens belonging to the German majority, but with Danzig citizens belonging to the Polish minority." [78]

Within the context of the present paragraph is is interesting that the Court then went on to observe: "... the text (of article 33) does not indicate between whom no discrimination is to be made. The Polish argument makes a very important addition, namely, a standard of comparison; this addition finds no support in the text of article 104(5)." [79] As we remarked above, a standard of comparison is essential to the very notions of "equality" or "inequality of treatment." Obviously the Polish contention did not "add" a standard; in fact, it is clear the Court itself employed such a standard too when it held that "the object of the prohibition (included in article 104(5) of the Treaty of Versailles) is to prevent any unfavourable treatment, and not to

[76] p. 28.
[77] p. 27.
[78] p. 29.
[79] *Ibidem.*

grant a special régime of privileged treatment."[80] The difference of opinion concerned the standards that were considered to be applicable.

Two conditions must at least be fulfilled in order to make a comparison possible. First of all, the legal positions of certain particular persons or groups can only be compared to the extent that they are subjected to one and the same legal system, i.e. when they owe the legal position involved to one system. Accordingly, a claim concerning "discrimination" must be addressed to the treating authority (e.g. a legislature) that these persons or groups have in common.

Second, only categories can be compared that are either at the same time subjected to the treatment concerned, or at different times if the mere course of time has not brought about relevant changes. Naturally, aspects of equality and inequality of the subjects treated constantly change with time.[81] The judgment whether equal or unequal treatment should be granted must be adapted accordingly. By "equal" or "unequal" we therefore presume: at a given time. Likewise, by "unequal treatment" we presume: treatment that is unequal to treatment granted either at the same time, or at an other point of time without the difference in time alone counting as a relevant change. (Or causing such a change, for example through the cancellation of a right as a result of prescription, or through the expiration of a treaty in which it was embodied).

[80] *Ibidem.*

[81] Since aspects of equality and inequality are constantly and necessarily changing in *time*, the time factor is always presupposed. Equality is: equality at a given time. We submit that Nef had a similar view and disagree with Kooymans' contention that Nef neglected the time factor. (P. H. Kooymans, *The Doctrine of the Legal Equality of States*, Leyden 1964, p. 10).

IV. DISCRIMINATION

24. *Terminological Aspects*

In the English language the verb "to discriminate" (and words derived from it: "discrimination," "discriminating," and so on) has two different meanings.[1] It can be used in a neutral sense: "to distinguish," "to differentiate" *between* (people, things, or whatever). In this original sense the word is found in learned dissertations, in works written in a scholarly style.[2] Occasionally it also appears in a literary work.[3] Secondly, the word can be used (and is most frequently used now) in a pejorative sense: to discriminate *against*, meaning "to make an adverse distinction," "to distinguish unfavourably from others." The Dictionary quoted gives examples of the expression employed in this sense, all in a social and political context[4]; and generally the term has this pejorative meaning when it is used in a social context, where it implies not an abstract distinction, but social action. In this latter sense it was adopted in other languages; in German for example, the word "Diskriminierung" can be used in this pejorative sense only[5] and the same is true for French,[6] Russian[7] and Dutch.

[1] This is true for old and for modern English, though in the notes we only refer to historic examples. See for the following *A New English Dictionary on Historical Principles*, Vol. III, D and E, edited by Dr. James A. H. Murray (Oxford 1897) p. 436–437. See generally W. A. McKean, "The Meaning of Discrimination in International and Municipal Law," in *British Yearbook of International Law* 1970, p. 177 ff.

[2] *Loc. cit.* For example Bacon (1626), Malthus (1789) and others quoted in the *Dictionary*.

[3] E.g. Prynne (1628), *ibidem.*

[4] "I did not propose to be discriminated against on account of my nationality" (Mark Twain, *A Tramp Abroad*, 1880); "The action of the German Government in discriminating againts certain imports from the United States..." (*Pall Mall*, 1885); "If the Police, as the Socialists declare, discriminate against them on account of their opinions..." (*Pall Mall*, 1886). *Ibidem.*

[5] Schindler, *op.cit.* p. 67; G. Jaenicke, *Der Begriff der Diskriminierung im modernen Völkerrecht* (Berlin 1940), p. 12.

[6] Jean Pictet: "... discrimination ... terme nouveau, toujours péjoratif..." *Principes du droit international humanitaire*, Genève 1966, p. 41.

[7] In the Commission on Human Rights the delegate from the Soviet Union explained that

From Anglo-American legal language and diplomatic practice the term has been adopted in international law. During this century English has become more and more important as a diplomatic language, along with French. One of the factors in this process was of course the fact that the United States took up its role as one of the great Powers of the world, especially after the First World War. The widespread use of the term "discrimination" is a direct result of this development.[8] Before the First World War we find "discrimination" employed only in Anglo-American relations. We mention for instance article III (1) of the Hay-Pauncefote Treaty (concluded in 1901), quoted above, at p. 43. In continental practice before World War I we could not find an example of the use of the word discrimination. The French diplomatic language still dominated. For example, we come across "traitement différentiel," as in article 3 of the Final Act of the Congo Conference (Berlin 1885):

"Les marchandises de toute provenance importées (...) n'auront à aquitter d'autres taxes que celles (...) qui, à ce titre, devront être également supportées par les nationaux et par les étrangers de toute nationalité. Tout traitement différentiel est interdit à l'égard des navires comme des marchandises."

But then, there was no general use of the term "discrimination" after the First World War either.[9] Again, the texts, mostly in French which is still employed frequently in the diplomatic intercourse of that time, speak of "traitement differentiel" that is prohibited, or of "distinctions"; sometimes "distinctions odieuses," "distinctions malveillantes" or "arbitraires."

However, occasionally "discrimination" figures also in French texts of this period. To give a few examples, the French version of article 18 (1) of the British Palestine Mandate, originating from the League of Nations (1922) runs in part as follows:

"the word 'discrimination' in Russian clearly referred to unfair, unequal treatment." (E/CN.4/SR.52, p. 11).

[8] Jaenicke, *op.cit.*, p. 10, points especially at the speeches of President Wilson during and after the First World War (and his activities at the Paris Peace Conference).

[9] For instance in Art. 4 of the Statute on the Régime of Navigable Waterways of International Concern (Barcelona 1921): "No distinction shall be made between the nationals..." (Text in Hudson, *International Legislation*, Vol. I, p. 645 ff.). Also Article 2 of the Statute on the Freedom of Transit (Barcelona, 1921): "No distinction shall be based upon the nationality of persons..." (Text in Hudson, *op.cit.*, Vol. I, p. 637 ff.). Compare also the Convention on the Revision of the General Act of Berlin (St. Germain, 1919), art. 2, 3 and 4: "No differential treatment shall be imposed upon the merchandise ..."; "Vessels ... shall be subject to no differential treatment"; "Nationals ... shall enjoy without distinction the same treatment"; "... no regulations ... shall admit of any differential treatment between the nationals ..." (Text in Hudson, *op.cit.*, p. 343 ff).

"Il appartiendra au Mandataire de faire en sorte qu'aucune discrimination ne soit faite (...) entre les nationaux d'un Etat quelconque Membre de la Société des Nations (...) et les nationaux de la Puissance mandataire ..."[10]

(But in the closing sentence of this first section of article 18 the French version says also:

"De même, il ne sera imposé en Palestine aucun traitement différentiel entre les marchandises originaires ..." etc.,

while the English text is again:

"Similarly, there shall be no discrimination in Palestine against goods originating ..." etc.

The French text is most probably a translation from the English). As a second example we mention Article 104 (5) of the Peace Treaty of Versailles, discussed above, in § 23, on the basis of which the Free City of Danzig was obliged ...

"De pourvoir à ce qu'aucune discrimination soit faite, dans la Ville libre de Danzig, au préjudice des nationaux polonais et autres personnes d'origine ou de language polonaise."

Another instance of the use of "discrimination" in French diplomatic language after the First World War can be found in Article 5 of the "Déclaration des droits internationaux de l'Homme," adopted in 1929 by the Institut de Droit International:

"L'égalité prévue (in the foregoing articles of the Déclaration) ne devra pas être nominale mais effective. Elle exclut toute discrimination directe ou indirecte."[11]

It can safely be maintained, however, that it was only after the Second World War, under the impact of the United Nations' efforts to realize a non-discriminatory protection of human rights, that "discrimination" became a generally employed expression.

25. *Some Definitions*

In this paragraph we shall compare a number of definitions of discrimination in international law; in the next we shall comment on some of them. As we remarked earlier, there is only little uniformity in the use of the term, and there is no general concensus as to its contents. We will pay attention to some different, representative interpretations

[10] Hudson, *International Legislation*, Vol. I, p. 116.
[11] Institut de Droit International, *Session de New York* (1929), Vol. II, p. 300.

arrived at by a few authors, rapporteurs, and international tribunals. Needless to say that this small collection is far from exhaustive.

It follows from our objectives that we must try to develop "discrimination" as a separate, independent legal concept. To call all possible instances of unequal treatment (as defined above, at p. 44) indiscriminately "discrimination" would deprive that word of its very *raison d'être*. If in the law a separate legal term is employed, then this term should denote something separate, that is, something with specific legal consequences. If a term has no distinct legal contents, *viz.* no such specific legal consequences, then the use of that term should be avoided as superfluous.

(a) We have earlier quoted the definition given in the *Dictionnaire de la Terminologie du Droit International*[12], which runs as follows:

"Traitement differentiel. Distinction consistant à refuser à çertains des droits ou avantages reconnes ou accordés à d'autres."

We already noticed the confusion of both the "distinction" element and the "treatment" element in this definition (p. 21). Our main objection is, however, that it suffers (not unlike a few others) from the deficiency just mentioned, namely that according to it discrimination differs in nothing from the countless legal, technical ("good") inequalities and classifications on the basis of which the law is build up. The description lacks the distinguishing elements which would justify the employment of "discrimination" as a distinctive legal notion; it covers *all* inequalities and classifications in the law. And what we are trying to find is precisely the specific element through which we can distinguish discrimination from the countless "technical," "reasonable" inequalities in the law. It is obvious that neither in municipal law systems, nor in international law and practice instances of such "good" unequal treatment are called discrimination (though this may occasionally occur; compare the award by the British American Claims Arbitral Tribunal of 9 November 1923, above at p. 25[13]). There is

[12] (Paris 1960), p. 217.

[13] As another example of this terminology the "discriminating concept of war" (compare G. Dahm, *Völkerrecht*, Vol. II, Stuttgart 1961, p. 328–331) could be mentioned, which refers to the position taken by third States with regard to an armed conflict. Given the validity of a rule prohibiting the use of force and consequently the distinction between "just" and "unjust" war, third States are no longer bound to observe strictly equal treatment of the aggressor and the party attacked by him, but should favour the latter. In the light of the prohibition to use force the unfavourable unequal treatment that is given to the aggressor, and frequently referred to as "discrimination," must be regarded as perfectly reasonable. See generally H. Meyrowitz, *Le Principe d'égalité des belligérants devant le droit de la guerre*, (Paris 1970).

more to discrimination than a simple unequal treatment. Why, for instance, would there otherwise be a Sub-Commission of the United Nations Commission on Human Rights for the "prevention of discrimination"? In the third meeting of the first Session of this Sub-Commision the representative of the United Kingdom suggested "that the word discrimination be used only in the case of unfair treatment, and that discrimination in favour of minorities necessary to their attainment of real equality should be called 'differential treatment'".[14]

(b) Sørensen gives the following definition:

"Discrimination is generally accepted as signifying any act or conduct which denies to individuals equality of treatment with other individuals because they belong to particular groups in society."[15]

Again we must object that there is no distinguishing characteristic in this definition establishing discrimination as a separate notion. The element "because they belong to particular groups in society" constitutes the very reason why classifications are made in the law. One could say that Sørensen's approach is sociological rather than juristic. Sørensen refers to the definition in the study "*The main Types and Causes of Discrimination*," a Memorandum submitted to the Sub-Commission on Prevention of Discrimination and Protection of Minorities by the Secretary-General of the United Nations at the request of the Economic and Social Council.[16]

(c) In this *Study* the following definition is given: discrimination is

"... a detrimental distinction based on grounds which may not be attributed to the individual and which have no justified consequences in social, political or legal relations (colour, race, sex, etc.) or on grounds of membership in social categories (cultural, language, religious, political or other opinion, national circle, social origin, social class, property, birth or other status)."[17]

(d) A definition in which quite a different criterion serves as distinguishing element was formulated by the Sub-Commission on Prevention of Discrimination and Protection of Minorities in its first Report to the Commission on Human Rights. This definition says:

"(Prevention of) discrimination is (the prevention of) any action which denies to individuals or groups equality of treatment which they may wish."[18]

[14] E/CN.4/Sub.2/SR.3 (1947), p. 6.

[15] M. Sørensen, "The Quest for Equality," *International Conciliation* No. 507, (March 1956), p. 293.

[16] E/CN.4/Sub.2/40/Rev.1 (1949).

[17] Paragraph 88 (p. 26).

[18] E/CN.4/52, p. 13.

We shall return to this remarkable definition later in more detail (see below, p. 138). From a *legal* point of view it is as insufficient as the definitions mentioned under (a) and (b). It is difficult to accept that the will of the individuals or groups in question would determine whether a given inequality of treatment constitutes discrimination – which the Sub-Commission would be obliged to prevent. The definition lacks a somewhat more objective element. But it hits the mark in this respect, that claims of alleged discrimination always originate from the "passive" side of the treatment, from those who are the "objects treated," and never – or nearly never – from those who are at the active side. This makes the wish of those treated important as the starting-point of investigations concerning discrimination.

(e) A definition that does not suffer from the deficiency we set forth under (a) is developed in Jaenicke's "*Der Begriff der Diskriminierung im Modernen Völkerrecht.*"[19] According to this definition discrimination is:

"... Basically the fact of unequal treatment in violation of international law."[20]

Twenty years later the same author stated in his article "Diskriminierung" in Strupp-Schlochauer, *Wörterbuch des Völkerrechts*:[21]

"Nowadays the practice of international law uses (the concept) to indicate an inadmissible unequal treatment."[22]

The precise nature of the inadmissibility, earlier indicated as a violation of international law, is not disclosed in the later article.

(f) An interesting definition which in our opinion is the most adequate of all mentioned here is the one given by H. Kipp.[23] It starts as follows:

"Discrimination can (...) be defined as: unequal treatment of equal objects or equal situations."

But then the author (with a reference to Nef's considerations) introduces an important proviso:

[19] Berlin 1940.

[20] "... Grundsätzlich der Tatbestand einer völkerrechtswidrigen unterschiedlichen Behandlung." *Op.cit.*, p. 14.

[21] 2nd ed., 1960, Vol. I, pp. 387–392.

[22] "Die Völkerrechtspraxis verwendet [den Begriff Diskriminierung] heute zur Bezeignung einer unzulässiger unterschiedlichen Behandlung."

[23] H. Kipp, "Das Verbot der Diskriminierung im modernen Friedensvölkerrecht," in: *Archiv des Völkerrechts*, Vol. IX, (1961/62), p. 137 ff. at p. 140/41.

"We can speak of discrimination or the unequal treatment of equal objects, *if there exists no meaningful connection between the inequality of the treatment and those aspects on which it is based.*"[24]

We will come back to this definition later, because we will base our own definition upon it.

(g) We know of only one judgment of an international arbitral tribunal in which a more or less explicit description can be found of what the tribunal means by "discrimination." It is an opinion of the French-Italian Conciliation Commission in a case concerning the treatment as enemy property of a French owned spinning-mill in Italy by Italian authorities during the Second World War.[25]
The Commission starts by expounding the general rule of the point at issue as follows:

"Pour qu'un mesure doive être qualifiée de discriminatoire point n'est nécessaire qu'elle consiste en un acte législatif ou réglementaire, faisant d'une manière générale la distinction entre le traitement, moins favorable, à réserver aux biens ennemis, et celui, plus favorable, à accorder aux autres biens ou, en tous cas, aux autres biens appartenant à des nationaux et sis sur le territoire national."

It then continues:

"Il suffit d'une mesure prise, dans la latitude de son pouvoir discrétionnaire, par l'autorité italienne, si ladite mesure a ou devait avoir des consequences préjudiciables pour les biens ennemis, et qu'aucun motif objectif ne peut raisonnablement être invoqué pour la justifier, de sorte qu'il faut en conclure qu'elle a été déterminée uniquemant par la qualité ennemie des biens en question."

(h) Several complaints based *inter alia* on "discrimination" reached the Permanent Court of International Justice. Apart from the *Oscar Chinn*-case these instances all originated from questions concerning the international protection of minorities. But the Court never described in general explicit terms what it understood by discrimination. Still for the purposes of this section some of the Court's considerations in the Advisory Opinion concerning the *Minority Schools in Albania* are noticeable.[26] We quote from these well-known passages:

"Equality in law precludes discrimination of any kind; whereas equality in fact may involve the necessity of different treatment in order to attain a result which establishes an equilibrium between different situations.

[24] Italics added. (Free) translation by the present author of "Diskriminierung kann (...) als ungleiche Behandlung gleicher Objekte oder gleicher Sachverhalte definiert werden." "Von diskriminierung oder unterschiedlicher Behandlung gleicher Objekte wird dann zu sprechen sein, wenn zwischen der Unterschiedlichkeit der Behandlung dieser Objekte, und jenen Gesichtspunkte, an denen sie sich orientiert, kein sinnvoller Zusammenhang besteht."

[25] *R.I.A.A.* Vol. XIII, p. 607. (*S.A. Filatures de Schappe*).

[26] P.C.I.J. *Series* A/B, No. 64 (1935), p. 19.

It is easy to imagine cases in which equality of treatment of the majority and of the minority, whose situations and requirements are different, would result in inequality in fact; treatment of this description would run counter to the first sentence of paragraph 1 of art. 5.[27] The equality between members of the majority and of the minority must be an effective, genuine equality; that is the maining of the provision."

The Court refers approvingly to an earlier Advisory Opinion, where it had said that:

"There must be equality in fact as well as ostensible legal equality in the sense of the absence of discrimination in the words of the law."[28]

We can deduce from the main passage just quoted that the Court did not consider "unequal treatment" to be the same as "discrimination." Rather, "discrimination" may result from equal treatment if the objects so treated are unequal. If an inequality is given, then unequal treatment is required in order to obtain "genuine equality" as the Court puts it.

The Court employed a somewhat awkward terminology: equality "in law" corresponds, it seems, with what we called "equal treatment." "Equality in fact" corresponds with what we referred to as "compensatory unequal treatment of unequals in order to reach equal social conditions." This latter notion is then described by the Court as the establishment of "an equilibrium between different situations."

The sudden appearance in this Opinion (also in the French text) of the word discrimination, the statement that "equality in law precludes discrimination of any kind," and also the requirement that the equality must be "effective," are remarkable. These elements strongly remind us of Article 5 of the "*Déclaration des Droits de l'Homme*" which the "*Institut de Droit International*" had adopted three years earlier: "L'égalité prévue ne devra pas être nominale mais effective. Elle exclut toute discrimination directe ou indirecte." We notice that all except three of the Judges of the Court were members of the Institut in 1929 and present at the Session during which the *Déclaration* was adopted.[29]

[27] Of the Albanian Declaration of October 2nd, 1921, made after its admission to the League of Nations, concerning the protection of minorities in Albania. The first sentence of Art. 5 (1) runs as follows: "Albanian nationals who belong to racial, linguistic or religious minorities, will enjoy the same treatment and security in law and in fact as other Albanian nationals." See below p. 145.

[28] Advisory Opinion of September 10th, 1923. *Series* B, no. 6. (*German Settlers*), at p. 24.

[29] See above, p. 50. Three members of the majority in the present Opinion had voted for the *Déclaration* in 1929 (Rolin-Jaecquemyns, Altamira and Schücking). So had one dissenter (Negulesco); the dissenting President Hurst had voted against the *Déclaration*. See *Annuaire de l'I.D.I. 1929*, Vol. II, p. 137–138. See on this leading case further below, p. 145 f.

(i) So far the European Court of Human Rights has had one opportunity to express itself on discrimination: in the *Belgian "linguistic" case* one of the issues concerned the meaning of article 14 of the European Convention on Human Rights.[30] In paragraph 10 of its Judgment the Court gives no definition, but offers some observations which, we think, are nevertheless illuminating:

"In spite of the very general wording of the French version ("sans distinction aucune"), Article 14 does not forbid every difference in treatment in the exercise of the rights and freedoms recognized. This version must be read in the light of the more restricted text of the English version ("without discrimination"). In addition, and in particular, one would reach absurd results were one to give Article 14 an interpretation as wide as that which the French version seems to imply. One would, in effect, be led to judge as contrary to the Convention every one of the many legal or administrative provisions which do not secure to everyone complete equality of treatment in the enjoyment of the rights and freedoms recognized. The competent national authorities are frequently confronted with situations or problems which, on account of differences inherent therein, call for different legal solutions; moreover, certain legal inequalities tend only to correct factual inequalities."

26. Comments on the Definitions

On the basis of the examples given in the previous paragraph we can distinguish between three types of definitions of discrimination. A representative of the first type is the definition given in the Study *"The Main Types and Causes of Discrimination."* The core element of these definitions is differential treatment, but this differential treatment is not further qualified in a legal sense. The additional elements do not by themselves separate the differential treatment in discrimination from the manifold forms of differential treatment that exist in the law anyhow. This is quite clear in Sørensen's definition, where the special element was simply: "because they belong to different groups in society." If this element is not further qualified, however, it would seem to imply that, for example, a legal technique such as progressive income taxation constitutes discrimination, or the taking of measures against delinquents. Both are directed at certain particular groups in society, as are innumerable other classifications, but are not held discriminatory.

As far as we know there exists only one specimen of what we list here as the second type: Jaenicke's definition. According to Jaenicke

[30] Judgment of 23 July, 1968. Text in *Case "Relating to certain aspects of the laws on the sue of languages in education in Belgium"* (Merits), Strasbourg 1968, p. 34.

the element to distinguish between simple, technical unequal treatment and discrimination was originally: "a violation of international law"[31] Discrimination is: unequal treatment in violation of international law, if the law contains a rule prescribing equal treatment applicable to the kind of treatment in the case at hand. He thus considers discrimination *only* in relation with a rule prohibiting unequal treatment, or prescribing equal treatment. Therefore he regards the action that constitutes discrimination as an international delict. Polemizing against the view that "arbitrariness" is a component of the concept, he contends that introducing so vague an element as "arbitrariness" into an international delict would entail the responsibility of the State for committing a delict each time the State acts "arbitrarily." This would result in too strict a limitation of the discretionary powers of the State in its conduct of foreign affairs.[32]

Jaenicke's view can only be correct if "discrimination" occurs in international practice merely in relationship with a prohibiting rule. And also: if such a prohibitory rule would be worded with so much accuracy and precision as not to include all kinds of legal inequalities of a technical ("good") nature.

Both presumptions are incorrect. The term discrimination is sometimes used to denote unequal treatment which is, let us say, undesirable, but not yet forbidden – not even by the treaty in question.[33] As an example we cite here Article I of the IMCO-Convention:

"The purposes of the organization are ... (b) to encourage the removal of discriminatory action ... by Governments."

And also art. 67 (1) of the Treaty Establishing the European Economic Community:

"Member States shall, in the course of the transitional period and to the extent necessary for the proper functioning of the Common Market, progressively abolish as between themselves (...) any discriminatory treatment based on the nationality or place of residence of the parties (...)."

Another example can be found in article 14 of the ILO Convention No 117 concerning Basic Aims and Standards of Social Policy (1962) which lays down in part that

[31] "Völkerrechtswidrigkeit." We do not think that Guggenheim intended to offer an explicit definition of the Jaenicke type with his repeated description of discrimination as a "distinction illicite." It comes close to it, but he does not say "illégale." (Paul Guggenheim, "Quelques remarques au sujet de l'article 14 de la Convention européenne des droits de l'Homme," in *René Cassin Amicorum Discipulorumque Liber*, Vol. I, *Problèmes de protection internationale des droits de l'Homme*, Paris 1969, p. 95 ff., at p. 98).

[32] *Op.cit.*, p. 16. The author discusses discrimination as between States.

[33] Compare also the criticism by Kipp, *op.cit.*, p. 138–139.

"It shall be an aim of policy to abolish all discrimination among workers on the grounds of race, colour, sex, belief, tribal association or trade union affiliation ..."[34]

As to the second presumption, many non-discrimination clauses are worded so loosely and in such an all-embracing manner, that a further specifying element is obviously called for. As an example we cite part of Article 26 of the International Covenant on Civil and Political Rights:

"... The Law shall (...) guarantee to all persons (...) protection against discrimination based upon any ground such as (...) property (...) or other status."

The advantage of Jaenicke's view is that it contains an objective criterion for the distinction between unequal treatment and discrimination: the violation of a rule of positive international law. But the price to be paid is an unacceptable simplification of the phenomenon we are dealing with. To reduce discrimination to unequal treatment in violation of a rule of positive law is to fail to appreciate the inherent meta-juridical, namely the moral aspect of the concept, which gives it its evasive character, but which also enables it to function as an instrument of criticism of positive law. We call this aspect "meta-juridical" and "moral" because it implies that discrimination in international law is to be considered as a *malum in se*, so to speak, and nor merely as a *malum prohibitum*, that is, a *malum* which owes this character only to its being *prohibitum* by a rule of positive law.[35] The latter point of view, such as the one originally taken by Jaenicke, is the outcome of consequent legal positivism.

Later on Jaenicke appears to have taken a position that is similar to ours, abandoning his earlier view. In his Article "Diskriminierung" in the "*Wörterbuch des Völkerrechts*"[36] he starts by saying that in his opinion the concept of discrimination is sufficiently defined as: the violation of an obligation to grant equal treatment. But then he asks himself whether qualifications should be added, whether the prohibition of discrimination is not in fact limited to "malevolent or arbitrary" discrimination. For the obscurity which he perceives he blames the "inaccuracy" (the "relativity," the "abstract nature," he adds by way

[34] Text in *U.N.T.S.*, Vol. 494, p. 250 ff.

[35] Compare on this distinction H. Kelsen, *Reine Rechtslehre*, p. 118; also *General Theory of Law and State* (Cambridge, Mass., 1946). p. 51–52.

[36] Strupp-Schlochauer, *Wörterbuch des Völkerrechts*, (2nd ed., Berlin 1960). Vol. I, p. 387 ff.

of explanation) of the specific prevailing notion of equality at the root of the rules prohibiting discrimination. After discussing the problem of equality and inequality the author comes to the conclusion that it must be examined each time (through careful interpretation of the wording of the rule in question) "in what relations – according to the intentions of the parties and the aim of the treaty – equal treatment is required." From his observation of international practice Jaenicke concludes that the word discrimination is used in case an obligation to grant equal treatment is violated (e.g. by a State as against another State), and also, *if no such obligation exists,* in case the unequal treatment must at least be qualified as "materially unjust" ("materiell ungerecht").

All this points at an important distinction that must be made, namely between on the one hand discrimination as unequal treatment which is *illegal* because it violates a rule prescribing equal or prohibiting unequal treatment, and on the other hand discrimination as unequal treatment which is regarded as undesirable, but as yet only condemned as *morally wrong*. In this second form it figures in legal rules which urge that it be abolished, which call for its elimination, but which themselves do not forbid it. In most cases we will find discrimination in prohibitory rules, in which it is forbidden because it is deemed undesirable, hence in both forms at once.

The conclusion must be that non-discrimination is not only a legal, but also a moral concept, and that as a legal concept it receives its contents from a moral rule, which prescribes that the right distinctions must be made so that justice will be done. That a legal concept sanctions a concept of morality, and can only be understood and implemented in the light of that moral concept is not an uncommon legal phenomenon: non-discrimination shares this characteristic with other evasive but pivotal legal notions such as "good faith," "equity," "due process," "abuse of right," and so on.

The third type of definition is represented in the small collection by the one that was developed by Kipp. From all approaches to discrimination it is clear that discrimination is regarded as wrongly unequal treatment. What is "wrong" about this unequal treatment is expressed in various ways. It may be said that "aucun motif objectif ne peut raisonnablement être invoqué" for the justification of the inequality or that it is "based on grounds which may not be attributed to the individual" and which have "no justified consequences in social ...

relations." Kipp's definition shows a more precise way to determine what is the "wrong" that turns unequal treatment into discrimination. Unlike the others it brings in the connection that must exist between the aspects of inequality on the one hand, and the character of the treatment on the other hand. This is important because it makes clear that the character of the treatment is a decisive factor in the qualification of a given unequal treatment as discrimination. We will try to develop Kipp's definition further in the following paragraphs.

27. Definition adopted in this Study

We start by saying that discrimination occurs when the equality or inequality of treatment results from a "wrong" judgment as to the relevance or irrelevance of the various human attributes that are taken into account. Therefore, discrimination will be provisionally defined as "wrongly equal, or wrongly unequal treatment." This is in agreement with international legal doctrine and with international practice, as is clear from the reasonings of the French-Italian Conciliation Commission, the Permanent Court, and from the views prevailing within the United Nations.

We choose the adjective "wrong" because it covers so many notions and can be used in such a great number of contexts; it covers everything from the illegal to the immoral, from the malevolent to the arbitrary.

From our discussion on the notions equality and inequality the conclusion can be drawn that it would not at all be helpful to explain what "wrong" means in this definition by saying that it refers to a situation in which equal treatment is accorded to "unequals," or unequal treatment to "equals," as is sometimes done.[37] This view results from our earlier discussion of equality and inequality, which was based most of all on Nef's considerations. The law, we contended, can in theory introduce, recognize or deny equalities or inequalities at will.

Though it may be true that there are no inherent logical limits to the capacity of human judgment to ignore or to constitute inequalities among men, there are of course moral and legal limits to the drawing or blurring of lines, to the creation or amalgamation of human categories.

As also appeared from the way Kipp described discrimination, the concept must be understood as a *combination*, namely of the equality

[37] Compare Jaenicke, *Der Begriff der Diskriminierung im modernen Völkerrecht*. p. 20.

and inequality aspects together with the treatment aspect. Equality and inequality go together in countless combinations but can only be appreciated within the context of a particular right or duty: what could be wrong with respect to one particular right or duty (e.g. voting, or education), might not be wrong within the context of another right or duty (e.g. taxation, or property rights). So we must emphasize the importance of the nature of the rights and duties involved (which constitute the treatment). It is by no means enough to say that red hair or blue eyes are irrelevant criteria for unequal treatment. Discussions sometimes concentrate somewhat on the attributes that are deemed morally acceptable or not as bases for legal classification,[38] but in problems such as this no decision can be arrived at *in abstracto*, that is, without taking into account the nature of the rights or duties concerned. Whether aspects of equality or aspects of inequality in the individuals treated must prevail is to be judged in relation to the nature of the subject matter regulated.[39] In the light of this side of the problem we can elaborate our definition, and clarify what we mean by the adjective "wrong" by saying that

discrimination occurs when in a legal system an inequality is introduced in the enjoyment of a certain right, or in a duty, while there is no sufficient connection between the inequality upon which the legal inequality is based, and the right or the duty in which this inequality is made.

The element "wrongly equal treatment" of our definition can be elaborated as follows:

discrimination occurs when in a legal system no inequality is introduced in the enjoyment of a certain right, or in a duty, and as a result thereof no sufficient connection exists between the unequalness of the subjects treated and the right or the duty.

Discrimination through inactivity, through the wrong abstention from differentiating between aspects of equality and of inequality – given the character of the rights or duties involved – will be discussed below in paragraph 31. We will first deal with discrimination through active differentiating.

28. The Element of the "Sufficient Connection"

What we call the "sufficient connection" is usually referred to as the

[38] Resulting in a definition such as the one given in *The Main Types and Causes of Discrimination*, reproduced above, in § 25 under (c).

[39] See further on this below, p. 133 ff.

"sufficient reason" that must be given in order to justify a deviation from the principle that equal treatment is the rule, and unequal treatment the exception.[40]

It may be observed that the sufficient connection apparently implies two different modes of reasoning. It is appropriate to distinguish between the cognitive aspect of the determination of a suffcient connection, and a volitive aspect of an evaluative, or even an emotional nature. The cognitive aspect, which might be contrasted to the other one by calling it the intellectual side of the problem, simply amounts to the requirement of the truthfulness of classifications. Or, more precisely, by the requirement that any classification must be based on considerations that conform to truth. This requirement is stressed especially by Arnold Brecht, who has done so within the context of his discussion of the "universal postulates of justice."[41] "An enormous field is covered by the postulate of factual truth in justice. In most cases in which justice is questioned the real issue is the truth of a factual statement," Brecht observes. And he goes on to say:

"The postulate of factual truth entails several procedural implications that have figured greatly in the history of justice. Here belong all those rules which are meant to facilitate the ascertainment of the true facts, such as the provisions to safeguard the evidence, and the demand that litigants be granted a fair hearing ("fair" meaning that they should be granted an adequate share in the ascertainment of all relevant facts), that they be allowed to prove their contentions, that the judge be unbiased."[42]

The element of truth thus involves the absence of prejudice; it demands that the factual aspects of the case at hand be investigated in an objective manner before choices are made. The remaining problem is how thorough and penetrating the factual research should be.[43]

Of equal importance is the volitive aspect of the determination

[40] See above, § 4.

[41] Arnold Brecht, *Political Theory* (Princeton 1959), p. 396, and especially Ch. XI, "Truth and Justice" (p. 404 ff).

[42] *Op.cit.*, p. 408, 409. Compare similarly Julius Stone's third "Quasi-absolute Precept of Material Justice": "It is always incumbent on an actor to discover with maximum possible accuracy all aspects of the situation in which he acts or fails to act." (*Op.cit.*, p. 341).

[43] A very interesting instance of this problem can be found in the *North Sea Continental Shelf Cases* (I.C.J., *Reports 1969*, p. 3 ff). In these cases one of the issues was how the "just and equitable share" of the Continental shelf, to which each coastal State is entitled, should be deliminated. Should only the geographical factors be taken into account, that is to say, should the delimination be based on the *surface* of the shelf, or should the notion of a "just and equitable share" be rested on a notion of opportioning the natural resources in the shelf? In the latter case, it might be argued, the already existing natural resources of the parties should also be compared. An additional problem was the fact that it was not quite clear how much information as to the exact quantities of natural resources in the shelf was available to the parties in the dispute. See on this aspect of the *Cases* the Separate Opinion of Judge Jessup, *loc. cit.*, p. 67 ff.

whether a sufficient connection has been established or not. This is a matter of will, it appears, of values recognized, not known.[44] The decision whether a connection is insufficient or completely lacking ultimately amounts to a subjective weighing, a choice made upon an emotional basis that often remains inarticulate. It is here that legal analysis must necessarily end.[45]

The difference between both aspects distinguished here can be illustrated by pointing at the difference between the sufficient connection in economics on the one hand and in law and politics on the other hand. In economic theory the notion exists that prices fixed at a given time for certain products must be the same for all customers, unless to serve a particular buyer involves higher costs than to serve the other buyers (e.g. extra costs for transportation, or for duties). If one particular buyer is asked to pay a higher price which is not related to extra costs, then economists speak of "price discrimination." Thus it can be said that

> "price discrimination occurs when a producer sells a specific commodity to different buyers at two or more different prices, *for reasons not associated with differences in costs.*"[46]

The terms "insufficient or completely lacking" imply the possibility of measurement. And indeed, in economics the connection can to some extent be measured; whether it is sufficient or not is to some extent a matter of figures that do or do not add up.

In law and politics this is of course much less true. Though the notions of equality and inequality, justice and discrimination in these fields likewise somehow presuppose the possibility of measurement, all this is much more elusive. The possibility of measurement as an essential problem of discrimination and the related notions we mentioned must be emphasized here, but it cannot be dealt with in any detail. Emge[47] has done so, demonstrating the manifold ambiguities and dangers that may stand in the way of justice: application of a measure to an outsider; no uniform measure; oversimplified measure; no measure at all; oversimplification of what is to be measured; measurement of the unmeasurable, and so on.

[44] G. Radbruch, *Rechtsphilosophie* (6th ed., Stuttgart 1963), p. 100.

[45] See also our Note on "Non-Discrimination and Justice," in *Archiv für Rechts- und Sozialphilosophie*, Vol. LVII (1971), p. 201.

[46] R. G. Lipsey and P. O. Steiner, *Economics* (New York and Tokyo, 1966), p. 273 (Italics in original).

[47] C. A. Emge, *Einführung in die Rechtsphilosophie* (Frankfurt a.M., Wien, 1956), p. 172 ff.

Whether a sufficient connection has been established in a certain case may not only be determined in a variety of ways, but also with varying degrees of severity. How scrutinizing the review of (for example) municipal legislation by an international institution will be is of course a matter of practice and procedure to be developed by the particular institution entrusted with that task.[48]

Marshall[49] has designed an interesting list of ten "increasingly high hurdles" of criticism that must be cleared by a particular measure involving unequal treatment in legislation. "It being agreed," he observes, "that legislators may select different persons or groups for different treatment, inasmuch as 'classification is inherent in legislation,'[50] various things may be said. To cite a few examples, it may be held:

1) that between classification and legislative objects there must be *some nexus;*
2) that classification must be based on an *intelligible* differentiation;
3) that classification must be based upon some *real and substantial* distinction;
4) that classification must be *relevant* to the object of the legislation;
5) that classification must be *rationally related* to the object;
6) that classification must be *fairly related* to the object;
7) that classification must not be *capricious or invidious;*
8) that classification must not be *arbitrary;*
9) that classification must be *reasonable;*
10) that classification must be *just.*"

It seems to us that the test of the sufficient connection is not satisfied with the first two requirements. That "some" nexus is easily established

[48] Such institutions are for instance the European Commission of Human Rights (art. 19 ff. of the Convention); the European Court of Human Rights (art. 38 ff. of the Convention); the Economic and Social Council of the U.N. (art. 16 ff. of the Convenant on Economic, Social and Cultural Rights); the Human Rights Committee (art. 28 ff. of the Covenant on Civil and Political Rights); the Committee on the Elimination of Racial Discrimination (art. 8 ff. of the Convention on the Elimination of All Forms of Racial Discrimination).

[49] Geoffrey Marshall, "Notes on the Rule of Equal Law," in *Nomos IX, Equality* (New York 1965), p. 268 ff.

[50] The author refers here to Mr. Justice Frankfurter's dissenting opinion in *Morey v. Doud,* 354 U.S. 457 (1957), at 472. In this case the U.S. Supreme Court held invalid under the Fourteenth Amendment a provision of the Illinois Community Currency Exchanges Act (1943) which excepted the American Express Company from the requirement that any firm selling or issuing money orders in Illinois must secure a licence and submit to State regulation. The Act intended to protect the public against the risks resulting from inadequate capital and insufficient safeguards of many small banking facilities; the excepted Company was regarded as of "unquestioned solvency and high financial standing."

may already have become clear from the ambiguous nature of "equality," from which it follows that classification is in nearly all cases to some extent "intelligible." But the sufficient connection can be regarded as involving any of the third and following requirements.

29. *An Example: Voting Rights for Women*

We illustrate our concept of discrimination here by giving just one example, and a relatively easy one, namely the time-honoured but not yet fully academic question of voting rights for women, also raised by Nef.

From his theoretical theses Nef[51] draws the proper conclusion that the necessary coexistence of equality and inequality makes it impossible to prove objectively that justice requires either that women should be granted voting rights (because they are equal to men with respect to voting), or that they should not have such rights (because they are not equal to men with respect to voting). Application of the test of the sufficient connection leads us to distinguish the following elements of the problem: the aspects of equality between men and women; the aspects of inequality between men and women; and the character of the right involved. If in a particular community the right to vote would be denied to women, then the sufficient connection should be shown to exist between the aspects in which women differ from men (who are entitled to vote) on the one hand, and the nature and function of voting rights on the other hand. In the light of the latter the distinguishing factors must therefore be weighed against the interests and capabilities of women as members of a politically organized community. In most civilizations physical differences (including those resulting from sickness or old age) have social consequences; e.g female workers are given special working conditions and extra health care; in most States women are excluded from compulsory military service (a fact that in such States may sometimes have been used as an argument for witholding voting rights from women). But physical differences, relevant as they may be to e.g. military service, are deemed less relevant as far as the role of women in a community is concerned, and their interests in the way the community is run. Most communities in which the problem plays a role have decided that there is no sufficient connection between physical differences and the nature of voting

[51] *Op.cit.*, p. 109–110.

rights. But some communities still think there is. To call the practice of the latter "discrimination" presupposes that a different, more or less authoritative choice has been made elsewhere. In this example we could mention as the result of such a judgment article I of the international Convention on the Political Rights of Women,[52] which runs in part: "Women shall be entitled to vote in all elections on equal terms with men ...."

30. "Arbitrariness"

Discrimination is usually approached in terms of "arbitrariness" rather than the broader "wrongfulness." However, arbitrariness is generally understood as a matter of irrationality, of whim and caprice. These expressions imply unpredictability as an essential element of arbitrariness. This element may to some extent be illustrated by the way the word "arbitrary" is used in the Universal Declaration[53 54] and in the Covenant on Civil and Political Rights: arbitrary arrest, detention or exile (article 9 Declaration, article 9 Covenant); arbitrary interference with privacy, family, home or correspondence (article 12 Declaration, article 17 Covenant); arbitrarily deprived of nationality, or property (articles 15 en 17 Declaration); arbitrarily deprived of right to enter one's own Country (article 12 Covenant). Nowhere is the word "arbitrary" employed in relation to matters of equality or discrimination.

It appears that the practices regarded as discrimination are generally by no means unpredictable and hardly ever a result of whim or caprice. This is especially true as far as discrimination in the form of legislation is concerned, which is, after all, the deliberate creation of general rules. The claim that a particular unequal treatment in a given community amounts to discrimination usually originates from those at the "passive side." Those who are at the active side choose and fix the standards for differentiation, and rationalize the differentiation

[52] Concluded in 1952. Text in *U.N.T.S.*, Vol. 193, p. 135 ff. Compare also article 3 of the Covenant on Civil and Political Rights: "The States Parties to the present Covenant undertake to ensure the equal right of men and women to the enjoyment of all civil and political rights set forth in the present Convention." See also below, § 40.

[53] See Parvez Hassan, "The Word "Arbitrary" as used in the Universal Declaration on Human Rights: "Illegal" or "Unjust"?" in *Harvard International Law Journal*, Vol. 10 (1969), p. 225 ff.

[54] Compare on the following also the similar view taken by a Committee of Experts on Human Rights, laid down in its Report of 12 may, 1969, to the Committee of Ministers of the Council of Europe (Doc. CM(69) 59) on "Problems arising from the coexistence of the UN Covenants on Human Rights and the European Convention on Human Rights," at p. 12.

within the context of their own culture.[55] The claim that discrimination is practised as a result thereof is raised by those who cannot or may not participate (fully or sufficiently, if at all) in this culture (illiterates, members of the lowest social classes, aliens), or who do not want to do so (like some minorities). The active, those who *do* participate sometimes may not even realize that they "discriminate."[56] At least they will certainly not agree that the social stratification in question is "capricious" or "arbitrary."

The changing of the standards comes when the arguments for their justification have come to fail and are no longer accepted. This change may be brought about through – among other things – the opposition against them that follows the emancipation of the lowest classes, or through addressing to the community rules that were developed in another, a larger community. For example, the standards of the international protection of human rights.[57]

From our description of discrimination it is clear that "arbitrariness," – or "unfairness," "malevolence" and other similar notions that are sometimes connected with it – have been absorbed by the concept as we understand it.[58] Therefore an expression like "arbitrary discrimination" is pleonastic in our terminology. As a matter of fact, such combinations are rarely found any more in treaty practice after the Second World War;[59] this is at least true for the human rights field in

[55] See also Brecht, *op.cit.*, p. 409 ff.

[56] Ernst E. Hirsch distinguishes between two types of discrimination, *viz.* discrimination on an emotional basis, related to a personal conflict and resulting from social prejudice, and intentional, rational discrimination, used as a weapon in a social conflict situation and aimed at exploitation and oppression (S.v. "Diskriminierung" in *Wörterbuch der Soziologie*, ed. by W. Bernsdorf, 2nd. ed., Stuttgart 1969, p. 191). See also M. Rehbinder, "Die Diskriminierung: ihre Ursache und ihre Bekämpfung," in *Kölner Zeitschrift für Soziologie und Sozialpsychologie*, Vol. 15 (1963), p. 6 ff.

[57] This is said without the implication that values which are developed and recognized in the international community are for that very reason morally superior to values of a smaller – national – community, as seems automatically to be assumed sometimes. See against this assumption W. Wengler, *Völkerrecht*, Vol. I, p. 98–99.

[58] This conclusion can also be drawn from the discussion in the UN Commission on Human Rights concerning a proposal submitted by the delegate of the Ukrainian S.S.R. to delete the adjective "arbitrary" from the expression "arbitrary discrimination" in the draft of what was to become article 7 of the Universal Declaration. After a lengthy discussion this proposal was adopted. U.N. Doc. E/CN.4/SR. 52, p. 8–13.

[59] Compare for the earlier period for example article 4 and article 20 of the Statute on the International Régime of Railways (Geneva, 1923): "... to refrain from all discrimination of an unfair nature..."; French version: "... toute discrimination qui aurait un caractère de malveillance..." (Text in Hudson, *International Legislation*, Vol. II, p. 1139 ff.). Similarly the interesting article 4 of the Convention on the Abolition of Import and Export Prohibitions and Restrictions (Geneva, 1927): "The following classes of prohibitions and restrictions are not prohibited by the present Convention, on condition, however, that they are not applied in such a manner as to constitute a means of arbitrary discrimination between foreign

which we are mainly interested. But of course we do not pretend that there is any degree of precision in international legal terminology: the rhetorics and vagaries of international law-creation may produce all kinds of expressions – some of which might, from our point of view, be called "atypical."

31. "Favourable"; "Unfavourable"

Very often terms such as "favourable," or rather "unfavourable" or "detrimental" are employed in descriptions of discrimination. In our opinion this is not necessary. Equality and inequality imply a comparison between two or more comparable cases. If, for example, rights are accorded to some individuals, but not to others, then each time there is unequal treatment that is favourable to some and unfavourable to others.[60] This can be expressed by saying that the first group is granted a "privilege" (compare "diplomatic privileges and immunities"), a "prerogative," or a "preference." Notions such as these are frequently used in this connection; and there are similar notions for the designation of the "unfavourable," the "detrimental" treatment at the other side: here it may be said that there is a "restriction," an "exclusion," or a "limitation." In most cases each favourable treatment of some individuals or groups constitutes at the same time the unfavourable treatment of other individuals or groups. This occurs necessarily whenever the treatment involves the distribution of a good (material or cultural) that is only available in limited supply. In such cases the latter groups must do without the extra that is granted to the former. But if this favour is justified (not "wrong"), then that same justification renders it impossible for the others to complain legitimately about "discrimination" against them. Likewise, if the favourable unequal treatment has no justification (is "wrong") then it will constitute a discrimination against the others. The sufficient connection works both ways.

What is involved here may be illustrated by a case in point, namely *Attorney-General of Palestine v. Abraham Altschuler.*[61] The case is reported as follows:

countries..." etc. The French version says: "discrimination arbitraire." Text in Hudson, Vol. III, p. 2164.

[60] See above, p. 44.

[61] Supreme Court of Palestine, May 1928. *Annual Digest of Public International Law Cases 1927–1928*, Case no. 35 (p. 55–56).

Altschuler, the respondent in the appeal, was charged before the Municipal Court of Tel Aviv (at that time "a Jewish suburb of Jaffa") with the breach of a municipal bye-law passed by the Local Council of Tel-Aviv which prescribed that no establishment other than a restaurant shall be open on the Jewish Sabbath day within the area of the Local Council, provided that the prohibition shall not apply to a shop owned by a Moslem or Christian, and that restaurants, other than those owned by Moslems and Christians, may be open at certain hours on the Jewish Sabbath day. The respondent was a Jew who opened his restaurant outside the prescribed hours, and was sentenced by the Court to pay a fine. On appeal, the District Court set aside the conviction, holding that the bye-law was invalid as being contrary to Article 15 of the Mandate for Palestine which lays down that "no discrimination of any kind shall be made between the inhabitants of Palestine on the ground of race, religion or language."

On further appeal to the Supreme Court it was held as follows:

The bye-law limits the freedom of action on the Jewish Sabbath of shopkeepers if they are Jews. It is none the less discrimination in favour of the small non-Jewish minority in the area of the Local Council. The bye-law is, therefore, invalid as contrary to the provisions of the Mandate and to Article 17 of the Palestine Order in Council, which prescribes that no legislation shall be promulgated which shall tend to discriminate in any way between the inhabitants of Palestine on the ground of race, religion or language.

The editor added a note which is particularly interesting:

"One of the judges of the Supreme Court gave a dissenting judgment, holding that where a law is made to be binding on the general public, but a certain class exempt from the operation of the law on the ground of religious belief, that is a privilege exceptionally granted on the ground of its religion, and is not a discrimination against the public at large. The bye-law granted a privilege to Moslems and Christians on the ground of their religion, so that they should not be compelled to close on the day of Sabbath in addition to their own day of rest. It cannot be regarded in any way as a discrimination against the Jewish inhabitants on the ground of their religion."

32. Discrimination through Equal Treatment

In paragraph 17 it was stated that treatment can also consist of "inaction." By legislative treatment through "inaction" we do not mean to indicate the total absence of legislation in a particular field. Nor do we mean by such legislative treatment legislation granting rights and freedoms that must be enjoyed without interference on the part of the organs of the State.

The notion rather refers to deficient legislation, to which additons should be made. "Inaction" refers, more precisely, to legislation that causes the coming into existence or the continuance of discriminatory social situations, which can be eliminated if the legislation in question is amended in the sense that differentiations are introduced in it so that inequalities that exist or that result from it are taken into account or compensated.[62] Thus, for the purposes of our discussion, the failure to act must be specified as a failure to differentiate within a particular type of treatment. This occurs for example when unequals are granted equal treatment.

From a legal point of view specific inaction is only relevant when there is a legal rule prescribing the very opposite specific action. Such a rule could be, in this example, a rule prescribing that "some" must be granted unequal treatment in proportion to the inequality between them and "others," instead of being subjected to the same treatment that is granted to the "others." This is the situation we had in mind when we described discrimination also as "wrongly equal treatment." We explained this description by saying that discrimination occurs when in a specific right or duty no inequality is made, and thus no sufficient connection exists between the unequalness of the subjects treated and the right or duty.

Discrimination has an aspect of "illegality" and an aspect of "immorality." This is true for both discrimination through action and for discrimination through inaction. In the light of this distinction it can be concluded that in the second case the "sufficient connection" is lacking because there existed a legal rule that prescribed active differentiation, or because there was a moral standard according to which the differentiation should have been introduced.

That discrimination can also occur through equal treatment is clearly expressed in article 5 of the "*Déclaration des Droits de l'Homme*" of the *Institut de Droit International,* quoted above in § 25 (h), where it was submitted that the formulation of this article had influenced the Permanent Court in its opinion concerning the *Minority Schools in Albania:* "L'égalité prévue ne devra pas être nominale mais effective. Elle exclut toute discrimination directe ou indirecte."

With the expression "discrimination indirecte" is denoted what is here referred to as "discrimination through equal treatment." "Indirect discrimination"[63] occurs when no specific classification has been made

[62] Compare the examples, taken from the case law of the German Constitutional Court, given by H. F. Zacher, "Soziale Gleichheit," in *Archiv des öffentlichen Rechts*, Vol. 93 (1968), p. 347–348.

[63] This term is also used by Schindler *op.cit.* p. 142 ff. ("indirekte Diskriminierung"). Sometimes the distinction is made between the law "on the books" and the law "as applied," like in the Peace-treaties concluded in 1947 with Hungary (article 2) and Rumania (article 3), quoted by Schindler (p. 143): "... the law in force ... shall not, either in their content or in their application discriminate *or entail discrimination*..." (italics added). We avoid the use

in a given regulation, but, because of the combination of the particular subject matter and particular elements of unequalness of the addressees of the regulation (a particular group in a particular situation), the regulation discriminates against this specific group of addressees. The discrimination is found in the effect of the rules rather than in their wording. As to voting rights, for example, it can result from devices like voting qualifications such as literacy tests and poll-taxes. Such requirements admittedly set equal standards for all voters.[64] Yet it is clear that such techniques deny, and are intended to do so, the enjoyment of voting rights to certain groups. And we think that Mr. Justice Douglass who delivered the opinion of the Court in the *Lassiter* case mentioned in note 64 was quite naive, if not obviously wrong, when he observed that "Literacy and illiteracy are neutral on race, creed, color and sex, as reports around the world show."[65]

In international law the problem is of course how international "equality clauses" relate to this type of "equal treatment." Has not a rule as mentioned above complied with an international obligation to grant "equal protection"? In a number of opinions the Permanent Court of International Justice has developed a consequent policy on the basis of which the above question was emphatically denied. In its Advisory Opinion concerning the *German Settlers in Poland*[66] the Court observed:

"The facts that no racial discrimination appears in the text of the law of July 14th, 1920 (which provided for the expulsion of German settlers from their

of this terminology here because "the law as applied" could be confused with discrimination by the administrative and judicial branches of government.

[64] Compare e.g. *Lassiter v. Northampton County Board of Elections*, 360 U.S. 45 (1959), in which the Supreme Court upheld a North Carolina law which prescribed a literacy test.

[65] In *Harper v. Virginia Board of Elections*, 383 U.S. 663 (1966) the Court declared Virginia's poll-tax inconsistent with the Equal Protection Clause of the Fourteenth Amendment. "The principle that denies the State the right to dilute a citizen's vote on account of his economic status or other such factors by analogy bars a system wich excludes those unable to pay a fee to vote or who fail to pay." The tax was US $ 1.50, but "The degree of discrimination is irrelevant."

In the joint dissenting opinion of Justices Harlan and Stewart we come across a remarkable passage which is worth quoting in this context: ... "Arguments have been and can still be made in favor of (property qualifications for voters). For example, it is certainly a rational argument that payment of some minimal poll-tax promotes civil responsibility, weeding out those who do not case enough about public affairs to pay $ 1.50 or thereabouts a year for the exercise of the franchise. It is also arguable, indeed it was probably accepted as sound political theory by a large percentage of Americans through most of our history, that people with some property have a deeper stake in community affairs, and are consequently more responsible, more educated, more knowledgeable, more worthy of confidence, than those without means, and that the community and Nation would be better managed if the franchise were restricted to such citizens."

[66] *Series* B, No. 6 (10 September, 1923), p. 24.

lands) and that in a few instances the law applies to non-German Polish nationals who took as purchasers from original holders of German race, make no difference .... There must be equality in fact as well as ostensible legal equality in the sense of the absence of discrimination in the words of the law."

Likewise, in its Advisory Opinion concerning the treatment of *Polish Nationals in Danzig* the Court observed:

"... The prohibition against discrimination, in order to be effective, must ensure the absence of discrimination in fact as well as in law. A measure which in terms is of general application, but in fact is directed against Polish nationals and other persons of Polish origin or speech, constitutes a violation of the prohibition ... Whether a measure is or is not in fact directed against these persons is a question to be decided on the merits of each particular case. No hard and fast rule can be laid down." [67]

Similar views were expressed in the Opinion concerning the *Minority Schools in Albania*, quoted above in § 25(h).

The Court puts the emphasis particularly on the fact that equality clauses require equality "in fact," and not only equality "in law." These terms were not introduced by the Court itself; it relied on the terminology that was already employed in the treaty provisions concerned, such as article 8 of the treaty on the protection of minorities concluded between the Allied and Associated Powers and Poland, [68] which states in part that

"Polish nationals who belong to racial, religious or linguistic minorities shall enjoy the same treatment and security in law and in fact as the other Polish nationals..."

These examples all relate to the protection of minorities. But there is nothing which would prevent a similar reasoning in other fields of the international protection of human rights, and international law in general. It is hard to assume that the Court's point of view could be different where other treaties than those concerning the protection of minorities would have been involved. The clearest examples to the effect that it is not enough to maintain standards that seemingly work out the same way for all parties involved, but in fact result in a detrimental position for one of them, can be found in the international practice concerning the law of aliens, the most-favoured-nation clause, and with respect to questions of tariffs and duties. In all these fields a material interpretation of equality clauses must be applied in order

[67] *Series* A/B No. 44 (February 4th, 1932), p. 28.
[68] Versailles, June 28th, 1919. Text in Hudson, *International Legislation*, Vol. I, p. 283 ff.

to comply with a non-discrimination clause.[69] The same conception prevails in the law of the European Communities, where the Court of Justice held that "The different treatment of non-comparable situations does not lead automatically to the conclusion that there is discrimination. An appearance of formal discrimination may therefore correspond in fact to an absence of material discrimination. Material discrimination would consist in treating either similar situations differently or different situations identically."[70]

We submit that the international non-discrimination principle rejects not only discrimination through unequal treatment, but also discrimination through equal treatment; it has replaced, or rather it incorporates the protection of minorities. The protection of minorities can be regarded as one of the ways in which the non-discrimination principle is to be implemented. As Wengler puts it[71]: "Der besondere Schutz der Minderheiten tendiert besonderes dahin, in dem Verbot "diskriminierender" Behandlung von Menschengruppen innerhalb eines Staates aufzugehen".[72] The principle requires not only legal but also factual, not only formal but also material equality.[73] It can be said that in the terminology of international legal practice the term "non-discrimination" is used to designate measures which are chiefly aimed at abolishing wrongly *unequal* treatment, while the expression "protection of minorities" is used to designate measures which are chiefly aimed against wrongly *equal* treatment and which purport to secure special

[69] Compare the examples, taken mostly from the practice of the League of Nations, especially of the *Comité Economique*, given by Jaenicke, *op.cit.*, p. 102–117.

[70] *Italian Government v. EEC Commission.* Case no. 13/63, *Common Market Law Reports* 1963, p. 289 ff, at p. 311–312. This case concerned a complaint lodged by Italy against a decision of the Commission authorizing France under article 226 of the EEC treaty to impose a special tax on the import from Italy of refrigerators and accessories for refrigerators which caused "serious difficulties" in that sector of the French economy. Italy asserted that the tax should also apply to imports of like goods from the other member-States.

[71] *Völkerrecht,* Vol. II, p. 1028, nt. 5.

[72] Compare for an identic opinion Peter Pernthaler, *Der Schutz der ethnischen Gemeinschaften durch individuelle Rechte* (Wien und Stuttgart, 1964), who observes: "Diskriminationsverbote, welche ... eigentlich die Grundlage des individual-rechtlichen Minderheiten-Schutzsystems bilden, gebieten rechtliche und faktische Gleichbehandlung von Mehrheits- und Minderheitsangehörigen" (p. 33). He refers to the same view set forth by Verdross in "Der Grundsatz der rechtlichen und tatsächlichen Gleichstellung der Volkstämme auf Grund der Kollektivverträge über den Minderheitenschutz" (in *Juristische Blätter*, 1936). Also Verdross regarded the prohibition of discrimination as the basic rule ("Grundnorm") of the minorities' protection. Very clear on this also Shigeru Oda in his discussion of the international protection of human rights in M. Sørensen, ed., *Manual of Public International Law* (London, New York 1968): "In fact, the treatment of minorities has now been replaced by the wider concepts of elimination of racial discrimination or apartheid and even of protection of human rights for all people without distinction as to race, sex, language, religion and so on" (p. 497).

[73] Thus also Jaenicke, "Gleichbehandlung," in *Wörterbuch des Völkerrechts*, Vol. I, p. 690 ff, at 692–693.

rights in the light of the special situation of the minorities. Both are forms of the non-discrimination principle, and both are directed at equal as well as unequal treatment. In the protection of minorities, the minorities must not only be granted special rights: they must also be given equal treatment, namely wherever rights are involved for the enjoyment of which the members of the minorities are held to be equal to the members of the majority. For example, Article 7 (1) of the Treaty between the Allied and Associated Powers and Poland lays down that

"All Polish nationals shall be *equal before the law* and shall enjoy *the same civil and political rights* without distinction as to race, language and religion." [74]

Likewise the non-discrimination principle may also require unequal treatment. [75] The difference is merely a matter of emphasis, which is put on equal treatment when non-discrimination is involved, and on unequal treatment when protection of minorities is involved.

33. *Discrimination and Social Rights*

At first sight it may seem that discrimination constituted by equal treatment poses extra difficulties, because in such a situation an obligation not to discriminate must be complied with through positive action instead of abstention. In many cases it may seem as if a non-discrimination clause, when aimed at the elimination of indirect discrimination, is not directed against particular human activities but rather against an indifferent, anonymous and indeterminate social situation, the modification of which requires purposeful intervention.[76]

It thus appears that the non-discrimination principle has two sides. On the one hand it contains an interdiction of positive discriminatory action on the part of the State, in particular legislative action. As such it appears to belong to the category of so-called "civil rights," or "freedom rights," that are traditionally intended to limit the power of the State over its citizens, and require State abstention. On the other hand the non-discrimination principle contains, as we submit in this paragraph, an interdiction of inaction on the part of the State as well,

[74] Italics added.

[75] See below, § 58 and § 60, especially p. 157 ff.

[76] In the *Study of Discrimination in Education* (E/CN.4/Sub. 2/181/Rev. 1, 1957, Charles D. Ammoun, Special Rapporteur), a distinction is made between "discriminatory practices resulting from *a policy evidently intended to originate, maintain or aggravate such practices*," and "discriminatory practices which are *economic, social, political or historic* in character." (p. 4).

namely if this inaction entails the continuance or the coming into existence of a discriminatory social situation. This inaction consists of a failure to recognize and react upon relevant social inequalities, e.g. by differentiating within a particular legislative treatment. As far as non-discrimination can also be regarded as a human rights principle which exhorts or obliges the State to take action under certain circumstances, it appears that it also belongs among those human rights which are usually referred to as "social rights."

Historically, social rights have come at the national level after the classic civil rights had become recognized if not ensured. At the international level, the social rights have been developed and adopted simultaneously or nearly simultaneously with civil and political rights. In this connection the International Labour Organization can be mentioned: since its foundation in 1919 it has been pre-eminently the agency that has created and promoted a comprehensive system of international labour and social law standards. After the Second World War the Universal Declaration laid down several social rights in the articles 22 to 28. Such rights have recently been codified in the European Social Charter of 18 October, 1961, and in the Covenant on Economic, Social and Cultural Rights.

That the concept of "social" rights is by no means precise, and that the designation "social" is quite inadequate needs no argumentation. It is not our concern here to discuss the concept of "social" rights at length, or to elaborate a neat distinction between "social" and "civil and political" rights. [77] However, within the context of this paragraph it is interesting to us that social rights are very often distinguished from civil rights on the basis of the view that while the latter require merely state abstention, the former can only be implemented through active public interference in the prevailing economic, social and cultural situation. [78] This is the traditional approach; however, in spite

[77] It seems best to follow the division created by the Covenant on Civil and Political Rights and the Covenant on Economic, Social and Cultural Rights. When we speak of "distinction" or "division" between social and civil rights, this of course does not mean that both types of rights are not closely linked as to their function and their purpose. Social and civil rights belong together as component parts of a unity, of one system of human rights. The parts are each without effect if one of them is enjoyed without the other. Only on the basis of social rights is it meaningful to grant civil and political rights. Therefore it would have been more appropriate, in our opinion, if only one comprehensive Covenant had been made, instead of two.

[78] See for instance H. Schambeck, *op.cit.*, p. 79 ff; Manuchehr Ganji, *International protection of Human Rights* (Geneva-Paris 1962), p. 204; Georges Burdeau, *Les Libertés publics* (3ième ed., Paris 1966), p. 343; Th. Tomandl, *Der Einbau sozialer Grundrechte in das Positive Recht* (Tübingen 1967), p. 6. As far as authors writing in German are concerned, references in support of this view are sometimes made to the theory of the four "status," developed by

of this classic distinction it appears that the difference between social rights and civil rights is in fact a relative one.[79] Relative not only because the difference between action and inaction is relative, but also because there is nothing in the nature of the rights to warrant such a clear-cut division into two types on the basis of State action or abstention. In some cases the granting of what are considered to be civil and political rights implies that the State takes measures, and in some cases the granting of what are considered to be social rights requires State abstention. For example, the Covenant on Civil and Political Rights opens with imposing on the State-Parties the obligation

Georg Jellinek in his "*System der Subjektiven Öffentlichen Rechte*," mentioned above in § 16. Compare e.g. Schambeck, *op.cit.*, p. 25–27, and Tomandl, *op.cit.*, p. 9–10. Also H. von Mangoldt and F. Klein, *Das Bonner Grundgesetz* (2nd. ed., Berlin and Frankfurt a.M. 1957), Vol. I, p. 58–60. In the discussion on article 3 of the Constitution, reproduced below in § 37, these authors remark that the right of the individual to "respect for equality" is a right belonging to the "negative status" (p. 195).

These four "status" that together constitute the whole legal relationship between the individual and the State are distinguished by Jellinek in the following way: first of all there is the "status subiectionis," also called the "passive status," in which the individual performs services for the State. Then follows the "status libertatis" or the "negative status," in which the individual enjoys freedom from the State; it constitutes what Jellinek designates as "eine staatsfreie, das Imperium verneinende Sphäre." Next comes the "status civitatis," also called the "positive status," in which the individual can claim that the State performs services for him. Finally comes the "active status" ("Status der aktiven Zivität"), in which the individual exercises political rights and functions, and is entitled to share in or bear state authority (*op.cit.*, p. 86–87).

The sharp distinction that is made between civil and social rights may in part have been caused by Jellinek's explicit distinctions between these status. Though the division between them was not intended as a historic but rather as a systematic one, they reflect to some extent the historical development of the position of the individual in the Western European state. The authors we mentioned interpret the transition from the "laisser-faire" State to the "social" State for the position of the individual as a transition from the "status libertatis," the "negative status" to the "status civitatis," the "positive status."

As to the equality principle, the classic right to formal legal equality is transformed into a social right to material equality. Tomandl notes this development in particular with respect to the equality principle: "Es sind also vor allem die Freiheitsrechte die den Negativen Status konstituieren. Bei näherem Zusehen erweist sich dagegen das zum klassischen Grundrechtsbestand zählende Gleichheitsrecht als über diesen status libertatis hinausragend und zumindest tendentiell in den positieven Status verweisend ... Solange die Gleichheitsverletzung nur negatorischer Wirkung begegnet, zur blossen Kassation des gleichheitswidrigen Aktes führt, wird die in den positiven Status zielende Richtung der Gleichheitsverbürgung freilich nicht sichtbar; sobald sich aber Tendenzen zeigen, und diese können wir heute deutlich wahrnehmen, den Gleichheitsanspruch nicht nur zur Beseitigung gleichheitsverletzende Regelungen, sondern auch zur Rechtsgrundlage ausgleichender Massnahmen und Regelungen zu verwenden, ist das Gleichheitsrecht bereits im status civitatis angesiedelt und schlägt die Brücke zu den sozialen Grundrechte." (*op.cit.*, p. 9–10). The author refers to several decisions of the German Constitutional Court in support of this view. See also H. F. Zacher, *op.cit.*

[79] See P. Schneider, "Social Rights and the Concept of Human Rights," in D. P. Raphael, ed., *Political Theory and the Rights of Man* (London 1967), p. 81 ff. Schneider states that the connection between "the classical and the modern doctrines of human rights" is not to be "interpreted in the sense of an *antinomy* but in the sense of a *gradual* differentiation" (p. 84; italics in original) See for a similar view also J. van der Hoeven, *De plaats van de Grondwet in het constitutionele Recht* (Zwolle 1958), p. 198.

to undertake the necessary steps to adopt "such legislative or other measures as may be necessary to give effect to the rights recognized" in the Covenant (article 2 (2)). The protection of children (article 24) and juvenile offenders (article 10) may be mentioned. To implement the citizens' right to vote (article 25) likewise requires a complex machinery, and so would at any rate the implementation of the standards set for the functioning of the judiciary, especially in criminal cases (article 14). Schneider remarks that "... one must not overlook the fact that giving effect to freedom of speech, for instance in the domain of television and radio, requires legislation in order to eliminate risks to the formation of opinion from public as well as private quarters." [80]

On the other hand, in some cases the granting of what are considered to be social rights does not call for action but for abstention. A very clear example would be the freedom to form and join trade unions (compare article 8(a) of the Covenant on Economic, Social and Cultural Rights), [81] and the right to strike (article 6(4) of the European Social Charter and article 8(d) of the same Covenant). The right to education, usually formulated as a basic social right [82] has also clear civil rights aspects, as article 13 of the Covenant on Economic, Social and Cultural Rights seems to indicate.

This mixed nature of both social and civil rights has been stressed here in order to show that no sharp division can be based on the amount of public interference for the implementation of a given right as the sole criterion. It is of course true that in general the implementation of social rights will demand more measures than the implementation of civil and political rights; but the difference is gradual. And it is also clear that implementation of the former will generally be more difficult: "... it is easier to *forbid* state measures ... than to *decree* them."[83]

The difference between social rights and civil rights is a gradual one, we contended, at least if it is based on the amount of State action. Consequently there is also only a gradual difference between on the one hand the non-discrimination principle as directed against dis-

[80] Schneider, *op.cit.*, p. 89.

[81] See generally C. W. Jenks, The International Protection of Freedom of Association for Trade Union Purposes (*Receuil des Cours*, Vol. 87, 1955, I, p. 7 ff) and on the ILO Conventions in this field, p. 19–31.

[82] Article 26 Universal Declaration; Article 13 Covenant on Economic, Social and Cultural Rights. In article 13 is said, among other things, that "education shall be directed to the full development of the human personality" and that it "shall strengthen the respect for human rights and fundamental freedoms." Similarly article 26 (2) of the Universal Declaration.

[83] Schneider, *op.cit.*, p. 89. (Italics in original).

crimination in the form of State action, and on the other hand the non-discrimination principle as directed against discrimination in the form of State inaction. Likewise there is only a gradual difference between non-discrimination and protection of minorities. From this point of view it can finally also be submitted that – on the basis of the traditional approach – a close relationship exists in international law between the legal institution of social rights and the legal institution of protection of minorities. Both require more State measures in order to be implemented than their component legal institutions, civil rights and non-discrimination (directed against unequal treatment) respectively.

The connection between non-discrimination and protection of minorities as ways to implement the postulate of "just treatment for all" is not quite clear in the practice of the United Nations' organs that are most directly involved in human rights matters. For example, in the Study "*The Main Types and Causes of Discrimination*" it is concluded from the definitions adopted by the U.N. Sub-Commission on Prevention of Discrimination and Protection of Minorities, that these texts "indicate the fundamental difference between the prevention of discrimination and the protection of minorities." [84] Yet, in the same study the opinion is expressed that both "represent different aspects of the same principle of equality of treatment for all." [85]

The problems involved in this ambiguity and in the practices of the U.N. concerning the relations between both forms will be dealt with later in more detail. [86] We shall then discuss the question whether there is between them indeed a high degree of similarity as we would assert, or a "fundamental difference."

34. Non-discrimination

What is meant by "non-discrimination," such as it is used in previous paragraphs, follows from the way we described "discrimination." Non-discrimination implies that aspects of equality and inequality are fully taken into account, and carefully weighed against each other in the light of the specific right involved, in such a way that the sufficient connection is established. As indicated above, the scrutiny can have varying degrees of strictness. And also, what would satisfy the test of the "sufficient connection" in one field of international law, might

[84] Paragraph 6 of that Study.
[85] Paragraph 9 *ibidem*.
[86] See below, § 60.

fail to do so in another. Whether the sufficient connection is established or not can be determined in a variety of ways. But even apart from that it seems fruitless to attempt to formulate in advance and *in abstracto* specific forms of "wrong" and specific standards for each field: one for trade, one for shipping, one for aliens, one for alien property, one for human beings as such, and so on.

In some instances an international regulation contains more or less precise criteria which facilitate the examination whether the sufficient connection can be established or not. For example, whereas articleI(a) of the I.M.C.O. Convention forbids discrimination in international shipping, article I (b) runs in part as follows:

"Assistance and encouragement given by a Government for the development of its national shipping and for purpose of security does not in itself constitute discrimination, provided that such assistance and encouragement is not based on measures designed to restrict the freedom of shipping of all flags to take part in international trade ..."

As a very complicated example we could also mention the General Agreement on Tariffs and Trade, which has the elimination of trade discriminations among its principal objectives, but spells out various froms of trade inequalities that are not regarded as discrimination: "The rule of non-discrimination ... embodied in GATT is a complex one, involving an interplay between the general principle and a mosaic of exceptions for various purposes." [87] And to return to the field of human rights: Sections (2) and (3) of article I of the International Convention on the Elimination of All Forms of Racial Discrimination (1965) run as follows:

(2) "This Convention shall not apply to distinctions, exclusions, restrictions of preferences made by a State Party to this Convention between citizens and non-citizens.

(3) Nothing in the Convention may be interpreted as affecting in any way the legal provisions of States Parties concerning nationality, citizenship or naturalization, provided that such provisions do not discriminate against any particular nationality."

These sections of this Convention, taken as a whole, cannot be understood otherwise than as implying that a governmental policy, based upon racial distinctions and directed against aliens and immigrants *in spe* on account of their race, is one of the "All Forms" of racial

[87] John H. Jackson, *World Trade and the Law of GATT. A Legal Analysis of the GATT* (Indianapolis etc., 1969), p. 264.

discrimination (as we will call it anyhow) not covered by this Convention, and excluded from its notion of "discrimination." A "sufficient connection" is seen between aspects of racial differences and unfavourable legal inequalities in matters of alienage and immigration.

The U.N. study *"The main Types and Causes of Discrimination"* contains a paragraph devoted to "legitimate distinctions which do not constitute discrimination," in which it is said that

> "Many distinctions, established by law, do not constitute discrimination because they are established on just grounds and apply to all alike, not merely to members of certain particular social groups. Examples of these include
> (a) Legal incompetence due to minority, to criminality, to insanity, or to absence from the country;
> (b) Restriction of liberty in virtue of lawful arrest or conviction;
> (c) Denial of political rights to foreigners;
> (d) Lawful expropriation with fair indemnity;
> (e) Diplomatic immunities;
> (f) Inviolability and immunities of members of Parliament, etc." [88]

This paragraph concludes with the remark that the list is not intended to be exhaustive. And indeed, it could be made much longer. It is interesting that in the passage quoted especially "just grounds" are mentioned, on which in general detrimental unequal treatment may be based. These "just grounds" can be contrasted with the human attributes on which detrimental unequal treatment may not be based, such as "race," "sex," "language," and "religion," which grounds are mentioned several times in the Charter as forbidden grounds for differentiation. The next chapter (V) will be devoted to a discussion of grounds of this character. It will appear that in some cases even on these forbidden grounds detrimental unequal treatment may nevertheless be based. This may for example occur in situations to which "special measures of protection" are applicable, such as are explicitly provided for in Article 5 of the Discrimination (Employment and Occupation) Convention, and Article 1 (4) of the Convention on the Elimination of All Forms of Racial Discrimination. These provisions will be dealt with later (see § 57), but they must be mentioned here within the context of this paragraph on "non-discrimination," since they represent a few more instances of treaty regulations that directly concern the question as to the possibility of establishing a sufficient connection – even on "forbidden grounds."

[88] § 126.

35. *Treaty Definitions*

"Discrimination" can be declared undesirable by a rule of general international law; it can be forbidden by a rule of general international law; it can also be forbidden by a specific non-discrimination clause. We described discrimination in order to indicate how we think it should be understood when the term is used in a treaty, a judgment or any other international legal document. There are also special conventions that are devoted to the elimination of discrimination in particular fields. These treaties are the Convention concerning Discrimination in Respect of Employment and Occupation and the Convention against Discrimination in Education. The international abhorrence caused by discriminatory practices based on racial differences led to the unanimous adoption by the General Assembly of the United Nations of the International Convention on the Elimination of All Forms of Racial Discrimination. These three Conventions contain each a definition of discrimination; though the validity of such a definition is explicitly limited to the purposes of each Convention, these definitions may of course be important for our discussion of the problem in general. We reproduce them accordingly.

Article 1 (1) of the I.L.O. Discrimination (Employment and Occupation) Convention runs as follows:[89]

"For the purpose of this Convention the term "discrimination' includes:
a) any distinction, exclusion or preference made on the basis of race, colour, sex, religion, political opinion, national extraction or social origin, which has the effect of nullifying or impairing equality of opportunity or treatment in employment or occupation;
b) such other distinction, exclusion or preference which has the effect of nullifying or impairing equality of opportunity or treatment in employment or occupation as may be determined by the Member concerned after consul tation with representative employers' and workers' organisations, where such exist, and with other appropriate bodies."

Article 1 (1) of the Convention Against Discrimination in Education[90] runs as follows:

"For the purposes of this Convention, the term 'discrimination' includes any distinction, exclusion, limitation or preference which, being based on race, colour, sex, language, religion, political or other opinion, national or social origin, economic condition or birth, has the purpose or effect of nullifying or impairing equality of treatment in education and in particular:

[89] Text in *U.N.T.S.*, Vol. 362, p. 31 ff.
[90] Text in *U.N.T.S.*, Vol. 429, p. 9 ff.

a) Of depriving any person or group of persons of access to education of any type or at any level;
b) Of limiting any person or group of persons to education of an inferior standard;
c) Subject to the provision of Article 2 of this Convention, of establishing or maintaining separate educational systems or institutions for persons or groups of persons; or
d) Of inflicting on any person or group of persons conditions which are incompatible with the dignity of man."

Article 1 (1) of the Convention on the Elimination of All Forms of Racial Discrimination runs as follows:

"In this Convention, the term 'racial discrimination' shall mean any distinction, exclusion, restriction or preference based on race, colour, descent, or national or ethnic origin which has the purpose or effect of nullifying or impairing the recognition, enjoyment or exercise, on an equal footing, of human rights and fundamental freedoms in the political, economic, social, cultural or any other field of public life."

36. Forbidden Grounds for Differentiation

One feature of these provisions is especially interesting: the listing of a certain number of specific human attributes on which the "distinctions," "exclusions," "limitations" or "preferences" may not be based. This is a characteristic that these treaty definitions share with the non-discrimination clauses in other recent human rights instruments.

The "sufficient connection" of our definition may be found lacking for various reasons, each of them representing a form of "wrong."Legal inequalities are based on human inequalities; it may be that the human attribute in question is deemed to be without social relevance (the well-known example of the red hair and the blue eyes). Or the right may be considered to be so basic that its enjoyment may not be denied to anyone, on any grounds (life). Or it may be that the human attribute in question is excluded (politically, morally, or legally, e.g. by a higher rule of law) as a ground for unequal treatment. Such an attribute may be for instance race, sex, language or religion. The non-discrimination clauses in recent human rights conventions usually contain quite a catalogue of such forbidden grounds for differentiation. This legislative technique reduces considerably the rather indeterminate character of our concept of discrimination, especially of the "sufficient connection" element in it. This is so because it can be said that generally on such forbidden grounds a sufficient connection cannot be established.

PART TWO

V. NON-DISCRIMINATION CLAUSES IN HUMAN RIGHTS CONVENTIONS

37. Forbidden Grounds for Differentiation (continued)

In this Chapter we intend to examine the various aspects of the elaborate non-discrimination clauses which appear in some conventions and documents on the international protection of human rights such as the Universal Declaration of Human Rights (1948), the European Convention on Human Rights and Fundamental Freedoms (1950), and the recent International Covenant on Civil and Political Rights, and the Covenant on Economic, Social and Cultural Rights (1966). The non-discrimination clause of the Covenant on Civil and Political Rights (article 26) is reproduced in full here as an example:

"All persons are equal before the law and are entitled without any discrimination to the equal protection of the law. In this respect, the law shall prohibit any discrimination and guarantee to all persons equal and effective protection against discrimination on any ground such as race, colour, sex, language, religion, political or other opinion, national or social origin, property, birth or other status."

Our attention will first of all be directed chiefly to what we referred to in the previous paragraph as "forbidden grounds for differentiation."[1]

The technique of spelling out some specific grounds on the basis of which differentiations are not allowed is not a new one, nor is it exclusively an international one.[2] In fact, if a certain type of unequal

[1] In a more sociological terminology these grounds have been called the "pretexts for prejudice" (*The Main Types and Causes of Discrimination*, § 58).

[2] Compare Article 3 (3) of the German Grundgesetz, which runs as follows: "No one may be prejudiced or favoured because of his sex, his parentage, his race, his language, his homeland and origin, his faith, or his religious or political opinions." (Text in Peaslee, *Constitutions of Nations*, Vol. III, The Hague 1968, p. 362). Article 15 (1) of the Indian Constitution lays down that "The State shall not discriminate against any citizen on grounds only of religion, race, caste, sex, place of birth or any of them." (Peaslee, *op.cit.*, Vol. II/1, p. 308). The Fifteenth Amendment to the Constitution of the United States runs in part: "The right ... of the Citizens of the United States to vote shall not be denied or abridged by the United States

treatment is likely to occur within a given society, but held to be wrong, it is only natural to forbid that precisely that type of differentiation be introduced into the law.

In a time when international law was not as "egalitarian" as it is nowadays, apart from the treatment of aliens it was religious inequality that was deemed the most undesirable form of unequal treatment within a society (or rather, this was the only form of unequal treatment deemed undesirable). Thus we find in some early treaties concern for the unequal treatment of individuals on the basis of religion. Since the beginning of the seventeenth century religion was a matter of utmost importance in European politics (Thirty years' War). Mandelstam[3] takes the Peace of Westphalia as the starting point. Also earlier dates are given; Wintgens[4] goes back to the Religious Peace of Nuremberg (23 July, 1532), one of the oldest examples mentioned.But Schindler[5] asserts that the Peace Treaty of Oliva, concluded in 1660 between Sweden and Poland is the first example worth mentioning: Catholic Poland ceded Livonia to protestant Sweden which undertook to quarantee to the population of the ceded territory the freedom to practice its faith. In the English translation article IV (2) of this Treaty runs as follows:

"As for what appertains to the Catholick Religion and the Exercise of it in *Swedish Livonia,* all the inhabitants and Subjects of *Livonia,* who are of that Religion, shall enjoy all manner of Security and Liberty of Conscience, and shall privately use their own Religion and Worship at home, without Examination and Animadversion." [6]

Religion did not stay the only human characteristic barred as a basis for unequal treatment; the number of such grounds has grown considerably since then. In the Treaty of Paris (1856) the "Christian" Powers of Europe made Turkey pledge to guarantee religious freedom to all its nationals. Article 8 of the decree ("Hatti-Humajun") states:

"Tout mot et toute expression ou appellation tendant à rendre une classe de mes sujets inférieure à l'autre, à raison du *culte,* de la *langue* ou de la *race* sont à jamais abolies du protocole administratif." [7]

or by any State on account of race, colour, or previous condition of servitude." Modern federal legislation in the United States, such as the Civil Rights Act (1964), mentions race, color, religion, sex and national origin (compare e.g. Title II, Section 201 (a), and Title VII, Section 703).

[3] A. N. Mandelstam, "La Protection Internationale des Minorités," *Recueil des Cours,* Vol. I (1923), p. 369 ff.

[4] H. Wintgens, *Der völkerrechtliche Schutz der nationalen, sprachlichen und religiösen Minderheiten* (Stuttgart, 1930) p. 67. See for many more examples up to the first World War, pp. 61–99.

[5] *Op.cit.* p. 104–105.

[6] Text in *Consolidated Treaty Series* (Parry, ed.), Vol. 6 (1660–1661), p. 10 ff., at p. 68.

[7] Wintgens, *op.cit.*, p. 77. Italics added.

These three grounds remained the only ones for a long period which ended with the outbreak of the Second World War. The international concern for group protection had its culmination point under the League of Nations in the international protection of *national, linguistic* and *religious* minorities in Europe after the First World War. Thus the treaty concluded on 28 June 1919 between the "Principle Allied and Associated Powers" and Poland on the protection of minorities in Poland, which served as a model for the later treaties on the protection of minorities lays down in article 7 (1):

"All Polish nationals shall be equal before the law and shall enjoy the same civil and political rights without distinction as to *race, language* and *religion.*"

And article 2 states that Poland shall assure all inhabitants protection of life and liberty "without distinction of *birth, nationality, language, race* or *religion.*"

In the Charter of the United Nations the formula "human rights and fundamental freedoms for all without distinction as to *race, sex, language* and *religion*" appears no less than four times.[8] From the Charter till the International Covenants on Economic, Social and Cultural Rights, and on Civil and Political Rights, concluded in 1966, the number of forbidden grounds has increased to the twelve we find respectively in articles 2(2) and 26 of these Covenants. And in the meantime three more weapons were forged for the battle against discrimination, two against discrimination in specific fields: employment[9] and education,[10] and one against discrimination based upon one particular ground: race.[11]

As to the grounds that can be found besides the four that appear in the Charter, article 2 of the Universal Declaration mentions (besides race, sex, language and religion) also colour, political or other opinion, national or social origin, property, birth or other status. Article 14 of the European Convention on Human Rights mentions all these, and adds "association with a national minority." Article 1, 1(a) of the Discrimination (Employment and Occupation) Convention contains the following: race, colour, sex, religion, political opinion, and national

[8] Articles 1, 13, 55 and 76.

[9] Discrimination (Employment and Occupation) Convention, 1958 (I.L.O. Convention no. 111).

[10] Convention against Discrimination in Education (adopted by the General Conference of UNESCO, 1960).

[11] International Convention on the Elimination of All Forms of Racial Discrimination (1965).

extraction or social origin, thus omitting language, property, birth or other status, and "other opinion." The Convention on the Elimination of all Forms of Racial Discrimination is limited to race and colour, and adds to these: "descent," and "national or ethnic origin" (article 1(1)). The grounds listed in the Covenant on Economic Social and Cultural Rights (article 2(2)), and on Civil and Political Rights (article 26) are identical to those of the Universal Declaration. In the following paragraphs some aspects of these grounds must be discussed: first, the meaning of the terms themselves, and what they stand for. And second, the legal relevance of these grounds, the function they have in the non-discrimination clauses in which they figure; and also, the possible role they play with regard to the concept of discrimination in general.

38. The Grounds of the Charter

The Charter of the United Nations mentions four grounds: race, sex, language and religion ("Charter grounds"). On the basis of these the grounds of Article 2 of the Universal Declaration[12]) were introduced ("additional grounds"); and it is after this provision that the non-discrimination clauses of later human rights conventions were copied.[13] Thus, apart from the Charter provisions, article 2 of the Universal Declaration is of prime importance for an investigation into the meaning of each of the grounds. It is obvious that some of them, though intended to clarify, are by no means very clear themselves. The *travaux préparatoires* may yield information as to their intended meanings.

During the drafting of the United Nations Charter at the Conference in San Francisco, May-June, 1945, many States submitted a great number of proposals concerning the protection of human rights. In the Dumbarton Oaks proposal itself it was only stated that "the Organization should (...) promote respect for human rights and fundamental freedoms."[14] The typical Charter formula "without distinction as to race, sex, language or religion" can be traced back to such proposals as the one submitted by Brazil, the Dominican Republic and Mexico.

[12] "Everyone is entitled to all the rights and freedoms set forth in this Declaration, without distinction of any kind, such as race, colour, sex, language, religion, political or other opinion, national or social origin, property, birth or other status."

[13] See also F. Ermacora, *Diskriminierungsschutz und Diskriminierungsverbot in der Arbeit der Vereinten Nationen* (Wien and Stuttgart, 1971).

[14] Ch. IX, Section A, 1. *Documents of the United Nations Conference on International Organization* (*UNCIO*), Vol. 3, p. 2-23.

These States proposed "the inclusion under Chapter I, Purposes, at any appropriate point, of the following paragraph:

"To ensure respect for human rights and fundamental freedoms, without discrimination against race, sex, condition, or creed."[15]

Most important in this respect was of course the joint amendment proposed by the governments of the United States, the United Kingdom, the Soviet Union and China, which was to become Article 1, Section 3 of the Charter after a few minor modifications. This amendment runs in part as follows:
The purposes of the Organization are...

"... promotion and encouragement of respect for human rights and fundamental freedoms for all without distinction as to race, language, religion or sex; ..."[16]

Especially some Latin-American States had been dissatisfied with the amount of attention given to the international protection of human rights in the Dumbarton Oaks proposal. At the Inter-American Conference on Problems of War and Peace of the Organization of American States (Mexico City, Chapultepec), February-March 1945, resolutions had been passed concerning the protection of human rights, proclaiming among other principles the abolishment of discrimination based on sex, race or religion.[17] On the basis of these developments these States took further action for the adoption of human rights provisions in San Francisco.

39. Charter Grounds: "Race"

In an Advisory Opinion of the Permanent Court of International Justice concerning minority-problems the Court employs the expression "the German race."[18] The term "race" had been introduced earlier, in articles 2 and 7 of the Polish minorities Treaty. "Race" was

[15] *UNCIO*-Documents, Vol. 3, p. 602.

[16] *UNCIO*-Documents, Vol. 6, p. 555. The same four States proposed similar amendments to what was to become Article 13 (*UNCIO*-documents, Vol. 10, p. 302), and to what was to become article 55 (ibidem, p. 305). On the basis of an American amendment the non-discrimination clause was added to (now) article 76 (*UNCIO*-documents, Vol. 10, p. 513).

[17] See Ruth B. Russell and J. E. Muther, *A History of the United Nations Charter; The Role of the United States 1940–1945* (Washington 1958), p. 567–569. In the proposal by Brazil, the Dominican Republic and Mexico reference was made to the Final Act of the Inter-American Conference.

[18] "The outstanding, fundamental point in the present case is the fact that the persons whose rights are now in question are as a class persons of the German race who settled in the lands ..." *Series* B, No. 6 (German Settlers in Poland, 1923), p. 24.

used in these instances to designate what otherwise was referred to as a "national" minority. The adjective "national" does of course not relate to the "nationality" of the minorities in the technical, legal sense. "Nation" refers to a group of people who through the combination of subjective factors (national consciousness) and a number of objective factors (a common language, religion, ethnic origin, history, and so on, in short: a common "culture") feel that they are different (and are regarded as different) from other such groups.[19] This implies that the characteristics that turn a community into a "nation" are much more complex than "race," and include such factors as "language," "religion," and "culture". With respect to the international protection of minorities under the League of Nations, no clear views prevailed as to what elements constituted a national minority. It is clear that, for instance, the German settlers in Poland were not regarded as first of all belonging to a different "race."

"Race" might not even have been an independent element at all in whatever made up a "national" minority: there was a consensus to the effect that "culture," including especially "language" were the most important (objective) factors. There was much more to a "national" minority than just a difference in "race."[20] In the study "*The Main Types and Causes of Discrimination*" it is observed: "While the concept of race as a definite human group appears illegitimate from the scientific standpoint, the concept of people or nation expresses a historical and sociological reality. This concept, however, is not based on natural factors, but rather on culture. A nation includes a great variety of physical and mental types, but it usually presents a relative unity in cultural heritage."[21]

Although in the minority treaties the term "race" was employed, such as in articles 2 and 7 of the Polish treaty, the notorious example in international politics after the First World War where it was felt that a truly *racial* equality was at stake was the Japanese proposal, made at the Peace Conferences in Paris in 1919, to insert in the Covenant of the League of Nations the following provision:

[19] Compare on this enormously complicated problem for example Oscar I. Janowsky, *Nationalities and National Minorities* (New York 1945) and especially C. A. Macartney, *National States and National Minorities* (1934), Chapters I–IV.

[20] See besides the authors mentioned in the previous footnote also e.g. Tore Modeen, *The International Protection of National Minorities in Europe* (Abo, 1969), Ch. I; Inis L. Claude, *National Minorities, An International Problem* (Cambridge, Mass., 1955), Introduction.

[21] *The Main Types and Causes of Discrimination*, § 63.

"The equality of Nations being a basic principle of the League of Nations, the High Contracting Parties agree to accord, as soon as possible, to all alien nationals of States members of the League, equal and just treatment in every respect, making no distinction, either in law or in fact, on account of their race or nationality."[22]

Though the equality envisaged was not even to be granted as between the nationals of the negotiating States, this proposal caused a profound embarrassment at the Conference. It was finally rejected, even in the later form of a harmless phrase that was to be inserted in the Preamble of the Covenant.[23]

"Race" as the single ground for "unfavourable unequal treatment" was pre-eminently the practice in National Socialist Germany. No other minority characteristics were taken into account; and no characteristics of assimilation could push aside the "race" factor.

After the Second World War, the drafters of the Charter of the United Nations employed the term "race" four times in this document. Since the Organization undertook to promote the international protection of human rights in a large part also as a reaction against the atrocities during the Second World War and the period immediately preceding it,[24] it can readily be assumed that in the terminology of the Charter the term "race" is used in the same biological sense as it was in the National-Socialist ideology before and during the War. It could no longer stand for a complex total of interdependent factors which made up a "national minority," as had been the case in the decade that followed the First World War. And as if to consolidate this terminological change article 2 of the Universal Declaration mentions "national origin" as a separate ground, while Article 27 of the Covenant of Civil and Political Rights speaks not of "national," but of "ethnic" minorities.

To this biological concept of "race" several studies have been devoted, especially under the auspices of UNESCO.[25] A UNESCO committee of experts on race problems found the following definition of "race": it "designates a group or population characterized by some concentrations, relative as to frequency and distribution, of hereditary particles

[22] David Hunter Miller, *The Drafting of the Covenant* (New York, 1928), Vol. I, p. 183. "Nationality" in this provision refers to the technical, legal concept.

[23] See for Miller's account of the unfortunate history of this proposal, *op.cit.*, Vol. I, p. 461–466, and Vol. II, p. 323–325, 387–392.

[24] E. Schwelb, *Human Rights and the International Community* (Chicago 1964), p. 24–25.

[25] See the *Special Study on Racial Discrimination in the Political, Economic, Social and Cultural Spheres*, by Hernán Santa Cruz, Special Rapporteur on Racial Discrimination; Doc. E/CN.4/Sub 2/307/Rev. 1 (1971), p. 11–13.

(genes) or physical characters, which appear, fluctuate, and often disappear in the course of time by reason of geographic and/or cultural isolation."[26]

In the United Nations "race" is meant in the biological sense of ethnic origin, and while it is made clear that "race" is not relevant as a biological concept, let alone as a scientific one, it is at the same time stressed that it is as a social concept that it causes problems in social relations:

"The human problems arising from so-called 'race' relations are social in origin rather than biological. A basic problem is racism, namely antisocial beliefs and acts which are based on the fallacy that discriminatory inter-group relations are justifiable on biological grounds."[27]

Thus, while on the one hand the concept of "race" is declared doubtful if not completely without substance, it has, on the other hand, to function at the same time as the main forbidden ground for differentiation in international conventions.[28]
Apart from a few exceptions – such as Jews in countries in Western and Eastern Europe, Chinese in several Asiatic countries – the racial factor that plays the main role in social relations is the colour of the skin.[29] The Convention on the Elimination of All Forms of Racial Discrimination mentions as factors that can be considered as included in the concept of race also: "colour," "descent," "national origin," and "ethnic origin."[30] It seems that with these grounds all the possible bases on which racial discrimination can be practiced are sufficiently covered.

40. Charter Grounds: "Sex"

"Sex" as a forbidden ground for differentiation is a relatively recent development in international humanitarian law. At the Sixth Conference of the Organization of American States (Havana, 1928) an Inter-American Commission of Women was constituted. The main legal

[26] UNESCO, *Statement on Race* (18 July 1950) § 4. Also referred to in the Study mentioned in the previous note, at p. 11.

[27] UNESCO, *Statement on Race and Racial Prejudice* (26 September 1967) § 4.

[28] Compare the remarks on this somewhat embarrassing paradox that were made by various representatives in the Commission on Human Rights on the draft of article 26 of the Covenant on Civil and Political Rights: E/CN.4/SR. 172 and 173, *passim*.

[29] On "Colour" see below, § 44.

[30] In Article 1 of the Convention, reproduced above, in § 35. See further Egon Schwelb, "The Convention on the Elimination of All Forms of Racial Discrimination," in *International and Comparative Law Quarterly*, Vol. 15 (1966), p. 996 ff.

outcome of the activities of this Commission was the adoption of two conventions at the Ninth Conference (Bogotá, 1948): the Inter-American Convention to Grant Political Rights to Women, ratified by seven Latin American States, and the Inter-American Convention to Grant Civil Rights to Women, ratified by nine States.[31] We mention these (Latin-) American developments because during the drafting of the Charter some Latin-American States were also particularly active in promoting women's rights.

In general (as contrasted to regional) international law "sex" was introduced as a forbidden ground for differentiation through the formula adopted in the Charter. Unlike race, language and religion it did not play a role in the international protection of minorities, nor did it figure in any of the older non-discrimination clauses. It can be said that the principle of non-discrimination on the basis of sex has been "a particular preoccupation of the United Nations."[32] Apart from the human rights clauses, also Article 8 of the Charter is to be mentioned as an affirmation of that principle. In San Francisco, Brazil, the Dominican Republic and Mexico proposed at one point to insert into the draft of (now) article 59 the following words:

"... and promote respect for human rights and fundamental freedoms and foster the democratic principle of equality of status, opportunity, and responsibility for men and women. Responsibility for the discharge of this function ... etc ...."[33]

This did not materialize; more successful was the Brazilian proposal to

"set up a special commission of women to study conditions and prepare reports on the political, civil and economic status and opportunity of women with special reference to discrimination and limitations placed upon them on account of their sex."[34]

This proposal resulted in the establishment within the Commission on Human Rights of a Sub-Commission on the Status of Women, which

[31] Both conventions contain only one operative provision; the Convention on Political Rights reads as follows:

"The High Contracting Parties agree that the right to vote and to be elected to national office shall not be denied or abridged by reason of sex."

The Convention on Civil Rights lays down that:

"The American States agree to grant to women the same civil rights that men enjoy."

See: *Convention on the Political Rights of Women, History and Commentary*. U.N. doc. ST/SOA/27 (1955), p. 3–5.

[32] Max Sørensen, "The Quest for Equality," p. 311.

[33] *UNCIO*-Documents, Vol. 3, p. 603.

[34] *UNCIO*-Documents, Vol. 8, p. 77; Vol. 10, p. 212–214.

shortly thereafter was made a functional Commission under the Economic and Cultural Council.[35]

In the second meeting of Commission II, June 11, 1945, at San Francisco, Dr. Bertha Lutz of the Brazilian delegation referred to "the amendment submitted by Brazil, Uruguay, Mexico and Santo Domingo jointly "at the request of the women of these delegations."[36] Miss Lutz called this amendment "the first mention of the basic rights of all human beings, regardless of race, creed or sex." She continued: "The fact that Field Marshall Smuts (the President of the Commission) also included the equality of men and women before the law in the Preamble,[37] and the magnificent support that we Latin American women have had from the men on all delegations, show that the world is thinking along these lines of elementary justice."[38]

The main legal achievements of the Commission on the Status of Women have been the adoption by the General Assembly of the Convention on the political Rights of Women, in 1952[39], and the adoption of the Convention on Consent to Marriage, Minimum Age for Marriage and Registration of Marriages, in 1962.[40] To these texts an important document was added as the General Assembly unanimously adopted the elaborate Declaration on the Elimination of Discrimination against Women in 1967.[41]

41. Charter Grounds: "Language"

In the protection of "national" minorities under the League of Nations language as distinctive factor was usually recognized as important but yet secundary. Language was regarded as the expression of nationality, and hardly or not as an independent characteristic of a group. Few groups were thought of as linguistic minorities without first of all being national minorities.[42] Language was rather one of the main

[35] See *U.N. Yearbook of Human Rights 1947*, p. 426–428; *Yearbook of the U.N. 1946–1947*, p. 528–531.

[36] See p. 87; the mentioning of Uruguay must be a mistake since this State is not named in any of the joint amendments involved.

[37] See the Preamble of the Charter of the U.N., § 2.

[38] *UNCIO*-Documents, Vol. 8, p. 57–58. See also the statements by the Australian representative, *ibidem*, p. 60.

[39] Entered into force on 7 July 1954, Text in U.N. *Yearbook of Human Rights* 1952, p. 375 ff. and *U.N.T.S.*, Vol. 193, p. 135 ff.

[40] Entered into force on 7 November 1962. Text in U.N. *Yearbook of Human Rights* 1962, p. 389 ff. and in *U.N.T.S.*, Vol. 521, p. 231 ff.

[41] Res. 2263 (XXII); text in *Yearbook of the United Nations 1967*, p. 521 f.

[42] Compare e.g. Wintgens, *op.cit.* p. 19, note 77.

factors on the basis of which it was to be ascertained whether or not an individual belonged to, or a group of individuals constituted, a national minority. Thus, article 9 of the Treaty between Austria and Czechoslovakia of 7 July 1920 runs as follows: "Les mots "par la race et la langue" veulent indiquer qu'en général, dans la pratique, c'est principalement la langue qui soit être prise en considération comme le signe le plus démonstratif du lien national (Volkszugehörigkeit)." [43]

As to the precise meaning of the term "language," however, in most minority-treaties no further indications were given concerning the language that was to be protected. From the fact that the language was protected as an element of the distinct culture of the minority, it may be concluded that only for the language that served as such the protection could be claimed; e.g. as the official language of instruction in the schools of the minority. This is of course of prime importance since languages directly affected the rights concerning minority education. [44] It would seem that the same consideration is valid for whatever similar cases to which the post-war non-discrimination clauses which mention "language" may be applicable.

The principle of non-discrimination on the ground of language, as far as it concerns individual persons instead of a national minority as a whole, is in many cases not applicable or without effect. Compare for example the case of an individual who speaks a language different from the one spoken by the people among whom he resides. His language is likely to cause "unfavourable unequal treatment" because it disqualifies him for a great many professions; and in most cases there will be a justification for this exclusion. It is not by accident that the non-discrimination clauses of U.N. Staff Regulation 4.3 and article 27 (2) of the "Statut des Fonctionnaires" of the European Communities, reproduced above in § 13, omit "language" from the four grounds mentioned in the Charter. A certain number of languages must be represented in the Secretariat of any international organization.

We conclude that "language" as a forbidden ground for discrimination is necessarily of limited significance. Whenever it involves the language of a group it is in most cases a secondary group-characteristic after nationality, expressing national characteristics rather than constituting them. [45] Whenever it involves the language spoken by

[43] Wintgens, *ibidem*.

[44] See on the connection between language and education also article 9 of the Polish Minorities Treaty (1919).

[45] Compare a relatively recent instrument such as the Agreement between Austria and Italy of 5 September 1946 concerning the German minorities in the Bolzano and Trento

an individual who lives among people speaking a different language, in most cases social or economic inequalities will be sufficiently connected with the linguistic difference.

The only clear cases are, it seems, offered by States in which different linguistic groups live together without constituting "national minorities" in the proper sense in which this term is employed in the protection of minorities. This may be so because none of these linguistic groups has a cultural preponderance or constitutes a clear numerical majority, or because the State in which they live has an appropriate federal structure. As examples we could mention Belgium, and Switzerland. In the *Belgian "linguistic" case,* decided by the European Court of Human Rights in 1968, we find such an instance of discrimination on the ground of language – as was alleged by the appellants and found by the Court – without there being involved individual qualifications or minority rights.

42. Charter Grounds: "Religion"

As we shortly discussed above in § 37, to prevent discrimination for reasons of religion is one of the oldest humanitarian concerns of the (European) international community.[46] The fact that religious beliefs tend, at least often tended, to dominate the whole social and political outlook of communities with moral and political claims of absolute validity, made protecting measures necessary, particularly in this respect.

Non-discrimination on the basis of religion is meaningful for religious minorities. The relationship that usually exists between the identity of a population group as a separate nationality and the language it speaks, is usually not as close where the relation between nationality and religion is involved. Therefore religious minorities do occur that are not at the same time also national (and linguistic) minorities.

There is also a difference between "religion" and "language" as far as the protection of individuals is concerned. Unlike linguistic differences, religious differences are much less likely to have a sufficient connection with the social and economic relations from which the

Provinces, which contains "special provisions to safeguard the ethnical character and the cultural and economic development of the German-speaking element," and which refers to the language as the only minority characteristic. Text in *U.N.T.S.* Vol. 49, p. 184–185.

[46] See generally Th. C. van Boven, *De Volkenrechtelijke Bescherming van de Godsdienstvrijheid* (Assen 1967).

"unfavourable unequal treatment" of the individual is to be eliminated. In fact, it seems that only in clearly religious matters social relevance can be attached to religious differences. The interdiction of discrimination on the basis of religion apparently intends to bar religious considerations from the public life except the fields which involve religion itself.[47] From this it can also be concluded that "religion" is not meant in the sense of purely internal religious convictions, but of socially perceptible religious practices and utterances. And also not only manifestations in an institutionalized form by groups, but by private individuals as well.[48]

As to the meaning of the term "religion" before the War, indications can be found in the protection of minorities, where the emphasis was put on the religion of the groups.[49] This excluded consideration of questions related to religious matters such as the possibility of discrimination particularly on account of agnostic or atheistic convictions, both of individuals and of groups. In this respect the articles 18 of the Universal Declaration of Human Rights and of the Covenant on Civil and Political Rights point at a broader notion of religion (or "religion or belief") than it has in its original sense: these provisions speak of a freedom of "thought, conscience and religion." Finally, the notion "religion" has been given its most recent interpretation within the system of humanitarian law as developed by United Nations bodies and affiliated organizations in the draft Convention on the Elimination of All Forms of Religious Intolerance, which is before the General Assembly for approval.[50] For the purposes of this Convention, according to its first Article, the expression "religion or belief" includes "theistic, non-theistic and atheistic beliefs."

[47] Thus, in the United States, we find in Title VII of the Civil Rights Act (1964) which is aimed against discrimination in employment, including discrimination on the basis of religion, section 702 which reads in part: "This title shall not apply to ... a religious corporation, association, or society with respect to the employment of individuals of a particular religion to perform work connected with the carrying on by such corporation, association, or society of its religious activities, or to an educational institution with respect to the employment of individuals to perform work connected with the educational activities of such institution."

[48] Compare the *Study of Discrimination in the Matter of Religious Rights and Practices* (U.N. Doc. E/CN.4/Sub.2/200/Rev. 1 (1960), Arcot Krishnaswami, Special Rapporteur), p. 20 ff., 29 ff.

[49] Compare e.g. article 8 of the Polish Minorities Treaty.

[50] Text in *Yearbook of the United Nations 1967*, p. 491 ff. The title of this draft Convention has been changed to "Draft Covenant on the Elimination of All Forms of Intolerance and of Discrimination Based on Religion or Belief." See the Note by the Secretary-General on *Elimination of All Forms of Religious Intolerance*, of 6 July, 1971 (A/8330).

43. Additional Grounds, General Remarks

The Universal Declaration of Human Rights has originated from a Declaration, originally drafted by a Committee of the Commission on Human Rights with the assistance of and on the basis of materials collected by the Secretariat of the United Nations. A great number of proposals and suggestions were provided for by members of the Organization, international organizations and several private bodies.[51] As to the forbidden grounds, the non-discrimination clause of the original draft prepared by professor Cassin[52] contained the four Charter grounds to which "opinions" was added (article 6).[53] However, at the request of the American member of the drafting Committee, (Mrs. E. Roosevelt), this ground was deleted;[54] the United States policy was to stick to the four Charter grounds.[55] The clause was put before the Sub-Commission on Prevention of Discrimination and Protection of Minorities, in the following form:

"Everyone is entitled to the rights and freedoms set forth in this Declaration without distinction as to race, sex, language, or religion."[56]

The Sub-Commission added several grounds again: besides the understanding that "race" also included "colour" it added "political or other opinion," "property status" and "national or social origin." This version of the Sub-Commission[57] was adopted by the Working Group on the Declaration on Human Rights of the Commission on Human Rights.[58] In the Commission itself, the Indian delegate proposed – as the Indian member of the Sub-Commission had done earlier – to insert "colour" after "race;" this proposal was adopted.[59] The Commission also added in the course of its deliberations the words

[51] On the drafting on the Declaration, see e.g. René Cassin, "La déclaration universelle et la mise en oeuvre des droits de l'Homme," *Recueil des Cours* Vol. 79 (1951, II), p. 237 ff, at p. 273 ff, and A. Verdoodt, *Naissance et Signification de la Déclaration universelle des droits de l'Homme* (Louvain and Paris, 1964); see p. 35 ff., especially p. 84 ff.

[52] A detailed account of the first stages of the drafting is contained in the Report of the Drafting Committee to the Commission on Human Rights, E/CN.4/21 (1 July, 1947).

[53] E/CN.4/21, Annex D, p. 51.

[54] E/CN.4/21, Annex F, p. 74; Verdoodt, *op.cit.*, p. 87.

[55] E/CN.4/AC 2/SR.9, p. 6, 10; similarly Belgium: E/CN.4/Sub.2/SR.4, p. 12.

[56] E/CN.4/52, p. 4.

[57] "Everyone is entitled to all the rights and freedoms set forth in this Declaration, without distinction of any kind, such as race, sex, language, religion, political or other opinion, property status, or national or social origin." *Ibidem.*

[58] E/CN.4/AC 2/SR.9, p. 11.

[59] See § 44.

"or other" to "property status." Finally, in the Third (social, humanitarian and cultural) Committee of the General Assembly, the ground "birth" was added in pursuance to a proposal of the delegate of the Soviet Union. In the next paragraphs we shall review in a succinct manner how these additional grounds were inserted in what was to become article 2 of the Universal Declaration.

44. *Additional Grounds: "Colour"*

At the time of the drafting of the Universal Declaration on Human Rights, the Cuban government submitted to the U.N. Commission on Human Rights a draft-declaration in which "colour" figured as a forbidden ground for differentiation; and the draft of the American Federation of Labour mentioned this ground too.[60] In the fourth meeting of the first Session (Geneva 1947) of the Sub-Commission on Prevention of Discrimination and Protection of Minorities (which hereinafter will be referred to as "the Sub-Commission") Mr. Masani, the Indian member, proposed, in pursuance to the wording suggested by the American Federation of Labour, to insert in the draft the word "colour" after "race".[61]

The reactions to this proposal varied among the members of the Sub-Commission. The remark was made by the United States' delegate, that it was "preferable to keep to the terminology of the Charter,"[62] a view generally held by the United States, as we remarked above. Some fear was expressed about the possible danger that inclusion of the word "colour" would lead to the *a contrario* conclusion that "colour" was not covered by the term "race" as used in the Charter or other international documents. It was also stated that since the idea of "race" generally covered differences in colour, the addition of "colour" was superfluous,[63] though otherwise not objectionable.

Other members of the Sub-Commission however, supported the proposal. It was remarked, *inter alia*, that the term "race" was not precisely and scientifically defined; therefore it was "urged that if there was the slightest doubt it was better to add the word 'colour'

[60] The draft international declarations and other proposals are collected in a documented outline. E/CN.4/AC.1/3/Add. 1. The texts of several drafts are also in the *U.N. Yearbook of Human Rights 1947*, p. 484 ff.

[61] E/CN.4/Sub.2/SR.4/p. 2.

[62] *Ibidem.*

[63] The same opinion is expressed by several authors. See e.g. Schindler, *op.cit.*, p. 130; H. Guradze, *Die Europäische Menschenrechtskonvention; Kommentar* (Berlin und Frankfurt a.M., 1968), p. 191; Kipp, *op.cit.*, p. 145.

than risk leaving out certain groups." Mr. Masani, who had submitted the proposal, pointed out that discrimination on the basis of colour not necessarily meant at the same time: on the basis of race. Referring to the United States immigration laws,[64] he remarked that in these laws "a distinction was made between Caucasian immigrants of the fair type and those of a darker one. The same thing occurred in South Africa." Among the racial characteristics that may exist, colour is the one that is the most easily perceptible in social relations. So racial discrimination is in practice mostly discrimination based on the different pigmentation of the skin.

We submit that "colour" is superfluous as a forbidden ground only when the discrimination occurs between coloured and non-coloured groups or communities. However, colour can be regarded as a meaningful ground as far as discrimination *within* racial communities is concerned,[65] (besides such cases as the Indian delegate mentioned). In such cases differences in colour take the place of what in relations with other ethnic groups are admittedly "racial" differences. The Commission decided not to mention "colour" as a separate ground, but that

"a note reading as follows should simply be added to article 6: It being understood that the term 'race' includes the idea of colour."[66]

In the 34th meeting, second session, of the Commission on Human Rights, Mrs. Mehta, the Indian delegate, proposed to insert the words "including colour," after "race" in the combined articles 3 and 6 of the Draft that was put before the Commission on Human Rights by the Working Group on the Declaration on Human Rights.[67] She based her proposal on the fact that in the Convention on Human Rights that was drafted by another Working Group of the Commission (and that was later to become the two comprehensive Covenants on Human Rights adopted in 1966) the term "colour" had been added. A similar amendment was proposed by the Chinese delegate.[68] Again, arguments ranged from the view that "race included colour" to the view that

[64] As existing at that time, in particular the quota system.

[65] As to colour differences within one racial community, compare the illustrative observations by a black American author, who spent his youth in the Harlem section of New York City: ... "It seemed as though under this new Muslim movement, everybody was becoming real black and becoming proud of it. Maybe this was a good thing. Maybe it was bringing all the shades together and making us realise that we're all coloured, regardless of complexion." Claude Brown, *Manchild in the Promised Land,* (New York, 1966), p. 336–337.

[66] E/CN.4/Sub.2/SR.4, p. 5.

[67] E/CN.4/SR.34, p. 10, 11.

[68] E/CN.4/SR.35, p. 5.

adding "colour" to "race" could imply that "colour" would otherwise not be covered by "race." Nevertheless, the addition of the words "(i.e. also colour)" after "race" was finally adopted by the Commission on Human Rights. [69] [70]

45. *Additional Grounds: "Political Opinion"*

During the fourth meeting of the First Session of the Sub-Commission Mr. Masani from India not only proposed to insert "colour," but also to add "political opinion" to draft article 6. [71] In order to explain his proposal he emphasized the importance of political minorities. He foresaw that in the future minorities "would be much more in the nature of political minorities than the traditional religious minorities, which tended to disappear." [72] The Chinese delegate remarked that political opinion was already recognized in the draft Declaration as a separate right and that political opinion was not "a qualification of those entitled to these rights." This is of course true but does not preclude that the "opinion" itself is used as a pretext to discriminate against those who hold it. It then functions in the same manner as race, sex and language and the other grounds that are qualifications of persons. The same applies to religion as well, and to some extent also to "property."

Mr. Borisov from the USSR regarded the proposal as possibly a dangerous one, he wondered whether the phrase "political opinion" covered nazi, fascist and racist opinions as well. But with respect to this problem the opinion prevailed in the Sub-Commission that it could not be the function of a non-discrimination clause in a Declaration to provide for and regulate also the safeguards against a possible abuse of the rights that were granted.

The French member moved an amendment to eliminate the adjective

[69] *Ibidem.*

[70] In this phase of the drafting of the Declaration the combined articles read now as follows: article 3
"1. Everyone is entitled to all the rights and freedoms set forth in this Declaration, without distinction of any kind, such as race (which includes colour), sex, language, religion, political or other opinion, property status, or national or social origin. 2. All are equal before the law regardless of office or status and entitled to equal protection of the law against any arbitrary discrimination in violation of this Declaration."
Report of the Commission on Human Rights to the Economic and Social Council. Official Records of the Economic and Social Council, Sixth Session, Supplement no. 1 (E/600, 17 December, 1947), p. 15.

[71] E/CN.4/Sub.2/SR.4, p. 2.

[72] *Ibidem*, p. 6.

"political" in order to give the addition a wider meaning.[73] He referred to the original text, drafted by Professor Cassin, which had also contained the term "opinions."[74] While emphasizing the importance of political opinions the text of article 6 should apply to any other opinion. Accordingly a compromise was suggested by Mr. McNamara from Australia, who proposed to insert the words "political or other opinion" in article 6.[75] The Indian amendment, as sub-amended by the Australian delegate, was adopted by the Sub-Commission.

46. Additional Grounds: "National Origin"

At the fifth meeting (First Session) of the Sub-Commission, the Russian delegate, Mr. A. P. Borisov, introduced a completely new and much more comprehensive wording for the (then) article 6 of the draft Declaration. This draft contained, *inter alia*, the words "national origin."[76] The French member moved an amendment to the effect that "national" would be deleted from the phrase, so that only "origin" would remain. The Soviet member disagreed with this version, since in his opinion "origin" did not necessarily include "national origin." The USSR, for example, "had various nationalities of the same origin." The Australian delegate thought that "national origin" was synonymous with "nationality" but that it might also have a wider meaning.[77]

A French-British amendment was then proposed which ran as follows: "... without distinction of any kind, whether of race, sex, language, religion, political or other opinion, property status, origin or class."[78] It was explained by the sponsors that "'national' had been omitted because 'national origin' was liable to be confused with 'nationality.'"

But Mr. Borisov did not consider that the words "or class" could be used to replace the words "national or social origin." He objected against the omission of the word "national"; in his opinion it was

[73] *Ibidem*, p. 7.

[74] See above, § 43.

[75] E/CN.4/Sub.2/SR.4, p. 7.

[76] E/CN.4/Sub.2/21. The text reads as follows: "All people are equal before the law and shall enjoy equal rights in the economic, cultural, social and political life, irrespective of their race, sex, language, religion, property status, national or social origin. Any advocacy of national, racial and religious hostility or of national exclusiveness or hatred and contempt, as well as any action establishing a privilege or a discrimination based on distinctions of race, nationality or religion, constitute a crime and shall be punishable under the law of the state."

Note that the words "political or other opinion" do not figure in this text.

[77] E/CN.4/Sub.2/SR.5/p. 7.

[78] *Ibidem*, p. 8.

important "in the interest of countries where people of different national origins lived together under the same government, that the word "national" should be specially mentioned."[79] In the next meeting various alternative versions were proposed which avoided the adjective "national," but these were withdrawn again because of other deficiencies. Hence some disagreement and misunderstanding concerning the expression "national" seemed to continue.[80] From the Report to the Commission of Human Rights, however, it appears that the Sub-Commission had finally reached a consensus with regard to the adjective "national." In this Report it is said: "... the Sub-Commission wished to make it clear that the words "national origin" should be interpreted by taking this conception, not in the sense of citizen of a State, but in the sense of national characteristics."[81]

The whole text of article 6 as proposed by Mr. Borisov was finally rejected; but instead an amendment tabled by the Australian and Chinese members was adopted in which the terms "property status, national or social origin" were taken over from the Soviet proposal, so that these elements were nevertheless maintained in Article 6.[82] And so was "political or other opinion," which had not been included in Mr. Borisov's proposal, though this addition had already been adopted by the Sub-Commission during a previous meeting.

[79] *Ibidem*, p. 8, 9.

[80] At one point also the Soviet delegate himself was somewhat confused in the presentation of his arguments. In the Summary Records this is related as follows: "Mr. Borisov (USSR) wished to clarify the meaning he attached to the word 'national.' He considered that within the same nationality there could be different origins. Article 6 defined equal rights for all. This meant that any citizen of the Soviet Union, were he Jew, Negro, Georgian, Caucasian, etc. could become a member or the president of the Supreme Council. He asked whether in the United States a Negro, a Jew or a naturalized Mexican could become President. If there was any discrimination in that field, there could be no equality of rights." Mr. Masani (India) remarked thereupon that the different categories to which Mr. Borisov had referred were ethnic or racial groups, whose rights were guaranteed by the word "race." (E/CN.4/Sub.2/SR.6, p. 6).

A list of Corrigenda was later issued which contained *inter alia* the following item: "Read as follows: Article 6 should define equal rights for all. In particular any citizen of the Soviet Union, were he Russian, Georgian, Ukrainian etc. could become a member or the President of the Supreme Council." (E/CN.4/Sub.2/SR.6/Corr. I). This rectification clearly indicates that the meaning of "national" in the proposal did not differ from the traditional meaning such as in the term "national minorities." (See above § 39).

[81] E/CN.4/52, p. 5. See on this meaning of the word "national" also the *Proceedings* of the "Seminar on the Multi-National State" (Ljubljana, Yugoslavia, June 1965), ST/TAO/HR/23 (1965). It is unfortunate, that some confusion between on the one hand this sociological, cultural and historical concept and on the other hand the legal "nationality" concept may again arise from the recent *Study on Equality in the Administration of Justice* (E/CN.4/Sub.2/296/Rev. 1), where, in para. 149, discrimination against *aliens* is discussed under the heading "National origin or nationality."

[82] E/CN.4/Sub.2/SR.6, p. 14.

47. Additional Grounds: "Social origin"

The expression "social origin" appeared for the first time in the Soviet proposal that was reproduced in the previous paragraph. The meaning of this element was discussed in the Sub-Commission in connection with the British-French amendment to the proposal. In this text "national or social origin" of the original proposal was replaced by "origin or class." In the ensuing debate the British delegate explained that the words "or class" had been included as a clearer version of "social origin."[83] Mr. Borisov, who had previously considered that the words "origin or class" could not be used to replace "national or social origin," now agreed that the words "or class" could be used to express "social origin." [84] (On a further role of the "class"-concept, see below, § 49, in which the element "birth" is discussed). Both the Soviet and the British-French drafts were eventually rejected[85]; but, as remarked in the previous paragraph, a Chinese-Australian amendment saved *inter alia* "social origin," so that the debate summarized here still has some relevance for the understanding of this element.

48. Additional Grounds: "Property," "Other Status"

When it was originally introduced by Mr. Borisov, the term was "property status"; as such it appeared again in the Australian-Chinese amendment via which the grounds of Mr. Borisov's proposal were adopted by the Sub-Commission. No comments were made on the meaning or significance of "property status," except for one single remark by the Belgian member. He pointed out that "there might be a political connotation in the word "property status," since in some countries income was one of the factors considered in determining the right to vote." [86] There were no reactions on the part of the other members of the Sub-Commission on this statement. In the Commission on Human Rights, Mr. Klekovkin from the Ukrainian Soviet Socialist Republic proposed the insertion of the concept "*soslovie*" after the

[83] E/CN.4/Sub.2/SR.5, p. 9.

[84] *Ibidem.* The delegate from the United States of America "objected to the use of the word "class" because it had some undesirable meanings which in his view made it unsuitable for inclusion in a Declaration of Rights."

[85] E/CN.4/Sub.2/SR.6, p. 15.

[86] E/CN.4/Sub.2/SR.5, p. 9 (We would say that such practices should necessitate rather than bar the inclusion of such a ground).

words "property status." [87] There appeared to exist no exact English equivalent for this Russian word, but the meaning of "*soslovie*" can approximately be rendered in English as "class" or "social status." The suggestion was then made to omit "property" so that only "status" would be left, which term would be "all-inclusive." However, Mr. Pavlov of the USSR objected to this idea. "The word 'property' should remain; it was most important that rich and poor should have the same rights." He added to this that "*soslovie*" in the Ukrainian amendment was directed against "feodal class privileges, which were generally determined by birth rather than wealth."

Thereupon Mr. Klekovkin accepted the suggestion of Mr. Chang, the Chinese delegate, to insert the words "or other" between the words "property" and "status," which would "meet the point he wished to make." [88] In this amended form the Ukrainian proposal was adopted.

49. *Additional Grounds: "Birth"*

In the 100th meeting of the Third Committee of the General Assembly the delegation of the Soviet Union submitted an amendment to the text of article 2 as it had been adopted by the Commission of Human Rights.[89] It was proposed to add the word "class" after "property or other status." [90] Mr. Pavlov of the Soviet delegation explained that the amendment aimed at the abolition of differences based on social conditions as well as the privileges enjoyed by certain groups in the economic and legal fields. (Such as the nobility, or the great landowners in a feudal system, the clergy, merchants, and so on, before the French and the Russian Revolutions). The Soviet delegate remarked, however, that the use of the word "class" to translate the corresponding Russian word ("*soslovie*") into English seemed defective to him, and should be revised.[91]

At the next meeting an informal drafting group that was formed to study the question reported to the Committee in part as follows:

"... The Group accepted a USSR amendment to article 2 providing for the addition, between the words "property or other status' (*situation de fortune ou autre*) and the words 'or national or social origin' (*d'origine nationale ou sociale*), of the word *soslovie* in the Russian text which is translated by the word *naissance*

[87] E/CN.4/SR.52, p. 5.
[88] *Ibidem.*
[89] E/800, p. 9.
[90] *Ibidem*, p. 32.
[91] A/C3/SR.100. G.A.O.R. 3rd Session, Part I, Third Committee, October 1948, p. 134.

in the French text and 'birth' in the English text. The literal translation of the word *soslovie* would be *état* in French and 'estate' in English, but the Group noted that those words, as currently used, no longer had their former meaning . . . ." [92]

Some delegates preferred other terms to express the meaning of the Soviet amendment, such as "class," "caste," "status," "social status," "social condition." But eventually the Committee voted in favour of the insertion of the word "birth" in article 2.[93]

50. *Other Grounds in International Instruments*

The catalogue of grounds in article 2 of the Universal Declaration is quite a long one and it seems that it can be regarded as almost exhaustive. Karl-Joseph Partsch spoke (with respect to the near-identic article 14 of the European Convention on Human Rights) of "*Kodifikationsperfektionismus*." [94] Still a few more grounds have been adopted in other international instruments. We will confine ourselves to a mere mentioning of some of these grounds here, since they are either connected to specific fields where the conventions in which they appear play a role, or are merely terminological variations which do not represent substantive changes or additions.

(i) In article 1 (1) of the Convention on the Elimination of All Forms of Racial Discrimination [95] "race" is supplemented by "descent" and "ethnic origin." Both are of course implied in "race." "Ethnic origin" appeared already in the several drafts of this provision, submitted by the delegates of the United States, England, and, jointly, by the Polish and Soviet delegates.[96] The term "descent" was added in the Third Committee of the General Assembly by the representative of India. The records do not disclose the intended meaning of the term. Schwelb [97] suggests that it includes the notion of "caste," which is a prohibited ground of discrimination according to article 15 of the Indian Constitution.[98] However in this provision "caste" is listed along

[92] A/C.3/SR.101 (*Ibidem*, p. 135).
[93] A/C.3/SR.102 (*Ibidem*, p. 141).
[94] K. J. Partsch, "Die Rechte und Freiheiten der Europäischen Menschenrechtskonvention," in *Die Grundrechte* I/1 (Berlin 1966), p. 326.
[95] Quoted above on p. 82.
[96] N. Lerner, *The Convention on the Elimination of All Forms of Racial Discrimination* (Leyden 1970), p. 39.
[97] *Op.cit.*, p. 1003.
[98] Text at p. 83, note 2, above.

with "race," from which it may be inferred that it is not regarded as included in "race." It appears that "caste" is generally not understood as a racial matter, however indetermined the notion of "race" may be. Nor can "descent" as such have any racial aspects of its own.

(ii) In article 1 (1) of the Discrimination (Employment and Occupation) Convention [99] the term "national extraction" is employed. For all practical purposes this term seems to be identic to "national origin."

(iii) The same can be said with respect to "economic condition" in article 1 (1) of the Convention against Discrimination in Education.[100] This term corresponds to "property" in article 2 of the Universal Declaration.

(iv) As an alternative of both "race," "national" and "ethnic origin" can be regarded "tribal association," which appears in article 14 of the I.L.O. Convention Concerning Basic Aims and Standards of Social Policy, quoted above, at p. 58. Also in this provision, "belief" replaces the more usual "religion." And finally, closely connected with the subject matter of this particular instrument is the ground "trade union affiliation" in the same article of the I.L.O.convention.

(v) The European Convention of Human Rights was drafted on the basis of the Universal Declaration. As far as the forbidden grounds are concerned, article 14 differs from article 2 of the Universal Declaration in this respect that in the former provision "association with a national minority" has been added. The proposal to include this ground was made by the Danish delegate in the Consultative Assembly of the Council of Europe, Mr. Hermod Lannung. The Danish action for minority rights was undertaken with a special eye to the Danish minority in South Schleswig (Germany).[101] Mr. Lannung himself[102] relates the matter – after having discussed the "disappointing experience" with the minority-issue in the United Nations[103] – as follows:

[99] Text at p. 81 above.

[100] *Ibidem.*

[101] See Council of Europe, Consultative Assembly, Reports of the first Session (1949) part II, p. 414, 420.

[102] H. Lannung, "The Rights of Minorities," in *Mélanges offerts à Polys Modinos* (Paris 1968), p. 184–185.

[103] See below, § 60. In the General Assembly the Danish delegation had suggested to insert the protection of minorities in art. 2 of the Covenant on Civil and Political Rights. GAOR, Tenth Session (1955), Agenda item 28 t 1), A/3077, para. 85

"When the Consultative Assembly made its proposals in September 1949 for the conclusion of the European Convention on Human Rights, it proposed to include in the Convention a "non-discrimination clause" based on the corresponding provision of the Universal Declaration. But on this occasion the minorities were not forgotten. On the proposal of the present author, a phrase ("association with a national minority") was added to the article in the Assembly's draft..."

For the understanding of the intended meaning of the addition it is interesting that the author remarks: "But this text was only designed to secure the first requirement of minorities, i.e. equality with the other nationals of the state. The harder task still remained, to ensure for them 'suitable means for the preservation of their racial peculiarities, their traditions and their national characteristics.'" This interpretation of the phrase is corroborated by the Report that was later submitted to the Consultative Assembly by the Committee on Legal and Administrative Questions dealing with the Establishment of a collective guarantee of Essential Freedoms and Fundamental Rights[104] of which Mr. Lannung was a member at that time. In paragraph 11 of this Report it is stated: "The resolution adopted by the Committee specified that the regime of guaranteed freedoms should prevent any discrimination based on membership of a national minority. After having heard a Report by Mr. Lannung on the problem of the *wider* protection of the rights of national minorities, the Committee unanimously recognized the importance of this problem."[105]

It must be noted that this forbidden ground is obviously redundant if it only intends to bar unfavourable unequal treatment based on minority characteristics. From our discussion of such grounds as "race," "language," "political or other opinion" and "national or social origin" it can be concluded that these were included with a similar purpose in mind, and with – hopefully – the same effect. A similar view was expressed by Professor Cassin with regard to the Danish proposal to insert this same ground in the draft of article 26 of the Covenant on Civil and Political Rights.[106]

[104] The so-called "Teitgen-Report," after the Chairman of the Committee. Council of Europe, Consultative Assembly, *Documents of the first session* (1949), no. 77, p. 197–209.

[105] Italics added.

[106] E/CN.4/SR.172, p. 11; SR.173, p. 5. See also below, §§ 59 and 60.

51. Classification of Grounds

In paragraph 38 we have distinguished between the four Charter grounds and an undetermined number of "additional grounds." This distinction is legitimate because on the basis of article 103 of the Charter the Charter grounds share in the higher status that this provision accords to Charter obligations generally in comparison with other obligations of the Member States.

A certain classification is also reflected in article 4 of the Covenant on Civil and Political Rights. In the first draft of the Covenant the text was as follows:

"In time of war or other public emergency, a State may take measures derogating from its obligations under article 2[107] ... to the extent strictly limited by the exigencies of the situation."[108]

It was understood that no derogations would be considered as lawful that could be repugnant to express Charter obligations. In this respect it was suggested earlier that exemptions should respect the principle of non-discrimination on the grounds of race, sex, language and religion.[109] In the 330th meeting of the Commission on Human Rights the British representative tabled an amendment which added to the (slightly modified) text of the draft article the words: "... provided that such measures are not inconsistent with their other obligations under international law and do not involve discrimination solely on the ground of race, colour, sex, language or religion."[110] At the request of the representatives from Chile, France and the Lebanon "social origin" was added to the English amendment.[111] During the next session this revised amendment was adopted.[112]

Through the enumeration of article 4 *in fine* the grounds that have not been included in it are put on a lower level of importance in the system of rules for the protection of human rights.[113]

[107] Art. 2 is a less detailed and less elaborated version of the wording of the definite art. 2 of the Covenant.

[108] Report of the Commission on Human Rights to the ECOSOC.E/600, p. 25.

[109] See e.g. Memorandum by the Secretary General, E/CN.4/528, § 81.

[110] E/CN.4/L. 139.

[111] E/CN.4/L. 139, Rev. 1.

[112] E/CN.4/SR.331, p. 6.

[113] In the opinion of the European Commission on Human Rights special legal consequences may be attached to *racial* discrimination. See below, § 53, *in fine*. Compare also section 703 (e) (1) of the U.S. Civil Rights Act (1964), reproduced in § 52 *in fine*, note 123. This same Act provides for a remarkable instance of "conflicting" grounds. Generally, it aims at

52. The Scope of the Clauses: The Rights

The clauses can generally be categorized according to their scope. In some of the clauses the interdiction of discrimination is general; it applies to the whole legal system (that is, as far as the affected rules concern the rights and duties of individuals). In some clauses the interdiction covers only a limited area of the law, a certain number of rights and duties. In some clauses the number of grounds that are listed is limited; in some we find a formulation such as "on any ground such as ..." (in French for instance "notamment"), indicating that the cataloque is enumerative. On the basis of the two essential elements of a non-discrimination clause, rights and grounds, we can come to the following categorization:

(i) Restricted as to both rights and grounds are the clauses of the I.L.O. Discrimination (Employment and Occupation) Convention,[114] and of the UNESCO Convention against Discrimination in Education.[115]

(ii) The Convention on the Elimination of All Forms of Racial Discrimination is restricted, according to its purpose, to race and related grounds, but covers in principle the entire legal order of a State-party, as appears from its article 5.

In this connection it may be noted that this Convention is quite remarkable among the other instruments on human rights. These

eliminating discrimination in employment based on race, colour, religion, sex or national origin. A curious conflict with what we would call "political opinion" results from section 703 (f), which runs in part as follows:

"... the phrase "unlawful employment practice" shall not be deemed to include any action or measure taken by an employer ... with respect to an individual who is a member of the Communist Party of the United States or of any other organization required to register as a Communist-action or Communist-front organization by final order of the Subversive Activities Control Board pursuant to the Subversive Activities Control Act of 1950." In his *Legal Restraints on Racial Discrimination in Employment* (New York 1966), Michael I. Sovern comments at p. 69: "Literally read this provision permits the very kind of discrimination prohibited by the Act – discrimination based on "race, color, religion, sex, or national origin" – as long as the person discriminated against is coincidentally a member of a Communist organization. So read, section 703 (f) is highly inappropriate in a bill designed to prevent discrimination. Congress does not feel compelled to demonstrate its patriotism by excepting Communists from the protection of (criminal) laws ... The practices proscribed are thought offensive enough to warrant prohibition no matter who the victim. It should be the same with racial discrimination."

[114] Text at p. 81 above.

[115] Text at p. 81 above.

instruments grant a number of substantive rights to individuals and add to these rights the stipulation that they must be ensured and enjoyed without discrimination. So the accessory character of the non-discrimination principle is brought out clearly. In contrast, the Convention on the Elimination of All Forms of Racial Discrimination puts the non-discrimination principle in the forefront, as an independent principle, as it were, while the rights to which the principle must be attached in order to come to legal existence are lumped together, so to speak, in article 5, which thus has become a curious "Bill of Rights in a Nutshell."[116]

The human rights provisions of the Charter of the U.N. also contain a limited number of grounds, while these provisions can be considered to aim at the whole legal system of the Member States – whatever their precise legal consequences may be.

[116] *Article 5.* "In compliance with the fundamental obligations laid down in Article 2 of this Convention, States Parties undertake to prohibit and to eliminate racial discrimination in all its forms and to guarantee the right of everyone, without distinction as to race, colour, or national or ethnic origin, to equality before the law, notably in the enjoyment of the following rights:

(*a*) The right to equal treatment before the tribunals and all other organs administering justice;

(*b*) The right to security of person and protection by the State against violence or bodily harm, whether inflicted by government officials or by any individual, group or institution;

(*c*) Political rights, in particular the rights to participate in elections – to vote and to stand for election – on the basis of universal and equal suffrage, to take part in the Government as well as in the conduct of public affairs at any level and to have equal access to public service;

(*d*) Other civil rights, in particular:
- (i) The right to freedom of movement and residence within the border of the State;
- (ii) The right to leave any country, including one's own, and to return to one's country;
- (iii) The right to nationality;
- (iv) The right to marriage and choice of spouse;
- (v) The right to own property alone as well as in association with others;
- (vi) The right to inherit;
- (vii) The right to freedom of thought, conscience and religion;
- (viii) The right to freedom of opinion and expression;
- (ix) The right to freedom of peaceful assembly and association;

(*e*) Economic, social and cultural rights, in particular:
- (i) The rights to work, to free choice of employment, to just and favourable conditions of work, to protection against unemployment, to equal pay for equal work, to just and favourable remuneration;
- (ii) The right to form and join trade unions;
- (iii) The right to housing;
- (iv) The right to public health, medical care, social security and social services;
- (v) The right to education and training;
- (vi) The right to equal participation in cultural activities;

(*f*) The right of access to any place or service intended for use by the general public, such as transport, hotels, restaurants, cafés, theatres and parks."

(iii) Not limited as to grounds ("without discrimination of any kind such as," "on any ground such as") but applicable only to "the rights enunciated in the present Covenant," "the rights and freedoms set forth in this Convention" are the non-discrimination clauses of respectively the Covenant on Economic, Social and Cultural Rights, article 2 (2),[117] and the European Convention on Human Rights and Fundamental Freedoms, article 14.[118] The same construction is employed in article 2 of the Universal Declaration of Human Rights. It is rather curious that also the Covenant on Civil and Political Rights contains a non-discrimination provision of this type, in its article 2 (1).[119] This clause appears to be redundant in the light of article 26 of the same Covenant.

(iv) Article 26 of the Covenant on Civil and Political Rights[120] is the non-discrimination clause that is the widest in scope of all; it is not confined either with respect to the rights or with respect to the grounds.

It seems sufficiently clear from our discussion of the forbidden grounds for differentiation that there will probably be no need for more grounds than those now figuring in the various catalogues. Thus, of the combinations rights-grounds set out here, the factor rights seems to be the more important as far as the determination of the range of applicability of the clause is concerned. If no restriction is made in this respect, the clause can function as a general principle of non-discrimination for the whole legal system in which it is incorporated or to which it is addressed. It can then be considered to be attached to all the rights and duties of the system, to be a part of all instances of treatment in the system.[121]

We remarked earlier (above p. 61) that the character of the rights in which the differentiation was made constitutes an essential element in our notion of discrimination, and that it would therefore be inap-

[117] Article 2 (2) reads as follows: "The States Parties to the present Covenant undertake to guarantee that the rights enunciated in the present Covenant will be exercised without discrimination of any kind as to race, colour, sex, language, religion, political or other opinion, national or social origin, property, birth or other status."

[118] Text reproduced above, p. 20.

[119] "Each State Party to the present Covenant undertakes to respect and to ensure to all individuals within its territory and subject to its jurisdiction the rights recognized in the present Covenant, without distinction of any kind, such as race, colour, sex, language, religion, political or other opinion, national or social origin, property, birth or other status."

[120] Text reproduced above, p. 83.

[121] This is said with the proviso made at p. 31 on legal relationships of a strictly private nature.

propriate to try to reach a decision concerning the occurrance of discrimination without an examination of the subject matter regulated. We have now come across the distinction between "forbidden grounds for differentiation" on the one hand, divided in "Charter grounds" and "other grounds," and "legitimate distinctions which do not constitute discrimination because they are established on just grounds" on the other hand (p. 80).

In the light of this distinction the question might be asked whether on the one hand certain rights can be distinguished with respect to which no differentiations are allowed on any grounds because of the very nature of the rights. And whether there are on the other hand also certain rights as to which all kinds of distinctions would be allowed for the same reason. Put in a more concrete way, the problem is for example whether so-called "civil rights" can be separated from other rights on the basis of some material criterion. And whether because of the nature of these rights any differentiation in such rights violates *eo ipso* the non-discrimination principle. Compare e.g. Mr. Justice Douglas' remark in *Harper v. Virginia Board of Elections:* "We have always been mindful that where fundamental rights and liberties are asserted under the Equal Protection Clause, classifications which might invade or restrain them must be closely scrutinized and carefully confined..."[122]

It seems indeed that in international practice some rights have become generally recognized as so "fundamental" that no differentiation as to these rights can be deemed sufficiently connected with any aspects of inequality in a subject treated. For example, the right to vote in elections is considered "essential," but not so much that it may not be denied to delinquents, or to aliens. A freedom such as freedom of religion is regarded as so "basic" that it may not be denied to any category of human beings. But again, as far as e.g. employment is concerned, it is usually not regarded as discrimination if certain employers (denominational schools and so on) employ only followers of their own religion. (See above, p. 95). Employment is also the particular field where the reasonableness of distinctions based on sex or language may be easily shown.[123] Freedom of speech is a funda-

[122] 383 U.S. 663 (1966), at p. 670.

[123] Compare for example also Sec. 703 (e) (1) of the U.S. Civil Rights Act of 1964: "... it shall not be an unlawful employment practice for an employer to hire and employ employees, for an employment agency to classify, or refer for employment any individual (...) on the basis of his religion, sex, or national origin in those certain instances where religion, sex, or national origin is a bona fide occupational qualification reasonably necessary to the normal

mental right, but it is by no means always granted to the members of the military forces. On the other hand the right to integrity of the body and the right to life are so basic that no differentiation in them could satisfy the test of the sufficient connection.

Clear cases of a division between types of rights can be found e.g. in the law of aliens. Alienage was in international practice a recognized ground for all kinds of unfavourable unequal treatment; yet in the so-called minimum-standard certain basic rights were reserved from such unequal treatment on otherwise so legitimate a basis. (And the same can be said of the minimum-standard embodied in the common article 3 of the Red Cross Conventions of 1949, quoted above in § 19 under (4). It may be true that the right concerned in this case can only be described as a "right to humane treatment" but it is accorded to members of the *enemy's* forces – another distinction that is otherwise a legitimate basis for unfavourable unequal treatment).

The division that we attempted to make here is not so important any more since rights of all types have been incorporated side-by-side in the instruments on the protection of human rights. Not only the grounds have been codified, so have the rights. Most important in this respect is of course the fact that in the concept of "human rights" a development has taken place which has resulted in the incorporation in that concept of both "civil and political" rights and "economic, social and cultural rights." Rights of the latter category traditionally did not or not fully belong to the rights that had to be accorded to "all."

Consequently, whether the range of applicability of the non-discrimination clauses is limited to "the rights set forth in this Convention," or not, the question that we discussed cannot come up any more. That is, if it arises the conventions answer it themselves. For example Article 4 (1) of the Covenant on Civil and Political Rights (quoted above in § 51) states that "in time of public emergency which threatens the life of the nation" the states parties to the convention may take measures which derogate from their obligations under the Covenant. But Section 2 stipulates that no derogation may be made from the right to life, (article 6), the prohibition of torture or cruel, inhuman or degrading treatment or punishment (article 7), the prohibition of slavery and servitude, (article 8), the freedom from imprisonment for insolvency (article 11), the *nulla poena* principle (article 15), the right to recognition as a person before the law (article 16), and

operation of that particular business or enterprise..." Note that "race" and "color," the two other grounds of the Civil Rights Act, are omitted from this particular section.

the right to freedom of thought, conscience and religion (article 18). A similar set of rules is laid down in article 15 of the European Convention on Human Rights.

53. The "Dependence" or "Independence" of Article 14 of the European Convention on Human Rights

Article 2 of the Universal Declaration of Human Rights limits its field of application to "all the rights and freedoms set forth in this Declaration." This limitation in the wording of the clause can be traced back to its earliest draft in the project of the Secretariat. The non-discrimination clause therein closed with the words: "There shall be full equality before the law in the rights enunciated in the Bill of Rights."[124] Similarly in the version drawn up by Professor Cassin, based on this draft: "... the rights and freedoms set forth in this Declaration."[125] Article 14 of the European Convention on Human Rights is copied from article 2 of the Declaration in as much as the whole Convention was based on the Declaration.[126] Thus the scope of article 14 is also limited to "the rights and freedoms set forth in this Convention." In our opinion the clause can consequently have no "independent existence" outside the Convention. In the case-law of the European Commission of Human Rights this problem of the "dependence" or "independence" of article 14 has nevertheless played quite a role.[127]

The "dependence" of the clause implies that a complaint concerning discrimination must always involve a double violation: the complaint must relate to a violation of a right or freedom as seth forth in the Convention, and it must also demonstrate that this violation infringed upon the non-discrimination clause of the Convention as well. It must not show that a State-Party applied or interpreted a provision in a

[124] Article 45. E/CN.4/AC.1/3/Add.1, p. 359.

[125] Professor Cassin's version is reproduced above at p. 96. In fact, the definite text of article 2 of the Universal Declaration speaks of "all" the rights. The addition of "all" resulted from an amendment submitted by the American delegate in the Sub-Commission. "All" had to make up for the deletion of the "economic, social and cultural" rights that were included in the rejected alternative text of (then) draft article 6, proposed by the delegate of the U.S.S.R. (See above, p. 100). E/CN.4/Sub.2/SR.5, p. 8.

[126] *Teitgen Report*, paragraph 6: "In approaching the general problem of the definition of rights and freedoms which are to be guaranteed ... the Committee considered that it was preferable ... to make use, as far as possible, of the definitions set out in the "Universal Declaration of Human Rights" ... It thus based itself, as far as possible, on this Document."

[127] See for a detailed survey of the cases in which the problem came up M. A. Eissen, "L''autonomie' de l'article 14 de la convention européenne des droits de l'Homme," in *Mélanges offerts à Polys Modinos*, (Paris 1968), p. 122 ff.

wrong manner which potentially affected the rights that all citizens enjoy under the Convention (or an undetermined number of citizens). It must rather show that a State Party did so with regard to a particular group of citizens in such a way as to introduce a wrongly (forbidden) unequal treatment of this group. The "dependence" of article 14 implies also that some complaints allegeing discrimination must be declared inadmissable by the Commission to the extent that they do not disclose violations of rights and freedoms set forth in the Convention, though these complaints may relate to treatment that is otherwise discriminatory (e.g. measures that – directly or indirectly – compel gypsies, but not other citizens, to abandon their caravans and to settle in fixed abodes).

Several authors have asserted that the European Commission, in dealing with affairs of this nature, has more or less denied this accessory character of article 14 in a number of occasions.[128] One author goes so far as to contend that one of the propositions concerning article 14 that are "clearly established" is that "Article 14 has an autonomous operation and a simultaneous breach of another article is not required."[129] These authors base their opinion on the Report of the Commission in the *Grandrath-case*.[130] In this connection the Commission's Report in the *Belgian "linguistic" case* can also be mentioned.

The *Grandrath case* concerned a complaint of a member of the "Jehova's Witnesses" who was denied the privilege of exemption from compulsory military service, (or, as was the matter in this case, substitute service) which German law accords to certain ministers of religion. Grandrath based his complaint on articles 4, 9 and 14. With respect to article 14 the Commission reasoned in part:

"... The application of Article 14 does not only depend upon a previous finding of the Commission that a violation of another Article of the Convention already exists. In certain cases Article 14 may be violated in a field dealt with by another Article of the Convention, although there is otherwise no violation of that Article."

The French text of the last nine words, however, is "bien que ce dernier n'ait pas été directement violé." The word "*directement,*" instead of

[128] See M. A. Eissen, *op.cit.*, p. 132 f; H. Guradze, *Die Europäische Menschenrechtskonvention*, p. 189; K. J. Partsch, *op.cit.* p. 328, 329; N. A. Antonopoulos, *Le jurisprudence des organes de la convention européenne des droits de l'Homme* (Leyde 1967) p. 215; see also J. E. S. Fawcett, *The Application of the European Convention of Human Rights* (Oxford, 1969), p. 233 ff. on this requirement of a "double complaint."

[129] W. A. Mc Kean, *op.cit.*, p. 185.

[130] Report of the Commission of 12 December 1966; text in *Yearbook of the Convention on Human Rights*, Vol. 10 (The Hague, 1969), p. 626 ff.

"otherwise," and the subsequent considerations, make clear that the Commission refers to the *restrictive clauses* in the second sections of the articles 8–11 of the Convention. The Commission continues as follows:

"In the present case, it is necessary to refer to the limitative provisions contained in various Articles of the Convention. For example, in each of Articles 8 to 11, a certain right is guaranteed by paragraph (1), but the contracting Parties are, under par. (2), allowed, subject to specific conditions, to restrict that right. When using this power to restrict a right guaranteed by the Convention the Contracting Parties are bound by the provisions of Article 14. Consequently, if a restriction which is in itself permissible under par. (2) of one of the above Articles, is imposed in a discriminatory manner, there would be a violation of Article 14 in conjunction with the other Article concerned. The situation under Article 4 is similar.[131] Although the types of work and service, enumerated in par. (3) of Article 4 are not expressly described as exceptions to the general prohibition against 'forced labour,' they nevertheless operate as such in the present context."[132]

The words "in conjunction with the other Article concerned" show that the Commission does not mean to say that article 14 is "independent" or autonomous. The Commission rather indicates that art. 14 is also applicable wherever the Convention seems not to be applicable in so far as it leaves the State a certain amount of discretion to restrict the rights and freedoms. We conclude from this that since in our opinion this discretion is completely determined and limited by the Convention, the Convention does in fact govern that "negative" field too. Consequently so does article 14, only not "directement."

In its Report in the *Belgian "Linguistic" Case*[133] the majority of the Commission expressed itself again and even in a more ambiguous way on the problem.[134] In Paragraph 400 of the Report[135] it is first stated:

"The question of the scope of article 14 does not arise when an applicant alleges discriminatory measures and the right or freedom claimed to be violated thereby is not guaranteed by the Convention or Protocol. In such a case art. 14 would not be applicable."

The Commission then remarks that the applicability is not in doubt when a measure passed by a Contracting Party violates a right of the

[131] Article 4 of the Convention forbids slavery, forced labour, etc. Section 3 excludes from these notions *inter alia* military service exacted from conscientious objectors.

[132] Par. 38 of the Report (*Yearbook*, p. 678).

[133] Text in European Court of Human Rights, *Series B, Pleadings, Oral Arguments and Documents*, "*Linguistic*" *Case*, Vol. I, Strasbourg 1967, p. 9 ff.

[134] "In den Belgischen Sprachenfällen hat sich die Mehrheit der Kommission in unglücklichen Formulierungen von der Akzessorietät noch mehr entfernt" ... (Guradze, *op.cit.* p. 189).

[135] *Ibidem*, p. 305–306.

Convention and "further entails some form of discrimination." It then goes on to say:

"Nevertheless ... the applicability of article 14 is not limited to cases in which there is an accompanying violation of another Article. Such a restricted application would deprive Article 14 of any practical value. The sole effect of the discrimination would be to aggravate the violation of another provision of the Convention. Such an interpretation would hardly be compatible with the wording of Article 14: this states that the enjoyment of the rights and liberties set forth in the Convention shall be secured (*doit être assurée*) without any discrimination. It thus places on States an obligation which is not simply negative."

(As to the "practical value," the Commission refers to *dicta* of the Permanent Court of International Justice and the International Court of Justice which affirm that texts must be interpreted in such a way as to give them full effectivity).

But of course this immediately raises the question to which cases article 14 is otherwise considered to be applicable.

The Commission states that a distinction must be made between the methods by which the rights and freedoms are defined in the Convention. First, some rights are precisely and exhaustively defined. Every infringement on the part of the State on the enjoyment of such a right by some individuals but not in the enjoyment of it by others has a discriminatory aspect, but this is at most only an aggravating circumstance. Second, the Convention contains some rights which leave the States a certain margin of appreciation with regard to the fulfilment of their obligations. Such a margin is also allowed under several articles which authorize restrictions on, or exceptions to, the rights guaranteed. Finally there are provisions in the Convention, which up to a point leave it to the State to choose the appropriate means to implement a right, e.g. by national legislation. In the opinion of the Commission Article 14 is of particular importance in relation to clauses of this type. The Commission concludes by saying that Article 14 is not "a normative provision of the same kind as Article 8 or Article 2 of the Protocol."[136] Rather Article 14

"... concerns the means or the extent of the enjoyment of rights and freedoms already stated elsewhere. It may happen that different measures taken by a State in respect of different parts of its territory or population entail no breach

[136] Article 8 guarantees the right to privacy; article 2 of the Protocol lays down that "no person shall be denied the right to education. In the exercise of any functions which it assumes in relation to education and teaching, the State shall respect the rights of parents to ensure such education and teaching in conformity with their own religious and philosophical convictions."

of the Article in the Convention defining the rights in question, but that the differentiation entails violation if the State's conduct is judged from the point of view of Article 14. The question would then arise of a violation not only of Article 14 but of the right in question as mentioned in the relevant article in conjunction with article 14: in fact, an individual who suffers prejudice as a result of a State's infringement of Article 14 does not enjoy the right or freedom in question on the conditions or to the degree laid down in the Convention viewed as a whole."

We find it hard to deduce from these passages the clear adoption by the Commission of an autonomous function of article 14, as is, apart from the authors mentioned, also done by Mr. Eustathiades in his Dissenting Opinion on this issue.[137] Rather we conclude from § 400 of the Report – as far as we can fully understand the reasoning therein – that the Commission considers the effect of the Convention to be limited to the "precisely and exhaustively" defined rights. Accordingly, in the opinion of the Commission, the Convention does not operate wherever rights are not clearly defined, and where restrictions or exceptions are authorized; in such cases the States are free. These are occasions to which article 14 would therefore not apply, were it not that the Commission by its broad interpretation makes it do so, in order to save the practical value of article 14. The reasoning seems then quite similar to that in the Grandrath-case Report. After all the Commission has not come to assert that article 14 has a function independent from the rights in the Convention, as it is often understood to have done; rather it has an unusually and curiously restricted notion of the field of application of the Convention. As we remarked with respect to the reasoning in the *Grandrath Report:* where a margin of appreciation is left to the State, either through the vagueness of the wording of the Convention or through the authorization of restrictions or exceptions, such a margin is constituted by the Convention itself, it is limited by it and therefore fully covered by it. Also, if the enjoyment of the rights and freedoms set forth in the Convention is restricted, it remains "enjoyment" as granted by the Convention, so that it is still governed by article 14. In fact it appears already from the opening lines of § 400 of the Report in the *"linguistic case"* that the Commission applies this provision only to the rights and freedoms of the Convention.

In the *Belgian "linguistic" case* the European Court of Human Rights approaches the problem in a slightly different manner, but with the same result. The Court starts by denying an "independent exist-

[137] Paragraph 454 of the *Report* (p. 345 ff).

ence" of article 14. However, in the opinion of the Court, a certain measure, which in itself is in conformity with a corresponding article of the Convention may still infringe this article when read in conjunction with article 14, because the measure is of a discriminatory nature. Thus Article 2 of the Protocol does not create a right to a particular kind of educational establishment; nevertheless when a State has set up such an establishment it may not draw up discriminatory entrance requirements within the meaning of article 14 (e.g. on the ground of language). The Court gives another example: if a State goes beyond its obligations under article 6 of the Convention by setting up a system of courts of appeal, it would violate article 14 "were it to debar certain persons from these remedies without a legitimate reason while making them available to others in respect of the same type of actions." The Court concludes: "... It is as though (Article 14) formed an integral part of each of the Articles laying down rights and freedoms."[138]

By stating that article 14 is an "integral part" of each provision of the Convention, however, the Court has at the same time recognized that the restriction in the wording of article 14 deprives the clause of much of its significance.[139] According to the provisions that embody substantive rights, the States Parties are bound to grant these rights to "Everyone," while the fundamental freedoms of the Convention may not be infringed upon with regard to "No one." And such terms are lacking in most legal systems exactly in those rights and freedoms that were not incorporated in the Convention, and would probably need them most. Of course, the broad interpretation adopted by the Commission and the Court of article 14 may provide for a remedy against the shortcomings of the wording; but not only are the reasonings of both organs not quite clear in our opinion, they appear to be also to some extent self-contradictory. The Commission and the Court endeavour to escape the restriction of the article, but they come somehow back within its confines after all.

Schindler draws the conclusion that a State party could bar a particular racial group entirely from e.g. trade or commerce without

[138] Judgment, § 9.

[139] Various authors have expressed the same view. Compare Schindler, *op.cit.*, p. 132; K. Doehring, "Non discrimination and Equal Treatment under the European Human Rights Convention and the West German Constitution with Particular Reference to Discrimination against Aliens," in *American Journal of Comparative Law*, Vol. 18, (1970), at p. 308; Ulrich Scheuner, "Comparison of the Jurisprudence of National Courts with that of the Organs of the Convention," in *Human Rights in National and International Law* (A. H. Robertson, ed., Manchester 1968), p. 261, 262.

violating the Convention.[140] (By the same token, it could be added, this might be done *vis à vis* any of the other groups identified by the grounds of article 14 as well). In principle this view seems to be correct, except for the fact that measures constituting such large scale discrimination are likely to involve violations of one or more rights and freedoms that are recognized in the Convention. And it should also be asked whether, and if so, to what extent the functioning of a specific ground such as "race" could transcend a limitation as imposed by the wording of article 14.

As a matter of fact, the European Commission on Human Rights has taken this step in its decision of 10 October 1970 on the admissibility of the complaints lodged by 26 "East African Indians" (*Samji M. L. Patel and 25 other applications v. the United Kingdom*). This case concerned complaints by citizens of the United Kingdom and British protected persons of Asian origin, who were expelled from Kenya and Uganda where they were born and where they had lived up till then. All of them were holders of British passports, but under the Commonwealth Immigration Act 1968 they were refused admission to the United Kingdom, or, if admitted, were not granted permission to remain permanently. The right to enter the territory of the State of which one is a national, and the right not to be expelled from such territory has not been included in the Convention itself, but in the fourth Protocol to the Convention. However, the fourth Protocol has not been ratified by the United Kingdom; consequently the British Government maintained that article 14 was not applicable. On this point the Commission reasoned as follows:

> "Whereas, however, the Commision is of the opinion that, quite apart from any consideration of Article 14, discrimination based on race could, in certain circumstances, of itself amount to degrading treatment within the meaning of Article 3 of the Convention; whereas the Commission considers that is is generally recognized that a special importance should be attached to discrimination based on race, and that publicly to single out a group of persons for differential treatment on the basis of race might, in certain circumstances, constitute a special form of affront to human dignity; whereas, therefore, differential treatment of a group of persons on the basis of race might be capable of constituting degrading treatment in circumstances where differential treatment on some other ground, such as language, would raise no such question."[141]

Apart from the European Convention, as far as race is concerned it could be possible to revert to the Charter itself. In its recent Advisory

[140] Schindler, *ibidem.*

[141] European Commission of Human Rights, *Collection of Decisions*, Vol. 36, p. 92 ff., at p. 117.

Opinion on the *Legal Consequences for States of the Continued Presence of South Africa in Namibia (South West Africa) notwithstanding Security Council Resolution 276 (1970)*, the International Court of Justice observes – with respect to "a territory having an international status" –:

"Under the Charter of the United Nations, the former Mandatory had pledged itself to observe and respect, in a territory having an international status, human rights and fundamental freedoms for all without distinction as to race. To establish instead, and enforce, distinctions, exclusions, restrictions and limitations exclusively based on grounds of race, colour, descent, or national or ethnic origin which constitute a denial of fundamental human rights is a flagrant violation of the purposes and principles of the Charter."[142]

We have discussed this problem of the "dependance" of the clause in the light of the European Convention. But as we said earlier, article 2 of the Universal Declaration is similarly restricted, and so is article 2 (2) of the Covenant on Economic, Social and Cultural Rights. The Universal Declaration was not designed as a binding instrument, so the consequences of the restriction are slight. The restriction of article 2 (2) of the Covenant, however, may have unfavourable consequences if a State is bound to this Covenant, but not to the Covenant on Civil and Political Rights. If a State is a party to both Covenants, article 26 of the latter Covenant covers the entire field, and thus cancels the restriction of article 2 (1) of the former Covenant.[143]

54. *Article 26 of the Covenant on Civil and Political Rights*

Earlier we reproduced article 26 of the Covenant on Civil and Political Rights as an authoritative, representative example of a non-discrimination clause of global applicability (at the beginning of paragraph 37). The grounds that figure in this clause have been discussed in some of the previous paragraphs. We must now shortly deal with the other elements of this provision. We have already seen that the provision has the broadest range both because of its affecting all rights and duties,

[142] I.C.J. *Reports* 1971, p. 16 ff., at p. 57 (paragraph 131). The Court employs partly the wording of article 1 (1) of the Convention on the Elimination of All Forms of Racial Discrimination. See on the significance of the Court's view in general, E. Schwelb, "The International Court of Justice and the Human Rights Clauses of the Charter," in *A.J.I.L.*, Vol. 66, (1972), p. 337 ff., especially p. 346 ff.

[143] In this connection article 60 of the European Convention may also be mentioned:

"Nothing in this Convention may be construed as limiting or derogating from any of the human rights and fundamental freedoms which may be ensured under the laws of any High Contracting Party or under any other agreement to which it is a Party."

and because of its enunciative rather than limitative list of grounds.

In the first drafts of the Covenant on Civil and Political Rights the clause was less wide in scope and much less complicated than it became later on. In the draft of the Convention contained in the Report of the 3rd Session of the Commission on Human Rights (1948) it was a relatively simple provision shaped after the corresponding article in the Universal Declaration.[144] But as the process of the drafting of the Covenants on Civil and Political and on Economic, Social and Cultural Rights went on the clause tended to become more complex. In its draft of 1951 the Commission on Human Rights offered the version (article 17) that in our opinion would have been the most satisfying of all both on account of its clarity and simplicity and its comprehensiveness regarding rights and grounds:

"All are equal before the law; all shall be accorded equal protection of the law without discrimination on any ground such as race, colour, sex, language, religion, political or other opinion, national or social origin, property, birth or other status."[145]

In 1954 the first part of the clause (then numbered article 24) had become:

"All are equal before the law. The law shall prohibit any discrimination and guarantee to all persons equal and effective protection against discrimination on any grounds such as ..." etc.[146]

This wording remained unchanged until the draft article was considered by the 3rd Committee of the General Assembly in November 1961, where it gave occasion to a very interesting debate.[147]

At the beginning several amendments were submitted to the draft article,[148] of which the following amendments were adopted by the Third Committee: India suggested to add at the end of the first sentence: "and are entitled to equal protection of the law." A sub-amendment moved by Argentina and Chile was to insert the words

[144] Article 20: "Equal protection of the law with respect to the enjoyment of any of the rights and freedoms set forth in this Covenant shall not be denied to any one on account of race (which includes colour), sex, language, religion, political or other opinion, property status, or national or social origin." Report of the Commission on Human Rights of its 3rd Session, ECOSOC, O.R. 7th Session, Supplement 2, (E/800), p. 26 (28 June, 1948).

[145] Commission on Human Rights, Report of the Seventh Session, Official Records of the Economic and Social Council, Official Records of the 13th Session, Supplement 9 (E. 1992), p. 22 (24 May 1951).

[146] Commission on Human Rights, Report of the Tenth Session (E/2573), p. 68.

[147] A/C.3/SR.1097–1103.

[148] See General Assembly, Sixteenth Session, Official Records, Annexes, Report of the Third Committee (A. 5000), p. 12.

"without any discrimination" between "are entitled" and "to equal protection of the law"; the Indian delegate accepted this sub-amendment and revised his amendment accordingly. He had preferred article 24 to be patterned after the first sentence of article 7 of the Universal Declaration on Human Rights and this would be achieved through his own amendment as subamended by the Chilean and Argentine delegations.

Finally, the United Kingdom, together with Greece, submitted an amendment which played an important role in the ensuing discussions as the "two-Power amendment" and which consisted of two parts. Of these, the latter was merely to add the word "such" to the word "discrimination" as appearing for the second time in the second sentence of the draft article between "against" and "on any grounds." This part of the British-Greek amendment was later withdrawn. The former, crucial part of the "two-Power amendment" was to insert the words "In this respect" at the beginning of the second sentence of the draft article.[149]

The insertion of "in this respect" was proposed as a replacement for the earlier suggestion by the United Kingdom to delete the entire second sentence of draft article 24. However, recognizing that the majority of the third Committee probably wished to retain this sentence, the United Kingdom now confined itself to suggesting merely a rewording of it – intended, we assume, to bring about the same effect. For the complete deletion of the second sentence the following reasons were given: the draft Covenant contained already a clause prohibiting discrimination (article 2, prohibiting discrimination, but only with respect to the rights recognized in the Covenant) and it was "inappropriate and unnecessary to repeat the same (sic) provision in other articles"; the proposed clause was too broad, unenforceable, and "contained obligations that no State could possibly meet"; finally, the second sentence of the draft article did not seem "to form a logical part of the article as a whole." This last reason was further explained as follows:

"The first sentence stated in simple terms a principle basic to all human rights, namely, that all persons were equal before the law. The purpose of the second sentence should be to explain and amplify that basic principle. Since article 2 (of the draft Covenant) already guaranteed non-discrimination, it would be appropriate to repeat that provision in a way designed to underline and strengthen the basic principle of article 24, which was equality before the law. The present

[149] A/C.3/L. 946.

wording introduced quite different ideas, concerned not with the guarantee of that equality, but rather with the relations and responsibilities of a State to those living within its jurisdiction."[150]

These same reasons now functioned as arguments for the inclusion of "in this respect." To insert these words would in the opinion of the British delegate not only "bring the second sentence in line with the first," but would also "amplify the idea of equality before the law."[151]

The debate that followed was devoted chiefly to the question what the consequences of the two-Power amendment would be, and whether these consequences were acceptable or not. The issue divided the Committee deeply and gave rise to a sometimes sharp debate, especially on the part of the opponents of the two Power amendment who subjected it to severe criticism. The two main positions taken by delegations in the Third Committee can be summarized in general terms as follows: The delegates who announced that they were prepared to vote for the two-Power amendment generally agreed with the British view that the purpose of the clause as a whole should be to guarantee "equality before the law." Thus the first sentence was regarded as the most important of the two, while the second sentence was considered as ill fitting or even redundant. From this point of view the second sentence of the original draft was not a logical part of the first, and failed to explain and amplify the principal of equality "before" the law, as it should.

The delegates who opposed the two-Power amendment likewise realized that the draft article dealt with two different notions, *viz.* equality "before" the law and non-discrimination both "before" and "in" the law. But in contrast to the supporters of the amendment, they emphatically wanted the article to do so. They denied that the non-discrimination principle was already sufficiently incorporated in the Covenant in draft article 2. The scope of that article was restricted to the rights of the Covenant, while article 24 was of general application. More important was the problem of the relation between the first and the second sentence. The opponents of the two-Power amendment did not wish to see article 24 reduced to a mere guarantee of equality "before" the law. The words "in this respect" would weaken the second sentence and render it an explanation of the first, and therefore subordinate and accessory to the first.

[150] A/C.3/SR.1097, §§ 27–29.
[151] *Ibidem*, § 31.

Although "equality before the law" was a principle of essential importance to any legal system, its limitations were not overlooked. As the delegate from the Philipines observed, States could still pass legislation under it "providing for separate but equal facilities such as housing, schools and restaurants for different groups. Since the facilities would be equal, such States could claim that they were applying the principle of the equality of all before the law."[152] It was recognized that equality before the law and non-discrimination are by no means necessarily opposite notions. On the contrary, they had common ground; non-discrimination covered fully equality before the law. This was brought out by the Indonesian representative as he informally suggested that the two-Power amendment could be reworded from "in this respect" to "therefore."[153]

Like other representatives[154] the Polish delegate, Mr. Szleper, expressed the view that the first sentence of article 24 "had become an abstraction which entailed no practical or legal obligations." Moreover, "discrimination of the most inhuman kind, such as the prohibition of any contact between races was entirely compatible with formal equality before the law. His delegation therefore favoured a second sentence making it clear that effective action must be taken to prohibit discrimination and to provide safeguards against it."[155]

The Polish statement was attacked by the Australian representative who remarked that his delegation "strongly disagreed with that interpretation, since the concept of equality for all in the application of the law was a corner-stone for good government, and accordingly should stand in article 24 as its operative principle."[156] The Polish representative felt justified to speak again in order to clarify his position: "In its original form, article 24 was the only one in the Covenants to make a frontal attack on discrimination as a whole. To reduce the prohibition to a statement of the principle that all were equal before the law ... would be tantamount to placing a serious limitation on that prohibition or to evading the question, or even, in some cases, to sanctioning discrimination as still practised in many countries."

Some speakers had said that the two-Power amendment would strengthen the prohibition of discrimination, but in the view of this

[152] A/C.3/SR.1098, § 25.
[153] *Ibidem*, §§ 1–3.
[154] E.g. Venezuela, A/C.3/SR.1101, §§ 27–32; India, *ibidem*, § 42.
[155] A/C.3/SR.1099, § 45.
[156] A/C.3/SR.1098, § 25.

delegate the reverse was the case. "Equality before the law had, as many representatives had pointed out, no substance from the standpoint of specific obligations assumed." And he continued:

"That substance lay in the second sentence of article 24, wherein the obligations of States were plainly enunciated. The statement that those obligations should serve to implement the principle set out in the first sentence would be similar to the mathematical proposition of multiplying a value by naught; the same result would be obtained, namely, naught."

In the remaining part of his statement the delegate demonstrated that several texts he cited from South African legislation were in conformity with the principle of equality before the law. These texts "were nontheless discriminatory. Moreover, they had to do with matters which were not dealt with in any of the draft articles of the Covenants." Finally, the Polish delegation could not believe that "... the General Assembly had the right to reject a general anti-discriminatory clause and accept instead a formula which, at best, committed States to nothing and, at worst, appeared to sanction every form – even the most outrageous – of discrimination."[157]

We have quoted extensively from Mr. Szleper's observations because they generally reflect the view of the delegates who opposed the two-Power amendment. These delegates regarded the non-discrimination principle as obliging the States that were bound to it to combat discrimination actively, e.g. to pass special legislation abolishing and redressing legal and factual discrimination that might still exist, and to safeguard against possible future discrimination that might develop. But then, so did obviously those who thought that the amendment contained a desirable restriction to the non-discrimination principle as originally conceived. When finally the vote was taken, the amendment was adopted by 36 votes to 30, with 11 abstentions.[158]

These discussions on the words "In this respect" of article 26 are of particular interest to us since we can draw two conclusions from them. Firstly, not only the opponents of the two-Power amendment were of the opinion that "non-discrimination" was a quite different notion from "equality before the law," but this was also the view of the proponents of the amendment. Secondly, not only the opponents of the amendment held the view that compliance with a rule prohibiting discrimination might require positive action on the part of the State (in contradistinction to the equality before the law principle), but also

[157] A/C.3/SR.1101, paragraphs 15–21.
[158] A/C.3/SR.1102, para. 63.

the proponents of the amendment thought so. This was precisely the reason why the amendment was proposed and adopted: it was admittedly designed to minimize or even to eliminate this element of the non-discrimination principle such as it was to be embodied in article 26. That also the delegations who favoured the two-Power amendment held this view can also be inferred from statements by several of them.[159]

The first sentence of draft article 24 of the Covenant on Civil and Political Rights was expanded by the Indian amendment, as subamended. As a result, the wording of the present article 26 is nearly the same as that of article 7 of the Universal Declaration. Since the way the first part of article 26 came into existence does not contribute to the understanding and interpretation of the concept of discrimination as is the case with the genesis of the second part, we shall not discuss it in any detail.

The starting point was, and remained, to provide a guarantee of "equality before the law." All later additions were proposed and adopted with the strengthening of this principle in mind. Each time the aim was to make guarantee more effective. Occasionally it was submitted that the clause became "repetitive", that certain insertions were "redundant," but this did not stop the process of enlarging it.

An analysis of the eventual text of article 26 would yield the following result: The final goal is equality before the law, as well as equal protection of the law. "Equal protection of the law" was introduced into the text of article 7 of the Universal Declaration by an American amendment in the working group that drafted the declaration[160], and adopted in article 26 through the Indian amendment. But the precise meaning and the intended scope of this formula is nowhere explained.

In article 26, the elements that follow "equal protection of the law" are designed – as we have seen – as explanations and specifications of the methods *via* which that goal can be reached. Equal protection, it appears from the text, can be realized in two ways, one formulated negatively, one positively. Negatively, namely resulting from a prohibition of "discrimination"; and positively, *viz.* resulting from a guarantee of what is again called "equal protection," now specified as a

[159] Apart from the United Kingdom and Greece we mention China (SR.1097, § 42); Chile (SR.1098, § 8–12, especially § 11; however, Chile, originally in favour of the amendment, abstained when the vote was taken); Ethiopia (SR.1098, § 13); Denmark (SR.1099, § 19); Canada (SR.1099, § 26); Cameroun (SR.1099, § 27); Turkey (SR.1099, §§ 31–33); Sweden (SR.1101, §§ 24, 25); Finland (SR.1101, §§ 44–46).

[160] E/CN.4/AC.2/SR.2, p. 8; E/CN.4/AC.1/SR.12, p. 4

protection "against discrimination," which must also be "effective." This latter discrimination is finally specified as to a number of grounds on which it may be based: race, colour, sex, etc. From this it can be concluded that article 26 prescribes that equal protection must be reached

(a) through the elimination of discrimination and

(b) through the guarantee of equal protection against discrimination.

Obviously all these elements of article 26 amount to a prohibition to "discriminate." Therefore, a provision such as article 26 – whether it is poorly or well drafted – shows that it is by no means superfluous to develop a more or less precise notion of discrimination. Such a notion is indispensable if a clause such as article 26, however elaborate and wordy, is to have any meaning at all.

In this connection it is interesting to note the lack of a common understanding among the members of the third Committee concerning the concept of discrimination: some representatives declared that they were in favour of the two-Power amendment because without it the non-discrimination clause of the second sentence would oblige the contracting Parties to the total elimination from legislation of all possible legal classifications. Especially, in this respect, some feared that the second sentence in its original form would rule out all differentiations between nationals and aliens, in particular with respect to the nationalisation of foreign investments. Both fears were emphatically declared baseless by the adversaries of the amendment.

55. *The Legal Function of the Grounds: Clarification*

In this paragraph we shall examine the legal significance and the rôle of the forbidden grounds for differentiation. This rôle can be regarded as a double one: first of all it is to clarify the non-discrimination principle in the human rights field. Secondly, in a more procedural context, the function – or rather: the effect – of the grounds is to shift the burden of proof. This function will be discussed in the next paragraph.

The Sub-Commission on the Prevention of Discrimination and the Protection of Minorities stated in its first Report to the Commission of Human Rights, that it

"... Considered that in extending by the words "political or other opinion, property status, or national or social origin," the enumeration given in article 6 as drawn up by the Drafting Committee ("without distinction as to race, sex, language, or religion"), it had not added to that enumeration, but had interpreted and clarified it by means of examples."[161]

In some of the previous paragraphs we have endeavoured to provide for some information that might further this clarifying function. (In many fields of international law the opinions that were voiced in the drafting bodies may have lost much of their relevance, two decades later, for the interpretation of the document in question. In matters of discrimination, however, the patterns are firm and enduring, so a historic interpretation is not quite out of place).

This clarifying function of the grounds is interesting in a historical context. As remarked earlier, a few centuries ago a different "religion" as a ground for unequal treatment constituted, as it were, the notion of discrimination. Later on, "discrimination" was a form of unequal treatment primarily conceived of as caused by a different "nationality." Beyond such grounds there was no reason or motive for equal treatment, or rather for a general prohibition of wrongly unequal treatment. In contrast, the notion of discrimination we are dealing with nowadays involves a *general* prohibition of discrimination. This development has reduced the different grounds to mere examples of the general principle. They no longer constitute but only clarify the notion of discrimination.[162]

The representative clauses go very far in this respect; the lists they

[161] E/CN.4/52, p. 4. The Sub-Commission added that its text ("without distinction of any kind such as race ..." etc.) was, moreover, intended to show that its enumeration was not exhaustive (*Ibidem*).

[162] It is remarkable to note that Jaenicke still seems to assert that only such forms of discrimination are forbidden, that are enumerated in the clauses: "Im Rahmen der Menschenrechte bedürfen die Gleichbehandlungs- und Nichtdiskriminierungsgebote wegen der Unschärfe des abstrakten Gleichheitsbegriffes in der Regel näherer Konkretisierung. Hier sind nicht Differenzierungen schlechthin, sondern zunächst nur solche Differenzierungen als Diskriminierungen verboten, die nach bestimmten, ausdrücklich aufgezählten unzulässigen Unterscheidungsmerkmalen (wie Farbe, Rasse, Sprache, Religion, politische Meinung) differenzieren." He therefore pleads for exhaustive catalogues if possible: "Sofern diese Aufzählung nicht erschöpfend sein soll, sondern darüber hinaus "jegliche Diskriminierung" (Artikel 7 der Menschenrechtendeklaration der Vereinten Nationen) verhindert werden soll, versucht man diese Lücke in der Weise zu schlieszen, dasz auch Differenzierungen nach sonstigen "unsachlichen" oder "willkürlichen" Unterscheidungsmerkmalen als Diskriminierungen gewertet werden, obwohl solche Kriterien als juristisch kaum faszbare Grenszfälle der praktischen Rechtsanwendung Schwierigkeiten bereiten. Es sollte deshalb mehr Wert auf eine möglichst vollstandige Aufzählung der unzulässigen Unterscheidungsmerkmale gelegt werden." "Gleichbehandlung," in *Wörterbuch des Völkerrechts*, Vol. I, p. 693 (See also our comments on Jaenicke's views *infra*, p. 56 ff).

Compare on this problem however Kipp, *op.cit.*, p. 145: "... eine festlegende Aufzählung unzulässiger Unterscheidungsmerkmale würde dann die Frage offen lassen, ob in eine solche Aufzählung nicht aufgenommene Merkmale nicht doch Grund wären, die gleichmäszige Zuerkennung der in der Deklaration (i.e. the Universal Declaration of Human Rights) enthaltenen Rechte an alle Menschen zu modifizieren."

contain are nearly all-embracing. This appears clearly from the discussions in the United Nations bodies that were involved in the drafting of these clauses. Especially the discussion in the third Committee of the General Assembly on the ground "birth" in article 2 of the Universal Declaration (to name just one example) illustrates the feeling that a ground such as this was already fully covered by other expressions that were earlier adopted and incorporated in the clause.[163] In various bodies occasional remarks were also made about the redundancy of other additional grounds.

However this may be, the enumeration of a number of grounds is an adequate device for clarifying and specifying the notion of discrimination, in particular the rather vague and indetermined element of the lacking "sufficient connection" as described above in § 27. A non-discrimination clause with a catalogue of grounds is directed against a number of symptoms that represent the attitudes through which a "discriminatory state of mind" of a group or an individual (or of a legal institution, c.q. a state organ) manifests itself. Such a clause is intended to do so because there appear to exist some regular patterns in discriminatory conduct; there are certain group characteristics towards which it is usually oriented: race, religion, national or social origin, and so on.

Still it is of course a typically juristic approach to distinguish neatly between kinds of discrimination according to the specific type of prejudice on which they are supposedly based, and thus to keep them apart in separate categories. This legal technique does not reflect the fact that discrimination hardly ever occurs on the basis of one particular ground only, but rather as a complex mixture of several types simultaneously. When we discussed such grounds as race, language, religion, national and social origin, it appeared already how closely connected these notions are, and how seldom any one of them will occur separately, at least in group relations. Thus Simson and Yinger state: "It is the contention of the present authors that the causes of antipathy between groups are *cumulative* and *interactive*."[164] This is clearly demonstrated in the example of the national, linguistic, and religious minorities. Noteworthy in this connection is also the question whether anti-semitism is a matter of racism or a form of religious intolerance, which played

[163] See above, p. 103.

[164] G. E. Simson and J. M. Yinger, *Racial and Cultural Minorities: an Analysis of Prejudice and Discrimination* (3rd ed., New York 1965), p. 12 (Italics in the original).

quite a role during the drafting of the Convention on the Elimination of All Forms of Racial Discrimination.[165]

Some types of discrimination generate other types, and are in turn reinforced by these.[166] A certain religion may lead people to a particular group of professions; the resulting economic conditions may produce a certain group-consciousness, which in turn may lead to different social attitudes, different political loyalties, may be even different linguistic usages, and so on. A process like his may start anywhere in the chain, but race, religion and national or social origin seem to be the most powerful factors, which generally produce the others.

What a non-discrimination clause containing an enumeration of forbidden grounds attempts to do is to eliminate a discriminatory social structure by aiming at its component parts, reaching its goal step by step, though it may seem to try to cure only symptoms.

56. *Idem: Shifting the Burden of Proof*

This concerns not so much a function, but rather an effect of the grounds. We would submit that the grounds shift the burden of proof wherever a violation (involving one or more of the grounds) of a non-discrimination clause is asserted (e.g. by an individual who claims that he is discriminated against), and denied by a State or one of its organs that are bound by the clause. This aspect of the forbidden grounds may come out not only in a typically procedural context, (such as in a procedure before the European Commission of Human Rights) but in fact in any dispute concerning possibly discriminatory measures. To demonstrate this submission we shall have to revert to illustrative instances of national rather than of international provenance.

In a municipal law context the grounds can have an impact on the procedural position of individuals before national courts in cases involving complaints about discrimination, subject to two conditions: (a) that there is judicial review of legislation, and (b) that the courts are authorized to take account of international conventions and to apply

[165] See Schwelb, *op.cit.*, p. 1011–1015, and Lerner, *op.cit.*, p. 78–82. The generally accepted conclusion is that anti-semitism constitutes racial discrimination within the meaning of the Convention.

[166] This is sometimes referred to as the "vicious circle" of prejudice and discrimination. Compare e.g. Rehbinder, *op.cit.* p. 10 ff., and *The Main Types and Causes of Discriminations*, p. 16–17. See generally on the sociological aspects of discrimination the book by Simson and Yinger.

an international non-discrimination clause to the case at hand (or that such a clause has been incorporated in municipal law and can be applied as such).

If these conditions are fulfilled, the outcome must be that any rule of national law which is partly or completely, directly or indirectly based on, or involves, a forbidden ground for differentiation, is "suspect." We borrow the expression "suspect" from Mr. Justice Black of the U.S. Supreme Court, who stated in his opinion in *Korematsu v. U.S.*:

"It should be noted ... that all legal restrictions which curtail the civil rights of a single racial group are immediately suspect. That is not to say that all such restrictions are unconstitutional. It is to say that Courts must subject them to the most rigid scrutiny ..."[167]

The same term was employed by Mr. Justice Warren in *Bolling v. Sharpe*, where he observed that:

"classifications based solely upon race must be scrutinized with particular care, since they are ... constitutionally suspect."[168]

The "shifting the burden of proof" can be brought forward in a different manner, namely as an obligation of the reviewing authorities – it must be added: whether they be "courts" or not[169] – to abandon the usual restraint in reviewing legislation. Generally the grounds should have

[167] *Korematsu v. U.S.*, 323 U.S. 214 (1944). This view was developed under the 14th Amendment, which admittedly, though not *expressis verbis*, concerns racial discrimination.

[168] *Bolling v. Sharpe*, 347 U.S. 497 (1954). This specific judicial attitude under the Fourteenth Amendment seems indeed limited to matters of race. In a chiefly *economic* context the main rule was formulated in a quite different manner, as follows: "1. The equal protection clause of the Fourteenth Amendment does not take from the State the power to classify in the adoption of police laws, but admits of the exercise of a wide scope of discretion in that regard, and avoids what is done only when it is without any reasonable basis and therefore is purely arbitrary. 2. A classification having some reasonable basis does not offend against that clause merely because it is not made with mathematical nicety or because in practice it results in some inequality. 3. When the classification in such a law is called in question, if any state of facts reasonably can be conceived that would sustain it, the existence of that state of facts at the time the law was enacted, must be assumed. 4. One who assails the classification in such a law must carry the burden of showing that it does not rest upon any reasonable basis, but is essentially arbitrary." *Lindsley v. Natural Carbonic Gas Co.*, 220 U.S. 61, 78–79 (1911), as quoted by the Court in *Morey v. Doud*, 354 U.S. 457 (1957).

[169] In this connection a "reviewing authority" may be a court of appeal, a constitutional court, a higher administrative authority, a parliamentary majority. At the international level it may be a court such as the European Court of Human Rights. But it could also be a quasi-judicial organ such as the European Commission of Human Rights, or e.g. the projected Human Rights Committee as provided for in articles 28 ff. of the Covenant on Civil and Political Rights and the Optional Protocol to that Covenant. Or the Committee on the Elimination of Racial Discrimination, provided for in articles 8 ff. of the Convention on the Elimination of All Forms of Racial Discrimination. (In these international instances the condition as to the applicability of international instruments is of course irrelevant).

the effect of laying the burden of proof that a contested measure does not involve discrimination on the authority that enacted it and seeks to enforce it. The burden should not be on the individual or group of individuals who seek to have such a measure condemned as discriminatory. In other words, and more in general (since the grounds are only examples), the legal effect of the grounds or of a clause in general should be to make it incumbent on him who introduces a classification, to show that the "sufficient connection" is established. A complaining individual should not be obliged to show that a measure constitutes "discrimination" because the connection is insufficient or completely lacking.

These views are corroborated by the doctrine concerning article 14 of the European Convention on Human Rights. Guradze states in his commentary on the Convention that a "presumption of irrationality" lies on the explicitly forbidden grounds.[170] Partsch speaks similarly about the suspicion that arbitrariness is involved whenever differential treatment based on race, language, religion etc. occurs.[171]

Interesting in this respect is also the theory developed by Podlech with respect to article 3 (1) of the German Constitution.[172] He regards article 3 (1) as a rule relating to the burden of proof, or rather, as he calls it, the "Argumentationslast." This rule on this burden has the effect of making unconstitutional any differentiation of which it cannot be argued, with constitutionally plausible arguments, that it is allowed under the constitution. The rule works to the benefit of those who claim that a differentiation violates the constitution. This rule requires that only when the constitutionality of a differentiation can clearly be shown it is valid; consequently it is not already valid when the unconstitutionality has not (yet) been established.[173]

To say that the grounds shift the burden of proof as to the legality of a differentiation based upon one of them carries the implication that the possibility is left open for the authority which enacted the rule introducting such a differentiation to prove the legality of that rule. This implication involves the "relative" nature of the grounds.

[170] "Die ausdrücklich verbotenen Unterscheidungsmerkmale haben die Vermutung der Sachfremdheit für sich" (p. 190).

[171] "Wenn eine unterschiedliche Behandlung nach Rasse, Sprache, Religion usw. stattfindet, besteht mindestens der Verdacht, dasz Willkür im Spiele sei." *Op.cit.*, p. 327.

[172] Paragraph 3 of article 3 is reproduced above, in § 37. The paragraphs 1 and 2 run as follows: "1. All persons shall be equal before the law. 2. Men and women shall have equal rights." English translation in Peaslee, *Constitutions of Nations*, Vol. III, 3rd ed. (The Hague 1968), p. 361 ff.

[173] Podlech, *op.cit.*, p. 87–90.

57. *The Relative Nature of the Grounds: "Special Measures of Protection"*

The question must be asked whether and if so in what circumstances the non-discrimination principle allows for classifications on the basis of forbidden grounds. Or is such a classification *eo ipso* "wrong," i.e. discrimination?

We submit that legislative differentiations on forbidden grounds do not necessarily violate the clause which contains the grounds. We have remarked earlier that *generally* on such grounds a sufficient connection cannot be established (§ 37 *in fine*). In certain circumstances, however, this can very well be the case. Compare for example article 5 of the Discrimination (Employment and Occupation) Convention, which runs as follows:

"1. Special measures of protection or assistance provided for in other Conventions or Recommendations adopted by the International Labour Conference shall not be deemed to be discrimination.
2. Any member may, after consultation with representative employers' and workers' organisations, where such exist, determine that other special measures designed to meet the particular requirements of persons who, for reasons such as sex, age disablement, family responsibilities or social or cultural status, are generally recognized to require special protection or assistance, shall not be deemed to be discrimination."

No less interesting an example of what we mean is section 4 of article 1 of the Convention on the Elimination of All Forms of Racial Discrimination:

"Special measures taken for the sole purpose of securing adequateadva ncement of certain racial or ethnic groups of individuals requiring such protection as may be necessary in order to ensure such groups or individuals equal enjoyment or exercise of human rights and fundamental freedoms shall not be deemed racial discrimination, provided, however that such measures do not, as a consequence, lead to the maintenance of separate rights for different racial groups and that they shall not be continued after the objectives for which they were taken have been achieved."

In the discussion of our definition of discrimination in § 27 *in fine* we stated that the concept must be understood as a combination of the equality and inequality aspects, and the treatment aspect. Only in the context of a particular right or duty can the meaning equality or inequality be appreciated. Accordingly the functioning of the grounds is closely related to the nature of the subject matter that is regulated.[174]

[174] This appears also from a provision like article 4 (1) of the Covenant on Civil and Political

This is why we speak of the "relative" nature of the grounds. In the two examples just quoted the specific circumstances, namely, the specific subject matter that is regulated is precisely and carefully described. This subject matter is such that it warrants for differential treatment even on otherwise forbidden grounds. In both cases it concerns extra assistance to, and the advancement of groups or individuals that are weak, backward, or handicapped in one way or another in comparison with other groups. They need "special measures of protection" as it is called in the I.L.O. Convention.

In this egalitarian epoch, the battle against the great inequalities among groups and individuals in about every society is fought with mainly "unequal treatment of unequals" as the most widely used weapon in order to reach "distributive justice." This seems to be simple enough; yet Professor S. I. Benn, discussing the problems of compensating welfare legislation for the back population in the United States notes "the ambiguous implications of equality and, in particular, of the "equal protection" clause of the Fourtheenth Amendment for the desegregation and the social integration of negroes."
He observes: "Even liberal friends of the Negro have been known to argue, it seems, that the law should be colorblind, and that compensatory legislation on the Negro's behalf is discrimination in reverse. If (it is said) color is irrelevant to eligibility for jobs, housing, education and social esteem, to make special provisions for the Negro as such would be to reinstate an irrelevant criterium, and so to treat equals unequally, or alternatively, to deny the human equality that it is so important to affirm."[175]

This "unequal treatment" is of course meant to be "favourable." What is the standard according to which this treatment can be granted? Is it possible to point at clear and unequivocal standards that

Rights, which, *in time of public emergency which threatens the life of the nation*, implies the possibility of lawful differential treatment based on "political or other opinion," "national origin," "property," "birth" or "other status." See on this provision also above, § 52 *in fine*.

[175] Stanley I. Benn, "Egalitarianism and the Equal Consideration of Interests," in *Nomos IX, Equality*, p. 74–75. The two international Conventions that were quoted obviously set aside the reasonings reproduced by Benn. Quite unclear is Podlech's discussion of the function of the forbidden grounds enumerated in article 3 (3) of the German Constitution. At p. 91 he states: "Unterschiede im Geschlecht, der Abstammung, der Rasse, der Sprache, der Heimat, der Herkunft, den religiösen und politischen Anschauungen sind *nie* ein Zureichender Grund für Ungleichbehandlungen, die zugleich Benachteilungen und Bevorzugungen sind." (Italics added). At p. 94, however, he states: "Art. 3 Abs. 2 und 3 G.G. verbieten den öffentlichen hoheitlich handelnden Gewalt nicht, nach den in diesen Absätzen genannten Merkmalen zu differenzieren. Sie verbieten vielmehr, etwaige Differenzierungen mit diesen Merkmalen zu begründen." The distinction between "to differentiate according to the grounds" and "to base the differentiation upon the grounds" is nowhere explained, and remains puzzling to us.

are also generally accepted, according to which certain inequalities are so relevant as to call for compensation?

The States Parties to the International Covenant on Economic, Social and Cultural Rights recognize, in the Preamble to the Covenant, that the ideal of free human beings enjoying freedom from fear and want can only be achieved if conditions are created whereby everyone may enjoy his economic, social and cultural rights, as well as his civil and political rights. This international ideal must, as nearly all international ideals in the field of human rights, be realized at the national level.

It involves therefore, at this level, the development of what can be referred to as conditions of social and economic equality, or at least really equal opportunities. Very often this requires compensation in one way or another: income policies, taxation, subsidies, all kinds of welfare programs, and so on.

In many cases the social realities expressed by the legal "forbidden grounds for differentiation" have caused the weakness or backwardness of the groups that require such compensation. Consequently, the compensation must be given according to the same criteria, on the basis of these same grounds. The same is true in the protection of minorities.

We have already observed that favourable unequal treatment for some – if compensation may be described as such – generally constitutes at the same time the unfavourable unequal treatment of others (see § 31). Thus, apart from the problem noted by Professor Benn, yet another problem arises from the granting of favourable unequal treatment to (economic, social or cultural) unequals: groups that are different from those that receive compensation are denied the favourable treatment on exactly the same grounds that characterize the especially protected groups. Yet the provisions we have quoted imply that such unfavourable unequal treatment against some does not constitute discrimination (even though it is, again, necessarily based on otherwise forbidden grounds) if the treatment is granted in order to compensate for the weakness or backwardness of others, as described above.

To give an example: if in a public housing development the rent is lowered for, say, a certain racial group, (or public educational institutions lower the admission-standards for that group, or that group is exempted from the payment of medical fees, and so on), such privileges are denied to those who do not belong to that particular group. They are denied the favours since they do not belong to that race, consequently, for racial reasons, that is, on the basis of race.[176] The international endeavours towards "conditions whereby everyone may enjoy his economic, social and cultural rights" provides for the justification of such unfavourable unequal treatment even on "forbidden" grounds. The standard that leads to these endeavours is the same that produces the sufficient connection.

In the light of the terminology we have adopted we would hesitate to employ such terms as "protective discrimination" or "favourable discrimination" to designate this state of affairs, as is done sometimes.[177] These terms may have come up because the situation was felt to be contradictory, which it is not if its elements (especially the character of the "treatment" in question) are properly defined and understood.

58. Special Measures of Protection: Allowed or Prescribed

The proviso with which article 1(4) of the Convention on the Elimination of all Forms of Racial Discrimination ends ("... provided, however, that such measures do not, as a consequence, lead to the maintenance of separate rights for different racial groups...") points at a problem that follows from each "compensation," that is in fact inherent in the very notion of "special" measures, "special" treatment. The seeming, formal equality that in a way may appear from equal treatment is replaced by an apparent inequality of treatment that is aimed at achieving "real," material equality – somewhere in the future. And this inequality of treatment is accorded precisely on the basis of the characteristics that made it necessary to grant it: race, religion, social origin, and so on. The two provisions which were quoted to illustrate the compensation problem *allow* special measures of protection to be taken ("... shall not be deemed discrimination ...," "... may ... determine that other special measures ..."; "... as may be necessary ...," respectively). They do not *prescribe* that such measures be taken.[178] Nowhere in the international law of human rights that is

[176] This would for example be the case (to refer back to Benn's observations) for the group of the "pour whites" in the United States.

[177] See e.g. Lerner, *op.cit.*, p. 45 and 51; F. Münch, "Volksgruppenrecht und Menschenrechte," in *System eines Internationalen Volksgruppenrechts* (Th. Veiter, ed.; Wien und Stuttgart, 1970), p. 98.

[178] Compare on this distinction Doehring's remark that "Since every legal order encounters factual variations, the only relevant question which remains is whether, in legal matters, these variations must be *dis*regarded, or *may* be regarded, or *must* be regarded." (*Op.cit.*, p. 306; italics in the original).

valid today can be found a rule prescribing compensatory unequal treatment to secure material equality for individuals or groups that are identified – as compared with other individuals or groups, treated by the same authorities – through otherwise forbidden characteristics.

This is what seems to constitute the main difference between the "non-discrimination principle" and the traditional "protection of minorities principle": it is frequently assumed that the latter *prescribed* that special measures for the protection of the minority were taken. Yet, if one closely examines the wording of the Polish Minorities Treaty of 1919, which is representative for the field as a whole, it appears that the Treaty nowhere clearly obliges Poland to take any specific *action* to the benefit of the minorities. The Polish obligations are formulated in quite general,[179] often even negative terms.[180] Article 8 lays down that minorities may establish, manage and control charitable, religious and social institutions, schools and educational establishments (one of the most important fields is minority education), with the right to use their own language and to exercise their religion freely therein; but this must be done "at their own expense." In the public educational system "adequate facilities" for instruction in the minority language shall be given to the children in the primary schools in minority regions, according to the first section of article 9. But then, the second section of this article says that in such regions the minorities shall be assured an equitable share in the enjoyment and application of the public funds for educational, religions or charitable purposes "which *may* be provided out of public funds under the state, municipal or other budget."[181]

We conclude – as we did earlier, in paragraphs 32 and 33 – that the difference between "non-discrimination" and "protection of minorities" is only a relative one (as is the difference between "civil and political" and "economic, social, and cultural" rights).

Consequently, the distinction between "allowed" or "prescribed" special measures of protection is not as sharp as it at first seemed to be. The protection of minorities contained both conceptions; and so does the non-discrimination principle, as has especially become clear from the debates on draft article 26 of the Covenant on Civil and Political

[179] Such as article 7 (1) and 7 (2) laying down general equality before the law and the equal enjoyment of civil and political rights.

[180] Such as in article 7 (3): "No restriction shall be imposed on the free use by any Polish national of any language in private intercourse, in commerce, in religion, in the press or in publications of any kind, or at public meetings."

[181] Emphasis added.

Rights in the Third Committee of the General Assembly, discussed above in § 54.

If "special measures of protection" may under both principles be both allowed or prescribed, then the attitudes and aspirations of the individuals or groups that are subjected to the treatment in question become pre-eminently important. This reminds us of the definition of discrimination (in terms of prevention), adopted in 1947 by the Sub-Commission on the Prevention of Discrimination and the Protection of Minorities, and accepted by the Commission on Human Rights:

"Prevention of discrimination is the prevention of any action which denies to individuals or groups equality of treatment which they may wish."[182]

With regard to compensatory unequal treatment and "special protection," roughly two different, subjective attitudes can be distinguished. Which of them prevails depends chiefly on varying conceptions of "equality"; varying as to the formal or material character of the equality, the "superficiality" or "reality" of the equality that should be attained.

First there is the view on "special protection" according to which compensation may seem to perpetuate the inequality that exists anyhow, but is not considered to consolidate this inequality: it is considered that the final result at which the special measures are directed can be realized, even if it initially brings only equality of opportunities. And the measures themselves are deemed to be adequate in view of this purpose. Then there is a second opinion, according to which special measures must necessarily consolidate what they should abolish. This more pessimistic approach may be based on different arguments. It may be held that equality is unattainable, for example because the existing social inequalities are beyond the reach of legal regulation. "Equality of opportunities," "equal chances" is regarded as a purely formal notion without much significance since it functions in a world in which some are Achilles, and some turtles, so to speak.

Besides, it may be that "equality" is rejected as an ideal – a view that may result from this particular conception of the inequalities involved. And if equality is not desired, compensatory measures are felt to be pointless if not degrading, especially since the compensation is granted on the grounds that otherwise qualify some forms of discrimination as the worst of all, such as race. Such measures may be experienced as attempts to thrust value standards upon a community

[182] E/CN.4/52, p. 13.

that are alien to it. Georges Kaeckenbeeck, who served from 1922 to 1937 as President of the Upper Silesian Arbitral Tribunal declares:

"The last thing a Minority is willing to accept is the loss of its character of a Minority. Refusal to be absorbed in the majority, tenacious maintenance of distinctive features is of the essence of Minorities." [183]

It appears that our discussion of non-discrimination clauses finally leads to the consideration of problems and situations that seem to belong rather to the protection of minorities than to non-discrimination. As we have asserted earlier, both fields of law are closely connected, and deal with identical questions. In the next Chapter we shall discuss the protection of minorities, and compare this legal institution to the non-discrimination principle.

[183] Georges Kaeckenbeeck, *The International Experiment of Upper Silesia* (London 1942), p. 250. Compare also e.g. the black minority in the United States, now no longer striving for "integration," but seeking "cultural independence," "black power," "separation."

VI. PROTECTION OF MINORITIES AND NON-DISCRIMINATION

59. *Protection of Minorities in the League of Nations*

An enormously important movement in European politics in the nineteenth century was nationalism. Originally a process of awakening national consciousness of peoples in a mainly cultural sense, nationalism gradually grew into a striving for political self-determination of peoples as well. At the Peace Conferences in Paris immediately after the First World War the majority of the Czechs and Slovaks, the Magyars, the Poles, the Croats and Slovenes, and others found their nationalism realised in political terms in the recognition of national (in a few cases: multinational) States. The same had happened to the majority of the Bulgarians, the Romanians and the Serbs some forty years earlier, at the Congress of Berlin in 1878. But parts of nearly all Central and Eastern European nationalities were left, with their national aspirations, as "national," "linguistic" or "religious" minorities within the territories and under the jurisdiction of national States that were not their own; in some cases newly established States, and in some cases ex-enemy States at that. Situations such as these admittedly necessitated a system of outside guarantees for the minority populations as a substitute for the protection that ideally should have been afforded by a national State.[1]

[1] C. A. Macartney, *National States and National Minorities* (London 1934), especially Part I, is indispensable for an understanding of the origins of the exceptionally complex ethnographical situation in Central and Eastern Europe, and consequently for an understanding of the historical and political backgrounds of the League of Nations régime for the protection of minorities in that region. See on the international protection of minorities under the League of Nations, besides Macartney, *op.cit.*, Part II, also e.g. Mandelstam, *op.cit.*; Wintgens, *op. cit.*; E. Flachbarth, *System des Internationalen Minderheitenrechtes* (Budapest 1937); J. Stone, *International Guarantees of Minority Rights* (London 1932); the three last mentioned are, with Macartney, the leading treatises from the later years of the functioning of the League system. See also Tore Modeen, *op.cit.*, and "*Definition and Classification of Minorities*," E/CN.4/Sub.2/85 (1949).

In 1919 it was not the first time that comprehensive political rearrangements in Europe caused the coming into existence of minorities. Neither was it the first time that the international community undertook to attempt the protection of those minorities against the possible oppression by the majority. We cited a few examples of such international rules of protection – all relating to religious minorities – above, in § 37. The most noticeable instance before the First World War was the Treaty of Berlin concluded in 1878, in which the Great Powers, as they recognized them as independent States, stipulated that Bulgaria, Montenegro, Rumania and Serbia grant religious freedom and legal equality regardless of religious differences to all citizens.[2]

But though the idea of international concern for the condition of minorities was not without precedent, the scope of the system of treaties[3] and unilateral Declarations,[4] constructed mainly in 1919 and 1920 and placed under the guarantee of the League of Nations, was unique indeed. A number of territories were recognized by the Allied and Associated Powers as independent States and admitted as members of the League subject to the condition that they accept obligations with respect to the treatment of the minorities under their jurisdiction (Poland, Hungary, Yugoslavia, Czechoslovakia). Among all States in Central and Eastern Europe – already existing as well as newly established – a number of transfers of territory were effectuated. As a result of these political developments all of them gained territory or were established on territory inhabited by peoples that were different from the bulk of the population.[5]

[2] See on this Macartney, *op.cit.*, p. 166–168.

[3] The treaty between the Allied and Associated Powers and Poland, concluded at Versailles, 28 June 1919, was the model for the other treaties and Declarations, with slight variations among them. That is why the Polish treaty is generally used as example. The other multilateral instruments are: Treaty with Austria, Saint-Germain-en-Laye 10 September 1919; with the Kingdom of the Serbs, Croats and Slovenes (now Yugoslavia), Saint-Germain-en-Laye, 10 September 1919; with Czechoslovakia, Saint-Germain-en-Laye, 10 September 1919; with Bulgaria, Neuilly-sur-Seine, 27 November 1919; with Romania, Paris, 9 December 1919; with Hungary, Trianon, 4 June 1920; with Greece, Sèvres, 10 August 1920. Bilateral instruments include the Convention between Poland and the Free City of Danzig, Paris, 9 November 1920; the Agreement between Sweden and Finland, concerning the Aaland Islands (27 June 1921), and the German-Polish Convention relating to Upper-Silesia, Geneva, 15 May 1922. For the texts see next footnote.

[4] Declarations, which were made before the Council of the League, include those made by Albania (2 October 1921), Lithuania (12 May 1922), Latvia (7 July 1923) and Estonia (17 September 1923). Texts in *Protection of Linguistic, Racial and Religious Minorities by the League of Nations* (L.o.N.Doc. C.L. 110, 1927 I, Annexe). Apart from a few exceptions these instruments are also reproduced in Hudson, *International Legislation*, Vol. I and II.

[5] Appendix III of Macartney's book (p. 510–534) contains a detailed survey of the minorities whose status was under the protection of the League of Nations.

For an understanding of the ideas that lay behind this League régime it is appropriate to revert to two most authoritative interpretations that were given, one of a political, one of a legal nature.

The former is embodied in the covering letter that Clemenceau wrote on behalf of the Supreme Council of the Allied and Associated Powers to Mr. Paderewski, the President of Poland, as he sent him the Polish Minorities Treaty for signature.[6] Clemenceau observed that the treaty did not "constitute any fresh departure." And he went on to say: "It has long been the established procedure of the public law of Europe that when a State is created, or even when large accessions of territory are made to an established State, the joint and formal recognition by the Great Powers should be accompanied by the requirement that such State should, in the form of a binding international convention, undertake to comply with certain principles of government." He pointed at the Congress and Treaty of Berlin of 1878 where "this principle ... received the most explicit sanction." The Powers have restored Poland to independence, and "It is on the support which the resources of these Powers will afford to the League of Nations that for the future Poland will to a large extent depend for the secure possession of (its) territories. There rests, therefore, upon these Powers an obligation, which they cannot evade, to secure in the most permanent and solemn form guarantees for certain essential rights which will afford to the inhabitants the necessary protection whatever changes may take place in the internal constitution of the Polish State."

Further down the reasons why this "necessary protection" must be given are elucidated more fully:

"The territories now being transferred both to Poland and to other States inevitably include a large population speaking language and belonging to races different from that of the people with whom they will be incorporated. Unfortunately, the races have been estranged by long years of bitter hostility. It is believed that these populations will be more easily reconciled to their new position if they know that from the very beginning they have assured protection and adequate guarantees against any danger of unjust treatment or oppression".

The other interpretation we mentioned has the same tenor; it expounds more specifically the nature of the rights evolving from the system of minorities' protection. It was given by the Permanent Court in its Advisory Opinion concerning the *Minority Schools in Albania*[7]:

"The idea underlying the treaties for the protection of minorities is to secure for certain elements incorporated in a State, the population of which differs from

[6] Letter of 24 June, 1919. English text in O. I. Janowsky, *op.cit.*, p. 179–184.
[7] P.C.I.J. *Series* A/B, No. 64 (1935), at p. 17.

them in race, language or religion, the possibility of living peacably alongside that population and co-operating amicably with it, while at the same time preserving the characteristics which distinguish them from the majority, and satisfying the ensuing special needs.

In order to attain this object, two things were regarded as particularly necessary, and have formed the subject of provisions in these treaties.

The first is to ensure that nationals belonging to racial, religious or linguistic minorities shall be placed in every respect on a footing of perfect equality with the other nationals of the State.

The second is to ensure for the minority elements suitable means for the preservation of their racial peculiarities, their traditions and their national characteristics.

These two requirements are indeed closely interlocked, for there would be no true equality between a majority and a minority if the latter were deprived of its own institutions, and were consequently compelled to renounce that which constitutes the very essence of its being as a minority."

Article 1 of the Polish Minorities Treaty, which Treaty we, too, employ as example, declared that the stipulations contained in articles 2 to 8 must be recognized as "fundamental laws." This implied that they prevailed over any form of national law. Articles 2 to 8, then, contained obligations that can be divided into four categories, according to the categories of individuals protected by them.

(i) Article 2 assured full and complete protection of life and liberty to *all inhabitants of Poland* (that is, all individuals under Polish jurisdiction, comprising also aliens, stateless persons, and so on) without discrimination on the basis of birth, nationality, language, race or religion.

(ii) The next provisions concerned *Polish nationals* (i.e. Polish citizens). It was essential that it was first determined who belonged to this category, and who did not. Articles 3 to 6 inclusive gave detailed provisions as to who were Polish nationals. From past experience, in particular from the Romanian practices vis à vis the Jews under the Treaty of Berlin [8] it had become clear that nationality provisions were especially important.

(iii) Article 7 stipulated that "*All Polish nationals* shall be equal before the law and shall enjoy *the same civil and political rights* without distinction as to race, language or religion." This was elaborated in the third, fourth, and fifth section of this article which laid down that no restriction was to be imposed on the use of languages in private intercourse, commerce, religion, the press, public meetings or in publications of any kind; that notwithstanding any establishment by the Polish

[8] Romania had been able to frustrate the protection due to the Jewish population by denying citizenship to large numbers of Jews. See Macartney, *op.cit.*, p. 169, 245.

Government of an official language, adequate facilities had to be given to Polish nationals of non-Polish speech for the use of their language, either orally or in writing, before the Courts.

(iv) Clemenceau asserted that article 8, no less than article 7 was "in accordance with precedent"; it prohibited any discrimination against *those Polish citizens who by their religion, their language or their race differ from the large mass of the Polish population.* This provision runs as follows:

> "Polish nationals who belong to racial, religious, or linguistic minorities shall enjoy the same treatment and security in law and fact as the other Polish nationals. In particular they shall have an equal right to establish, manage and control at their own expense charitable, religious and social institutions, schools and other educational establishments, with the right to use their own language and to exercise their religion freely therein."

The special rights that were conferred on the minorities, such as those granted in article 8 of the Polish Treaty, varied according to the specific minority situation in the respective countries. Special minority rights covered essential fields of the public life; a systematic survey of "special protective measures" might contain any of the following: grants of local autonomy; political representation of minorities; protection of nationality; protection of family law or personal status; instruction in public primary schools in the minority language; use of language in general intercourse, in the courts, in social, charitable, religious or educational institutions, and in various media of information; the establishment and control of such institutions, including museums and sacred places, and the publication of such media of information.[9]

It may be stressed again that it was precisely on the traditional grounds for discrimination and oppression that these rights were granted.

Already in its first Advisory Opinion in a dispute involving the protection of minorities[10] the Permanent Court availed itself of the opportunity to give the broad interpretation of provisions such as article 8, to which interpretation it adhered throughout. It did so, as the Court

[9] See also the "Memorandum listing and classifying special protective measures of an international character for ethnic, religious, or linguistic groups," E/CN.4/Sub.2/221/Rev.1 (1963).

[10] *German Settlers in Poland. Series* B, No. 6 (10 September 1923).

explained five days later in its next Advisory Opinion, in order to safeguard the effectiveness of the system of minorities protection:

"... in the Advisory Opinion on the questions put concerning the German colonists in Poland, the Court has already expressed the view that an interpretation which would deprive the Minorities Treaty of a great part of its value is inadmissable."[11]

In the *German Settlers* case the Polish law in dispute would have had as its effect that a number of former German colonists, who had become Polish nationals in 1919, were divested of the rights they had as owners of their lands under the former Prussian regulations for the Germanization of the West Prussia and Posen provinces, and that they would have been expelled from their farms. The Court attached no importance to the fact that the law did not explicitly single out the former Germans as the group that would be chiefly affected by it, nor to the fact that it also applied to some non-German Polish nationals who had earlier succeeded Germans in the rights to the real estate.

The strongest expression of its view was given by the Court in its opinion on the *Minority Schools in Albania;* the pertinent passages from this Opinion are quoted in full above, in par. 25 under (h), since they also contain clear indications of what the Court understood by "discrimination." This case, which for the purposes of our argument may be regarded as a leading one, concerned the treatment of – in particular – the Greek (Orthodox) minority in Albania with respect to minority education. The rights of the minorities in Albania had been laid down in a Declaration, made by Albania before the Council of the League of Nations on the 2nd October, 1921, after it was admitted as a Member of the League.[12] This Declaration was, except for a few additions, modeled after the Polish Minorities Treaty. The provision of the Declaration that played the principal part in the dispute was article 5 (1), which stipulated:

"Albanian nationals who belong to racial, religious or linguistic minorities will enjoy the same treatment and security in law and in fact as other Albanian nationals. In particular they shall have an equal right to maintain, manage and control at their own expense or to establish in the future, charitable, religious and social institutions, schools and other educational establishments, with the right to use their own language and to exercise their own religion therein."

[11] Advisory Opinion on the *Acquisition of Polish Nationality, Series* B, No. 7 (15 September 1923), p. 16–17.

[12] Text in Hudson, *International Legislation*, Vol. I, p. 733 ff.

Up to 1929, as appears from statements made by Albania before the Court, education had varied according to religion: "the Moslems attended the Ottoman schools; the Orthodox, the Greek schools, and, in the districts adjacent to the Slavs, the Serbian or Bulgarian schools; the Catholics attended the Italian or Austrian schools."[13] In 1929 secular education was introduced; the creation of a system of public education and the abolition of private schools culminated in 1933 in the modification of the pertinent provision of the Constitution, which from then on read as follows:

"The instruction and education of Albanian subjects are reserved to the State and will be given in State schools. Primary education is compulsory for all Albanian nationals and will be given free of charge. Private schools of all categories at present in operation will be closed."[14]

Albania contended that, as the abolition of private schools constituted a measure applicable to the majority as well as to the minority, it was in conformity with article 5 (1) of the Declaration. The Court rejected this view on the basis of its interpretation of the words "the same treatment in law and in fact" in article 5. "This special conception finds expression in the idea of an equality in fact which in Article 5 supplements equality in law," the Court observed.[15]

The minorities enjoy, according to the instruments for their protection, two types of rights. Equal rights with the majority in those fields where their needs are considered to be equal to the majority (e.g. civil rights), and "special" rights where minorities are considered to have special needs (e.g. education). Such "special" rights are frequently referred to as "positive minority rights,"[16] "prerogative measures," "privileged treatment," and so on. This is a somewhat curious terminology, though, since such guarantees merely place the minority on a footing of equality with the majority with respect to those rights. If such special guarantees would not be granted, the result would not be an equal, but an inferior position of the minority. As to the establishment of educational institutions, for example, such guarantees do not secure the minority a better position, in comparison to that of the majority, since the result is only that both have – equally – their "own" schools. Such institutions "... are indispensable to enable the minority to

[13] *Minority Schools in Albania*, p. 10.
[14] *Ibidem*, p. 12.
[15] See further on the case-law of the Court in this field H. Lauterpacht, *The Development of International Law by the International Court* (London 1958), p. 257 ff.
[16] This is the term employed – among others – by Claude, *op.cit.*

enjoy the same treatment as the majority," as the Court put it. By the same token, therefore,

> "The abolition of (educational institutions of the minority itself), which alone can satisfy the special requirements of the minority groups, and their replacement by government institutions, would destroy this equality of treatment, for its effect would be to deprive the minority of the institutions appropriate to its needs, whereas the majority would continue to have them supplied in the institutions created by the State."[17]

"Special rights" meant consequently no more than an equal right to have or to do what the majority has or does. "Special rights" brought about "effective, genuine equality," as the Court put it in the same Opinion, not privilege, not compensation.

As to the nature of the "special rights," they did not consist in conferring on the minorities the benefits of active State protection;[18] they rather consisted in guarantees of State abstention. They demanded an attitude of *tolerance* on the part of the majority with regard to communities that are culturally different; this tolerance in itself is of course already of enormous importance. The "special rights" did not provide for the advancement of the minorities. This is so because the minorities were not regarded as culturally backward, compared to the majority, but – except in a mere numerical sense – as essentially equal and equivalent in every respect. (Which was even why they were protected in the first place. Originally, e.g. in the constitutional law of the Austro-Hungarian Monarchy, minorities protection was intended as a device to remedy the necessary and perpetual inequality in terms of numbers of voters in a democratic State.[19])

Thus the minority rights belong – in accordance with the "spirit of the time" in which they were formulated – essentially to the category of what are traditionally referred to as civil rights, rather than to the category of economic and social rights.

It is in our opinion spurious to call the granting of those rights in which the minority is held to be equal to the majority "non-discrimination," and to call, in contrast, the granting of "positive minority

[17] *Minority Schools in Albania*, p. 19, 20. See on this point also J.-W. Bruegel, "A Neglected Field: the Protection of Minorities," in *Human Rights Journal*, Vol. IV (1971), No. 2–3 (In honour of Egon Schwelb), p. 413 ff, at p. 435–436.

[18] See above, par. 58.

[19] Compare on this aspect of the problem E. Viefhaus, *Die Minderheitenfrage und die Entstehung der Minderheitenschutzverträge auf der Pariser Friedenskonferenz 1919* (Würzburg, 1960), p. 13 ff.

rights": "protection of minorities," as is generally done in the United Nations.[20] This strict distinction between the two notions in the practice of the United Nations will be discussed in the next paragraph.

60. Protection of Minorities and Non-Discrimination in the United Nations

The discussion of the League of Nations System for the protection of minorities was restricted mainly to the nature of the rights evolving from it; no attempt was made to describe the system as a whole in detail. The same restriction applies to the following discussion of the work done by the United Nations in the field of minorities protection. We shall not examine in detail the ways in which the proper United Nations organs have dealt with the minorities problem since the Organization was created.[21] We are, again, chiefly interested in the United Nations' conception of the nature of minorities rights and how they relate to the non-discrimination principle.

We shall first shortly indicate the various ups and downs experienced by the cause of minorities in United Nations politics. Secondly, some attention must be given to the only legal result of the efforts on the part of the champions of the cause of minorities: article 27 of the Covenant on Civil and Political Rights. Finally, we shall examine the views that prevail in the U.N. on what is involved in minorities protection as compared with the requirements of the non-discrimination principle.

United Nations politics on minority questions may be qualified as essentially ambiguous. For this ambiguity several reasons can be given. The Organization is committed, as is professed at several occasions in its constituent document, to promoting and encouraging human rights and fundamental freedoms for all "without distinction as to race, (sex),

[20] Thus also Claude, *op.cit.* p. 33: "Some groups desired only guarantees of nondiscrimination, and looked upon differential treatment as a disability; others were preoccupied with resistance to assimilation and strongly demanded the maximum enjoyment of positive minority rights." Similarly in "Definition and Classification of Minorities", E/CN.4/Sub.2/85, §§ 4–12.

[21] A very detailed and fully documented account of the U.N. activities with regard to minority problems is F. Ermacora, *Der Minderheitenschutz in der Arbeit der Vereinten Nationen* (Wien and Stuttgart, 1964). See also Claude, *op.cit.*, p. 144–213; J.-W. Bruegel, *op.cit.* p. 424 ff., R. Hiscocks, "The Work of the United Nations for the Prevention of Discrimination," in *Die Moderne Demokratie und ihr Recht* (Festschrift G. Leibholz, Tübingen 1966), Vol. I, p. 713 ff; John P. Humphrey, "The United Nations Sub-Commission on the Prevention of Discrimination and the Protection of Minorities," *A.J.I.L.*, Vol. 62 (1968), p. 869–888, and W. A. McKean, *op.cit.*, p. 178 ff.

language and religion." It is as though, through the very wording of this purpose of the Organization (art. 1(3) of the Charter), it took up, as it were, the thread that had been lost by the League of Nations somewhere during the decade that preceded the outbreak of the Second World War. The League's fatal experiences with the minority system during that period, however, made it highly expedient, politically, for the new Organization to keep aloof from minority questions.

But the way the human rights provisions have been formulated is of course no less a reaction to the atrocities that took place during the War. Also after the War, therefore, the protection of minorities remained a matter of great importance. It was obvious that the minorities problem persisted. However reluctant States are to settle minority questions in international agreements, ample evidence of their persistence is given by the considerable number of international instruments on the subject, multilateral and bilateral, that have been concluded after the War.[22] Examples of such instruments[23] include the Genocide Convention,[24] the I.L.O. Convention (No. 107) concerning

[22] See e.g. E/CN.4/Sub.2/214/Rev.1 (1963): "Compilation of the texts of those international instruments and similar measures of an international character which are of contemporary interest and which provide special protective measures for ethnic, religious or linguistic groups."

[23] Often also the human rights clauses of the Peace treaties with Bulgaria, Finland, Hungary, Italy and Romania are mentioned as belonging in this category. The texts of these Treaties, concluded on 10 February 1947, in *U.N.T.S.*, respectively Vol. 41, p. 21 ff.; 48, p. 203; 41, p. 135; 49, p. 3; 42, p. 3. These clauses are identic, and run as follows: "Bulgaria (Finland, etc.) shall take all measures to ensure to all persons under Bulgarian (Finnish etc.) jurisdiction, without distinction as to race, language or religion, the enjoyment of human rights and of fundamental freedoms including freedom of expression, of press and publication, of religions worship, of political opinion and of public meeting." These articles, however, contain scarcely minorities provisions. Only in the Treaties with Hungary and Romania a second section is added, which comes somewhat closer to a minority provision: "Hungary (Roumania) further undertakes that the laws in force in Hungary (Roumania) shall not, either in their content or in their application, discriminate or entail any discrimination between persons of Hungarian (Roumanian) nationality on the grounds of their race, sex, language or religion, whether in reference to their persons, property, business, professional or financial interest, status, political or civil rights or any other matter."

[24] See also above, § 20. Originally, in the draft of this Convention prepared by the Secretariat, three types of genodice were distinguished: not only physical genocide (destruction of the group) and biological genocide (prevention of births within the group), but also *cultural* genocide was suggested, which designated "... any deliberate act committed with the intent to destroy the language, religion or culture of a national, racial or religious group on grounds of the national or racial origin or religious belief of its members such as: 1) prohibiting the use of the language of the group in daily intercourse or in schools, or the printing and circulation of publications in the language of the group; 2) destroying or preventing the use of libraries, museums, schools, historical monuments, places of worship or other cultural institutions and objects of the group." Text in E/447, and in the Report of the Ad Hoc Committee on Genocide, E/794 (1948), p. 18. This form of genocide could have turned a harsh policy of assimilation into a most serious international crime, and it met with strong resistance, especially on the part of immigration countries. After a long struggle it was deleted from the final text of the Convention. See further Bruegel, *op.cit.*, p. 426 f., and Claude, *op.cit.*, p. 154–157.

the Protection and Integration of Indigenous and other Tribal and Semi-Tribal Populations in Independent Countries[25], the European Convention of Human Rights (article 14), the Agreement between Austria and Italy on the German speaking inhabitants of the Bolzano and Trento Provinces, and the Statute of Trieste,[26] the Agreement between India and Pakistan concerning their respective minorities,[27] and the Austrian State Treaty, article 7 of which lays down the rights of the Slovene and Croat Minorities.[28] Minority problems were also dealt with, but eliminated rather than regulated, in the Protocol of Potsdam, which provided for the transfer to Germany of German minorities in Poland, Czechoslovakia and Hungary.[29]

Apart from the Genocide Convention, none of these instruments was the result of direct United Nations activities. Within the organization, various bodies that were engaged in the drafting of the Universal Declaration considered proposals to insert a provision on minority rights in the Declaration. The oldest version was the one in the Secretariat's draft (art. 46):

'In States inhabited by a substantial number of persons of race, language or religion other than those of the majority of the population, persons belonging to such ethnic, linguistic or religious minorities shall have the right to establish and maintain, out of an equitable proportion of any public funds available for the purpose, their schools and cultural and religious institutions, and to use their own language before the Courts and other authorities and organs of the State and in the press and in public assembly."[30]

In a later phase, the drafting Committee of the Commission on Human Rights proposed a slight but important rewording: it omitted "out of an equitable proportion of any public funds available for the purpose," but inserted instead: "as far as compatible with public order."[31] The

[25] Geneva 27 June 1957; text in *U.N.T.S.*, Vol. 328, p. 248 ff.

[26] Paris, 5 September 1946 (Annexes IV and VI of the Treaty of Peace with Italy); text in *U.N.T.S.*, Vol. 49, p. 184–185.

[27] New Delhi, 8 April 1950; text in *U.N.T.S.*, Vol. 131, p. 4 f.

[28] Vienna, 15 May 1955; text in *U.N.T.S.*, Vol. 217, p. 229 f. Other instances relate to *inter alia* the Malay minority in Singapore, the Turkish minority on Cyprus, the German minority in Denmark and the Danish minority in Germany.

[29] Section XII of the Protocol of 1 August, 1945, in which the Governments of the USSR, the United Kingdom and the United States "recognize that the transfer to Germany of German populations, or elements thereof, remaining in Poland, Czechoslovakia and Hungary, will have to be undertaken . . ." in an "orderly and humane manner." Text in E/CN.4/Sub.2/367 (1950), p. 34, and Claude, *op.cit.*, p. 115.

[30] Article 46 of the Draft Outline of an International Bill of Rights. Text in E/CN.4/AC.1/3/Add 1, p. 380, and in *U.N. Yearbook of Human Rights 1947*, p. 486.

[31] Report of the Drafting Committee, E/CN.4/21, p. 81; also in *U.N. Yearbook of Human Rights 1947*, p. 503.

Committee advised, "in view of the supreme importance of this article (article 36) to many countries" that it be studied by the Sub-Commission "for examination of the minority aspects." This advise was followed, and the Sub-Commission – in an attempt to save the provision, whatever the cost, one might say – narrowed the wording further down so as to forestall as much as possible the objections that were bound to be raised against it. The restrictive formulations are so characteristic for the problem as a whole (and also the replacement of "minorities" by "groups,") that it may be reproduced in full:

"In States inhabited by well defined ethnic, linguistic or religious groups which are clearly distinguished from the rest of the population and which want to be accorded differential treatment, persons belonging to such groups shall have the right as far as is compatible with public order and security to establish and maintain their schools and cultural or religious institutions, and to use their own language and script in the press, in public assembly and before the courts and other authorities of the State, if they so choose."[32]

Not only the Sub-Commission, but also the other U.N.organs that were involved in minority rights struggled with questions that kept coming back, aroused serious disagreement, and defied formulation and regulation acceptable to all: the definition of minorities; cultural pluralism *versus* the building of unitary States; the necessity of assimilation and the idea of the "melting pot"; closely related to this the problem of immigration; the question whether protection of minorities involved individual or group rights; the loyalty of minorities to the State, and the security of the State; and so on. As the Universal Declaration finally reached the General Assembly for adoption, article 36 formed no longer part of the text. In the Third (Social, Humanitarian and Cultural) Committee of the Assembly no compromise was reached; thus no minority provision was incorporated in the Declaration.[33] By way of compensation the General Assembly passed a resolution[34] on the same day the Declaration was adopted, which kept the minority issue alive. It did no more than just that, however, despite the aspirations of the champions of the cause, which are mainly based on its first sentence:

"The General Assembly, *Considering* that the United Nations cannot remain indifferent to the fate of minorities...."

[32] E/CN.4/52, p. 9.
[33] For details see Ermacora, *op.cit.*, pp. 24–36.
[34] Res. A/217 C(III) of 10 December 1948, "Fate of Minorities." Text in G.A.O.R. 3rd Session, part I, Resolutions, p. 77, and in Ermacora, *op.cit.*, p. 17.

The operative part of this resolution merely requests the ECOSOC to ask the Commission on Human Rights and the Sub-Commission "to make a thorough study of the problem of minorities," though the final aim is stated as: "... in order that the United Nations may be able to take effective measures for the protection of racial, national, religious or linguistic minorities." Here again an illustration of the ambiguity we mentioned earlier.

For a long time, the making of studies of minority questions was about the only thing the Sub-Commission was able to do indeed, that is, as far as the minorities part of its mandate is concerned; in the field of prevention of discrimination it was more successful. It found itself in an embarrassing situation, because although the U.N. was unable and unwilling to do anything for the minorities, from the Resolution on the "Fate of Minorities" appears that it was equally unwilling to drop the matter altogether.[35]

The only tangible result of the Organization's occupations with minorities protection is article 27 of the Covenant on Civil and Political Rights, which runs as follows:

"In those States in which ethnic, religious or linguistic minorities exist, persons belonging to such minorities shall not be denied the right, in community with the other members of their group, to enjoy their own culture, to profess and practice their own religion, or to use their own language."

The draft of a comprehensive Covenant on Human Rights that was prepared by the Commission on Human Rights did not contain any provision relating to minorities.[36] It had before it, however, a proposal for such a provision, submitted by the Sub-Commission, which read:

"Persons belonging to ethnic, religious or linguistic minorities" ... and so on, dentic to the wording of the final versi on of article 27.[37]

In 1953 the Commission came to a conclusion with regard to this proposal, which up to then had merely enjoyed the status of an "Additional Article."

In the Commission, the Soviet Union and Yugoslavia – who had both tabled draft minorities provisions of their own (which were rejected) in addition to the one prepared by the Sub-Commission – acted as the advocates for an article on minorities; one of their main opponents was

[35] Particulars on the weal and woe of the Sub-Commission may be found in the literature cited at the beginning of this paragraph. See also "Activities of the United Nations relating to the Protection of Minorities," E/CN.4/Sub.2/194 (1958).

[36] *U. N. Yearbook on Human Rights 1947*, p. 546 ff.

[37] Text in E/2256, Annex II, Section A, III (p. 54).

Chile. The resistence on the part of the Chilean representative, among others, was based on the familiar arguments: there existed no national minorities in the "European" sense in large areas of the world. Whatever minority problems existed in the world outside Europe, it was highly doubtful whether a "European" and a uniform solution would do them justice. In immigration countries such as on the American Continent the preservation of the previous national characteristics of immigrants should not be furthered. Preserving and developing minority characteristics would necessitate the granting of privileges to such groups. This might be prejudicial to the unity of the State, especially for States that were still in a process of nation-building; it might even breed separatism. "The recognition by the State of what he would describe as 'super' rights would imply the provision of special services and special institutions at extra expense, and entailing special legislation. That process might well culminate in a minority's claiming autonomy within the State. His delegation was fully prepared to concede the principle of non-discrimination, but it was firmly opposed to the grant of special prerogatives ..."[38]

As appeared throughout the debates, very much depended on the way the notion "minority" was to be defined.[39] In the 370th meeting the Chilean delegate submitted an amendment,[40] according to which, as modified by him in the next meeting, the Sub-Commission's text would be preceded by the words "In those States in which ethnic, religious or linguistic minorities exist" ...[41] This proposal was accepted. It was the Sub-Commission's text, which, thus amended, was finally adopted by the Commission on Human Rights.[42] This version remained unaltered during the later stages of work at the Covenants, and the same text constitutes what is now article 27 of the Covenant on Civil and Political Rights. Obviously, the effect of the Chilean amendment is to place the judgment whether there exist ethnic, religious or linguistic minorities at all in a State entirely in the hands of that State. Whatever protection article 27 may be intended to afford, the obligation

[38] E/CN.4/SR.368, p. 8–9.

[39] Thus e.g. the remarks of the delegate of the USSR, *inter alia* that the Sub-Commission's text would have the effect of protecting "groups" which might never become "national minorities" (E/CN.4/SR.369, p. 13–14).

[40] E/CN.4/L.261.

[41] E/CN.4/SR.371, p. 4. Earlier, the same delegate had drawn the Commission's attention to the definition given by the Sub-Commission which began with the words: "In States inhabited by well-defined ethnic, linguistic or religious groups ..." etc. (E/CN.4/SR.368, p. 10).

[42] *Ibidem*, p. 6–7.

to secure that protection depends at any rate on the answer the State chooses to give to that preliminary but decisive question.

So far, mainly the political sides of the protection of minorities in the United Nations have been discussed. Now, the views must be examined that prevail within the Organization regarding the legal nature of the matter, as contrasted with the principle of non-discrimination. As to the nature of the rights that evolve from protection of minorities, the definitions arrived at by the Sub-Commission in the Report of its First Session to the Commission on Human Rights[43] are of course of prime importance. They may therefore be reproduced here in full:

"1) Prevention of discrimination is the prevention of any action which denies to individuals or groups of people equality of treatment which they may wish.
2) Protection of minorities is the protection of non-dominant groups which, while wishing in general for equality of treatment with the majority, wish for a measure of differential treatment in order to preserve basic characteristics which they possess and which distinguish them from the majority of the population. The protection applies equally to individuals belonging to such groups and wishing the same protection. It follows that differential treatment of such groups or of individuals belonging to such groups is justified when it is exercised in the interest of their contentment and the welfare of the community as a whole. The characteristics meriting such protection are race, religion and language. In order to qualify for protection a minority must owe undivided allegiance to the Government of the State in which it lives. Its members must also be nationals of that State.
If a minority wishes for assimilation and is debarred, the question is one of discrimination and should be treated as such."

We are not unsatisfied by what seems to be the core of the protection of minorities: granting in general equality of treatment with the majority, but granting "a measure of differential treatment" in order to preserve distinguishing characteristics. The relationships between both are not brought out clearly, however. In this connection it is illuminating also to quote from a Memorandum submitted by the Division of Human Rights of the Secretariat to the Sub-Commission. In this Memorandum "Definition of the Expressions 'Prevention of Discrimination' and 'Protection of Minorities,' "[44] the question is asked whether the two expressions have meanings that can be distinguished from each other:

"It might be said that to prevent discrimination on grounds of race, language or religion, is to protect racial, linguistic and religious minorities. It might be

[43] E/CN.4/52, Section V (6 December 1947), p. 13–14.
[44] E/CN.4/Sub.2/8 (29 October 1947).

argued, therefore, that there is no essential difference between the two expressions, and the Sub-Commision may decide to consider the prevention of discrimination and the protection of minorities as a single problem."

The reason why it is nevertheless believed that "the two expressions have different meanings" is merely based in this Memorandum on the origins, and on the terms of reference of the Sub-Commission, in which the expressions figure separately so as to designate, as it were, separate tasks.[45] (We find these reasons inconclusive; and, after all, only one Sub-Commission was in fact created. In the Memorandum the differences between both tasks are further discussed on the basis of the assumption that the distinction made in it between prevention of discrimination and protection of minorities is correct).

The same ambiguity with regard to the relationship between both concepts can be found in the Secretariat's Memorandum "*The Main Types and Causes of Discrimination.*" The texts adopted by the Sub-Commission for the clarification of the concepts (quoted in full above at p. 154) are said to "indicate the fundamental difference between prevention of discrimination and protection of minorities." It is pointed out that for the prevention of discrimination inequality of treatment must be suppressed or eliminated, "aiming at the prevention of any act or conduct which implies that an unfavourable distinction is made between individuals solely because they belong to certain categories or groups of Society." Why a "fundamental difference" between this notion and protection of minorities is seen can be readily explained by quoting the conception of minorities protection that is then expounded in this Memorandum:

"The protection of minorities, on the other hand, although similarly inspired by the principle of equality of treatment for all peoples, requires positive action: concrete service is rendered to the minority group, such as the establishment of schools in which education is given in the native tongue of the members of the group. Such measures are of course also inspired by the principle of equality: for example, if a child receives its education in a language which is not its mother tongue, this might imply that the child is not treated on an equal basis with those children who do receive their education in their mother tongue. The protection of minorities therefore requires positive action to safeguard the

[45] Originally the ECOSOC had empowered the Commission on Human Rights to establish two Sub-Commissions, one for each field, but eventually only one Sub-Commission was set up. The Sub-Commission's terms of reference, at that time, asked it to examine "what provisions should be adopted in the definition of the principles which are to be applied in the field of the prevention of discrimination on grounds of race, sex, language or religion, and in the field of the protection of minorities..." See E/CN.4/Sub.2/194, "Activities of the United Nations relating to the Protection of Minorities," p. 5–6.

rights of the minority group, provided of course that the people concerned ... wish to maintain their differences of language and culture."[46]

It is hard to appreciate on the basis of what minority-régime, previously or actually in force, this conception could have been developed. As remarked earlier, the protection of minorities was in essence a matter of tolerance; it was conceived of as a way to observe civil rights. No "positive action" was required, no legal obligation to render "concrete service" to minorities was imposed on a minority State, not even under the League of Nations minorities system.

In the light of the loose, if not confusing terminology that is frequently used with respect to "equality," "equal treatment," and similar notions, it is appropriate to point at four different situations among which, we think, must be distinguished. But before we do so it must first be pointed out that for a view on protection of minorities as implied in these United Nations statements on the subject, apparently an essentially formal conception of equality[47] has served as point of departure. We found that protection of minorities generally boiled down, in practice, not to "special measures," "positive action" and similar notions, but to a permissive attitude on the part of the dominant group, which in most cases controls the State. Formal equal treatment for all is set aside to the benefit of the minority, and instead a simple form of differential treatment is introduced. Of these types of differential treatment innumerable instances can be found in any developed system of law; however, in those cases in which they favour minorities, such differentiations are referred to as "privileges," "super rights," "special services," etc. But, in fact, no real prerogatives are granted to minorities; to mention just one example, the rights granted amount to no more than such usual "human rights" as free speech, a free press, and freedom of assembly, that must be accorded – in an attitude that is favourable to human rights in general – to e.g. political minorities. (We refer back to the holdings of the Permanent Court to that effect, cited in the previous paragraph). In so far the generally accepted United Nations philosophy that the observance of human rights in a strictly non-discriminatory manner is as good as a system securing minority rights, makes sense indeed. In so far, also article 27 of the Covenant on Civil and Political Rights can be regarded as securing minorities protection. (But even then, why insist on minority rights as "special" rights and at the same time point at so weak a text

[46] E/CN.4/Sub.2/40/Rev.1 (7 June 1949), § 7.
[47] This term is defined above, in §§ 4 and 5.

as article 27 as an achievement in the field of the protection of minorities?).

In this connection a distinction may be made, as said, among four different situations:

A) The "denial of human rights situation": individuals (or groups, for instance minority groups) are placed in an inferior position in comparison with others (resp. in comparison with the majority group). If we stick to the example of education this situation would e.g. occur whenever members of a particular group are debarred for that reason from attending available educational facilities, and are forced to content themselves with inferior education, or no education at all. Such individuals are subject to discrimination in the narrow sense of this concept.

B) The "inchoate," the "incomplete civil rights situation": individuals or groups are granted the same treatment as other individuals or other groups (e.g. the majority). Such equal treatment is discriminatory *vis à vis* those individuals or groups, if any, whose specific situation would call for *differential* treatment, inasmuch as justice requires unequal treatment of unequals.

C)The "genuine civil rights situation": in order to cure the invidious consequences of B, a further refinement in the law is made. Differential treatment is introduced wherever specific individuals or groups in different situations ask that this be done. An attitude of tolerance, of accepting cultural pluralism, of willingness to preserve diverse cultural patterns prevails. So-called "positive minority rights" are granted and guaranteed against the forces of oppression and assimilation. Deviations from such an attitude of tolerance and acceptance constitute discrimination against those individuals or groups, who should be given full enjoyment of human rights and fundamental freedoms, on a basis of "genuine equality," as the Permanent Court put it in the *Minority Schools in Albania-case.*[48]

D) The "social rights situation": individuals or groups who find themselves in a position of social and economic weakness are accorded special rights. It is most important to note that this situation concerns equals in an inferior position, in contrast to situation C, which concerns both equals and unequals, who are in a different, rather than in an inferior position. Such special rights are intended to compensate

[48] See also our comments on the meaning of the words "association with a national minority" in article 14 of the European Convention of Human Rights, above, in § 50 under (e). And compare art. 5,1, c of the Convention against Discrimination in Education.

disabilities. Privileges are granted to stimulate advancement, to help overcome existing backwardness, and to attain conditions of economic, social and cultural equality as compared with the other individuals and groups in a given society. As a matter of fact this view has already actually been introduced into the non-discrimination concept.[49] Such ideas raise the problem of "social" or "economic" discrimination; of "social" or ' economic" minorities.

On the basis of these distinctions it can be established that in practice protection of minorities amounts to protection of human rights in combination with the non-discrimination principle as we interpret it, and that this specific form of protection of human rights is not necessarily more comprehensive, or more active than what should normally be ensured for the purposes of protection of human rights in general.[50] Although, as we observed earlier (above, § 32 *in fine*), there is a difference of emphasis (for instance, a situation as distinguished under B will not be regarded as specifically related to minorities protection, while it can be said to belong to the protection of human rights), this conclusion fits with our view that the non-discrimination principle, operative in a system of human rights, also fully covers a situation such as indicated under C. Non-discrimination requires, no less than protection of minorities, the kind of differentiations in treatment as referred to in situation C; therefore it comprises whatever standards are regarded in the United Nations as part and parcel of protection of minorities. (That is, in the current conception of it; so broad a conception as is set out in § 7 of the Study "*Main Types and Causes of Discrimination*" is not the commonly accepted one in the United Nations. This broad conception relates rather to "situation D").

Views on the implication of protection of minorities in non-discrimination, as set forth here, may bring on a somewhat more effective protection of minority rights, realised through the granting of human rights in combination with the non-discrimination principle such as we think it should be interpreted, while no references to "protection of minorities" need to be made. This final element is important because the latter institution enjoys a poor reputation in the United

[49] Compare above, p. 133.

[50] If the granting of a certain degree of local autonomy is regarded as typically belonging among minority rights (compare e.g. articles 10–13 of the Minority Treaty with Czechoslovakia of 1919, on the Ruthenes, and art. 2 of the Agreement between Austria and Italy, of 1946, on the German speaking communities in Italy), a reservation must be made here with respect to local autonomy.

Nations. In fact, we think that it is possible to do justice to minority problems through the application of the non-discrimination rule. Discrimination also occurs – according to the definition given of it above, in paragraph 27 *in fine* – when in a legal system no inequality is introduced in the enjoyment of a certain right, or in a duty, and as a result thereof no sufficient connection exists between the unequalness of the subjects treated and the right or the duty. This implies, in a minority situation, that the denial to allow the establishment of for instance minority educational facilities, or the abolishment of such facilities, constitutes a violation of the non-discrimination principle.

Via this principle the needs of minorities, recognized by the United Nations, could be reconciled with the not quite unjustified aversion to an international system of protection of minorities, clearly manifested in the United Nations. Professor Humphrey, who for a long time has been Director of the Division of Human Rights of the Secretariat, and a member of the Sub-Commission, states outright: "In the higher bodies of the United Nations, at least, there has never been any serious intention of doing anything about minorities."[51] It seems indeed highly unlikely, at the moment, that a full-fledged international system in this field (in contradistinction, that is, to the kind of international protection afforded by article 27 of the Covenant on Civil and Political Rights) will be constructed by the United Nations, and will also be explicitly termed: "protection of minorities." Not only such a system, but even the very name has too many unfavourable political connotations.[52]

Historically, the term "protection of minorities" is linked to the political troubles which contributed to the failure of the League of Nations. It recalls the dangers of Balkanization, disruption of the unity of the State, separatism, disloyalty to the State, irredentism incited and exploited by co-national States, and so on. All this resulting in serious international tensions, and possibly in armed conflict.[53]

[51] J. P. Humphrey, *op.cit.*, p. 872.

[52] In 1967, however, the Sub-Commission adopted a Resolution (Res. 9 (XX) approved by the ECOSOC, on recommandation by the Commission on Human Rights) in which it decided to initiate a study on "the implementation of the principles set out in article 27 of the International Covenant on Civil and Political Rights with special reference to analysing the concept of minority taking into account ethnic, religious and linguistic factors and considering the position of ethnic, religious or linguistic groups in multinational societies." See on this new development the preliminary report "Study of the Rights of Persons belonging to Ethnic, Religious and Linguistic Minorities" by Mr. F. Capotorti, Special Rapporteur, (E/CN.4/Sub.2/L.564, 27 June 1972).

[53] See further the political analysis of the problem given by Claude, *op.cit.*, especially p. 203 ff.

In contemporary world politics, "protection of minorities" may be scorned in the light of the "bipolarization" that is felt to have its effects everywhere. Since, as we observed earlier (paragraph 55 *in fine*) in many cases minority characteristics cannot realistically be separated from economic and social characteristics of the minority groups in question, minorities may look out for support not only to co-ethnic, co-religious or co-linguistic States, but also to the State, or the bloc, that seems to be the most sympathetic to the way in which they want to further their social and economic position. However that may be, a particularly important political factor that militates against the designing of an international régime for the protection of minorities in the United Nations is the fact that many of especially the newly established and developing member-States are struggling with serious minority problems at the same time when each of them is engaged in the building of a unitary State. Humphrey observes: "Today, with the emergence of the new countries in Africa and Asia and their preoccupation with nation-building, the forces favoring assimilation are even stronger, notwithstanding the fact that it is precisely in these countries that minority problems are the greatest."[54]

Against these political drawbacks of "protection of minorities," most of which are attributed to it on account of the League's experiences with it, the advantages of an equivalent protection through the implementation of a materially interpreted non-discrimination principle in a system of human rights may be set. If protection of minorities proves to be unattainable, politically, the full potentialities of the non-discrimination rule in the protection of human rights should be brought out so as to see whether it can effectively substitute minorities' protection, as it was designed to do. The non-discriminatory granting of human rights is not an obligation that is imposed on a few States and not on others, as was the case in 1919, but it is a world-wide undertaking in which all U.N.members participate. Non-discriminatory human rights do not refer to the building and maintaining of separate groups; consequently no specific rights are singled out of a whole set of protected human rights and granted to some groups, but not to others. Rather, rights for such groups remain completely embedded in a larger framework of human rights protection. Thus it will be much less felt as a restriction of sovereignty. It is not tied up exclusively with national, linguistic or religious groups, but forms part of a total

[54] *Op.cit.*, p. 870.

of measures for the protection and support of disadvantaged or deprived groups or individuals of all sorts. Also, again in comparison with the situation in 1919, the non-discriminatory granting of human rights is not regarded as a predominantly political device, that must serve as a means to a political end, namely to help keep the peace in a specific tension area.[55] It is an end in itself and it hardly involves risks of intervention by co-national, co-religious or co-linguistic States. Since no explicit reference need to be made to particular minority groups, non-discriminatory granting of human rights does not bring along possible implications of separatism, self-determination, union (or reunion) with the co-national, co-religious, or co-linguistic State, if any, or minority autonomy within the State.

On the other hand, the non-discrimination principle in a system of human rights can help to preserve any form of existing cultural pluralism that may exist in a State, and thus help safeguard a State from the uniformity and sameness brought forth by policies of assimilation. It is clear that this opinion is based upon the hypothesis that cultural diversity is a valuable asset which deserves to be furthered and protected, if such furtherance and protection is desired by the minorities concerned.[56]

61. Social and Economic "Minorities": a Speculation

In his famous Dissenting Opinion in the *South-West Africa*-Case,[57] Judge Tanaka observes:

"To treat unequal matters differently according to their inequality is not only permitted but required."

[55] See also the Final Observations in Chapter XIV of the "*Study of the Legal Validity of the Undertakings Concerning Minorities,*" E/CN.4/367(1950), p. 70.

[56] The only clear and explicit rejection of our idea that non-discrimination is to be regarded as implying protection of minorities that we know of is made by Georges Kaeckenbeeck, *op.cit.*, p. 249–250, where he observes, under the heading "Equality": "This central and essential aspect of minority problems is all pervading. Protection of minorities is throughout protection against differentiation, on national, religious, or linguistic grounds. In one way, therefore, it might be thought, and it is sometimes asserted, that the full realisation of the principle of non-discrimination would set aside all minorities questions. I think that a close observation of these questions in actual life is bound to dispel such vain hopes. Theoretically, of course, one may give non-discrimination such an extended meaning as to be able to read into it whatever one apprehends as a minority issue. But this is no help in practice and we may dismiss the attempt as futile." In our opinion, however, the reasons for this assertion are not sufficiently stated.

[57] International Court of Justice, *Reports* 1966, p. 248 ff., at p. 306.

Earlier he had said that

"To treat different matters equally in a mechanical way would be as unjust as to treat equal matters differently."[58]

It is this view, so clearly stated by Judge Tanaka, that will serve as point of departure for our considerations of the question to what extent the rule of non-discrimination requires that differential treatment be granted not only to unequals who are in a culturally different position (such as national minorities), but also to unequals who are in an inferior social and economic position.

Most traditional notions of minorities protection implied that it involved some sort of support for the minority on the part of the State. It has appeared, however, that no actual financial obligations were imposed on the State to the benefit of the minorities. In the U.N. Memorandum "Definition and Classification of Minorities" a distinction is made, accordingly, in the "positive services" that minorities must have "if their equality within the State is to be real." It is observed in this Memorandum that "the rendering of 'positive services' may take either of two forms: (a) Provisions effected at the expence of the minority; or (b) Provisions effected out of public funds and facilities."[59] It may be recalled, in this connection, that in an early stage of the drafting of article 27 of the Covenant on Civil and Political Rights the phrase "out of an equitable proportion of any public funds available for the purpose" was deliberately deleted from the original version prepared by the Secretariat (see above, p. 150). It would seem that if the above question would be answered within the confines of the traditional conceptions of non-discrimination and protection of minorities in the United Nations, one would be bound to reply in the negative.

It remains to be seen, however, whether the traditional conception of minorities is still fully valid, and also whether there are other ways *via* which an answer to that question can be given. Thus, first of all a widening concept of minorities must briefly be discussed. Secondly, chiefly in the light of the Covenant on Economic, Social and Cultural Rights, it may be asked whether it is not more appropriate to approach the matter from the angle of the granting, on a basis of non-discrimination, of economic, social and cultural rights as laid down in that Covenant.

[58] *Ibidem*, p. 305.
[59] E/CN.4/Sub.2/85 (27 December 1949), § 9.

As to the widening concept of the minority, it may be submitted that through the interaction and cumulation of the forbidden grounds for differentiation [60] in many cases "national" and similar minority characteristics coincide with "economic and social" [61] characteristics. The doubts that are felt in many regions of the world concerning the characteristics that are usually regarded as constituting minorities in the traditional sense, may lead to a shift away from the traditional national, linguistic or religious minority, to the "social and economic minority." A shift away from the traditional characteristics to the social and economic factors that underlie minority problems. At the United Nations Seminar on the Multi-National Society (Ljubljana, June 1965), the agenda item "Equal treatment of economic regions within a country" was felt to have "special significance," since economic freedom was held to be "the key to the realisation of all the other (minority) rights" discussed by the seminar. "Experience had shown that the suppression of various groups had often been accompanied by economic oppression carried out by more powerful forces ... within ... a given society. Examples were given of administrative discrimination between regions within a country, evidenced by economic and social repression, by exploitation of minority groups ... It was therefore agreed that the deliberate diversion of assets from any given region would constitute oppression." [62] In the "national" State it is the "national" minority that needs to be protected; likewise, in the "social" State it is the "social" minority that calls for such protection.[63] Consequently, the forms of social and economic support enjoyed by the majority should similarly be afforded to the minority.

Occasionally one comes across references to other than "national" minorities. Thus, already in the first meeting of the Sub-Commission, reference was made to the existence of "intellectual and political minorities." [64] During the third meeting the Indian representative mentioned "vocational minorities," consisting of "workers who refused to belong to the State-recognized union." [65] As the Commission on

[60] See above, § 55 *in fine*.

[61] The term "social" is used here, as elsewhere, in the same sense as it is used in "social rights."

[62] ST/TAO/HR/23(1965), p. 30.

[63] For the purposes of this paragraph the term "social State" may be taken as referring to a State that endeavours to implement the rights set forth in e.g. the European Social Charter and the Covenant on Economic, Social and Cultural Rights.

[64] E/CN.4/Sub.2/SR.1, p. 9.

[65] E/CN.4/Sub.2/SR.3, p. 4.

Human Rights discussed the draft of article 27 of the Covenant on Civil and Political Rights, the Chilean representative stated that "it would certainly be logical that the Covenant should contain an article on minorities, despite the fact that non-discrimination formed, so to speak, the *Leitmotiv* of both Covenants." He continued to say: "But such an article should properly cover not only the cultural, but also the juridical, political and economic aspects of life ..." [66]

More interesting than slight indications such as these is, we think, the clause on "special measures of protection or assistance" in the I.L.O. Discrimination (Employment and Occupation) Convention; such measures are designed to meet the particular requirements of persons who need them for such reasons as "sex, age disablement, family responsibilities, or social or cultural status." But most important is of course the impulse originating with the non-discrimination principle as operative in the Covenant on Economic, Social and Cultural Rights. Article 2(2) of this Covenant runs as follows:

"The State Parties to the present Covenant undertake to guarantee that the rights enunciated in the present Covenant will be exercised without discrimination of any kind as to race, colour, sex, language, religion, political or other opinion, national or social origin, property, birth or other status."

If to this non-discrimination clause the same material interpretation is applied that was applied to the related "civil rights" provisions on non-discrimination, the result must be that it requires differential treatment wherever equal treatment would place groups or individuals in an inferior position in the social and economic field. National, linguistic and religious minorities should then – just as should be done in the field of civil and political rights – be accorded differential social rights. But then, should not a similar differential treatment be granted on the basis of "property"? When it was suggested to delete this term from the catalogue of forbidden grounds for differentiation, it was remarked that "property" should remain, for it was "most important that rich and poor should have the same rights." [67] Groups or individuals that are *not* distinguished from other groups or individuals by their national origin, their language, or their religion, but *only* by their social and economic backwardness, should be given a similar "special protection" in the economic and social fields as might be given

[66] E/CN.4/SR.368, p. 8. It may safely be assumed, however, that these suggestions were made in an attempt to thwart the setting up of minorities protection by demanding that it be made universal.

[67] Above, § 48 *in fine*.

to national minorities in the chiefly cultural field. For groups or individuals in an economically or socially exceptional position the non-discrimination principle requires special measures of an economic and social character that are capable of ensuring economic and social compensation and development: "genuine" economic and social equality.[68]

Differential treatment for groups or individuals in disadvantaged or differential positions does not constitute, then, a privilege; according to the criteria laid down by the Permanent Court it merely would bring forth economic and social "equality in fact," which is, we submit, the only form of equality that corresponds with the traditional international equality standard.

The fact that the Covenant on Economic, Social and Cultural Rights was produced and adopted by the United Nations points in the same direction: it is only after compensatory unequal treatment has been accorded in compliance with the non-discrimination rule that legal equality, i.e. formal equal treatment, will also constitute material equal treatment, will produce "genuine equality." Lauterpacht observed with respect to the attitude of the Permanent Court *vis à vis* the – then newly created – system for the protection of minorities, that the Court made important and progressive contributions to the system because it proceeded from the assumption that its task was to secure the effectiveness of the minorities Treaties. The result would have been different if the Court's starting point had been different: the Court might then have interpreted the minorities Treaties – in comformity with the parallel, negative, developments in the political sphere – within the traditional limits of the sovereignty of States, "instead of being bent on the full development of a new institution created in the interest of protection of human rights and international peace ..."[69]

We submit that less decided views on the – now recently adopted – non-discrimination principle than these would violate this principle and the standards of international protection of human rights that are implied in it.

[68] See on this also the Preliminary Study on Issues Relating to the Realisation of Economic and Social Rights contained in the Universal Declaration of Human Rights and the International Covenant on Economic, Social and Cultural Rights. E/CN.4/988 (20 January 1969), especially §§ 110–114.

[69] *Op.cit.*, p. 261.

VII. CONCLUSION

The hypothesis underlying this inquiry into the concept of discrimination in international law was that the international endeavours to protect human rights are aimed at the attainment of justice in the relations between community and individual, i.e. between States and those who are subjected to their jurisdiction. As point of departure functioned the important and generally recognized aspect of justice according to which equal treatment must be granted to equals, and, likewise, unequal treatment must be granted to unequals in proportion to the inequality.

Discrimination is regarded in this study as a violation of either one of these postulates of justice; consequently the non-discrimination principle is regarded as a safeguard not only against unequal treatment of equals, but also against equal treatment of unequals. Condemning the former the principle may be referred to as "formal non-discrimination," while the "material non-discrimination principle" condemns the latter. Compliance with this material principle may, as the case may be, necessitate a more refined, that is a more complicated legal regulation than is required by the formal principle, which is satisfied by simply equal treatment. Hence the material principle may call for action, that is, for the introduction of differentiations into the law, instead of for State abstention. (It thus would seem that the formal non-discrimination concept corresponds to the traditional notion of "civil rights" and "fundamental freedoms," while the material conception of non-discrimination would correspond to what are usually referred to as "social" ("economic" and "cultural") rights).

The formal non-discrimination principle aims at "formal equality," which is typically the "legal" equality. The material principle, which may require unequal treatment as well, dependent on the nature of whatever is treated, aims at attaining material equality, i.e.

equality not only as to legal, but also as to social and economic conditions. In the United Nations this broad non-discrimination principle, which is the principle as we think it should be understood in international law, is narrowed down to its formal component. Thus it is regarded as a safeguard for supposed equals, who are protected by it against measures that would put (some of) them in an inferior position as compared to other members of the same community. It is not seen as a protection that likewise requires special rights for individuals or groups who are in a special position (e.g. national minorities), so as to put them not in a seemingly (merely formal) equal position with others, but in a position of "effective, genuine equality." In the United Nations this latter notion is called "protection of minorities," and as such it is kept separated from the "narrow" non-discrimination principle, because it is generally repudiated as requiring "special rights," "privileged treatment." The traditional protection of minorities, however, requires no more "special" rights or "privileges" – in a cultural sense – than are accorded, in a human rights system, to e.g. political dissenting groups (freedom of the press and freedom of association for political minorities). It is one of the faults of the United Nations approach to protection of minorities that no clear distinction is made between granting different rights to essentially equal, yet (culturally) different groups (such as in the protection of minorities) on the one hand, and the granting of compensatory unequal treatment to individuals or groups who are in an inferior position, e.g. in an economic and social sense, on the other hand (such as may be the case with social rights).

In the United Nations, the creation of a system of rules for the protection of minorities appears to be politically unfeasible for the moment. It was one of the aims of this study to show that the non-discrimination principle can accomplish the same task, can afford a similar protection. From our assumption that the protection of human rights aims at the realisation of justice resulted the broad, material non-discrimination concept to which we adhered throughout. But that this is not merely our own conception of non-discrimination appears from the fact that in the United Nations the view prevailed that it had first to be restricted before it could be adopted in United Nations instruments for the protection of human rights. In our opinion, however, the cultural heritage of national, linguistic and religious minorities is so much worthy of protection against the postulates of the monolithic nation-State, if they so desire, that in the light of the history of the international protection of human rights, in particular the attitude of the Permanent Court of International Justice, the granting of differential treatment to different individuals or groups must be considered as part and parcel of the non-discrimination concept in international law.

A present day development, that also affects international law, is the shift away from the preoccupation with the *national* State to the preoccupation with the *social* State. This development raises the question to what extent the international non-discrimination principle protects not only the culturally different, but also the socially and economically backward individuals or groups in a given community. "Property" figures as a forbidden ground for differentiation. Some instruments mention "special measures of protection" for *inter alia* social groups. Most important of all, the non-discrimination concept is also made operative in the Covenant on Economic, Social and Cultural Rights. On the basis of these new elements it is submitted, finally, that the non-discrimination concept in international humanitarian law implies compensatory unequal treatment of individuals and groups who do not differ from the majority of the population by their nationality, language, or religion, but only by their social and economic backwardness.

BIBLIOGRAPHY

Antonopoulos, N. A., *La Jurisprudence des organes de la convention européenne des droits de l'Homme*, Leiden 1967.

Benn, S. I., "Egalitarianism and the Equal Consideration of Interests," in *Nomos IX, Equality*, New York 1965.

Boutros-Ghali, B., "Le Principe d'égalité des Etats et les organisations internationales," *Receuil des Cours*, Vol. 100 (1960, II), p. 1ff.

Boven, Th. C. van, *De Volkenrechtelijke Bescherming van de Godsdienstvrijheid*, Assen 1967.

Brecht, A., *Political Theory*, Princeton 1959.

Brierly, J. L., *The Law of Nations*, 6th ed. by H. Waldock, Oxford 1963.

Briner, R., *Zur Funktion der Gleichheit in der menschlichen Gerechtigkeit*, Wädenswill 1948.

Brown, C., *Manchild in the Promised Land*, New York 1966.

Bruegel, J.-W., "A Neglected Field: the Protection of Minorities," *Human Rights Journal*, Vol. IV, 1971, no. 2-3 (In honour of Egon Schwelb), p. 413 ff.

Burdeau, G., *Les libertés publiques*, 3ième éd., Paris 1966.

Cassin, R., "La déclaration universelle et la mise en oeuvre des droits de l'Homme," *Receuil des Cours* Vol. 79 (1951 II), p. 237 ff.

Chaumont, Ch., "La Signification du principe de specialité des organisations internationales," *Mélanges Henri Rolin*, Paris 1964, p. 55 ff.

Claude, I. L., *National Minorities, an International Problem*, Cambridge, Mass. 1955.

Consolidated Treaty Series, ed. by C. Parry, Vol. 6, Dobbs Ferry, N.Y., 1969.

Dahm, G., *Völkerrecht*, 3 Vols., Stuttgart 1958–1961.

Detter, I., "The Problem of Unequal Treaties," *International and Comparative Law Quarterly*, Vol. 15, 1966, p. 1069 ff.

Dictionnaire de la terminologie du droit international, Paris 1960.

Doehring, K., "Non-discrimination and Equal Treatment under the European Human Rights Convention and the German Constitution, with Particular Reference to Discrimination against Aliens," *American Journal of Comparative Law*, Vol. 18, 1970, p. 305 ff.

Eissen, M.-A., L''autonomie' de l'article 14 de la Convention européenne des droits de l'Homme," *Mélanges offerts à Polys Modinos*, Paris 1968, p. 122 ff.

Emge, C. A., *Einführung in die Rechtsphilosophie*, Frankfurt a.M., Wien 1956.

Ermacora, F., *Die Minderheitenschutz in der Arbeit der Vereinten Nationen*, Wien and Stuttgart 1964.

– *Diskriminierungsschutz und Diskriminierungsverbot in der Arbeit der Vereinten Nationen*, Wien and Stuttgart 1971.

Fawcett, J. E. S., *The Application of the European Convention of Human Rights*, Oxford 1969.
Flachbarth, E., *System des Internationalen Minderheitenrechts*, Budapest 1937.
Fleischmann, M., *Völkerrechtsquellen*, Halle a. S. 1905.
Ganji, M., *International Protection of Human Rights*, Geneva and Paris 1962.
Ginsberg, M., *On Justice in Society*. London 1965.
Glastra van Loon, J. F., *Norm en handeling*, Haarlem 1957.
Guggenheim, P., "Quelques remarques au sujet de l'article 14 de la Convention européenne des droits de l'Homme," *René Cassin, Amicorum Discipulorumque Liber*, Vol. I, *Problèmes de protection internationale des droits de l'Homme*, Paris 1969, p. 95 ff.
Guradze, H., *Die Europäische Menschenrechtskonvention; Kommentar*, Berlin and Frankfurt a.M., 1968.
Hackworth, G. H., *Digest of International Law*, Vol. III, Washington D. C., 1942.
Halle, L. J., *Men and Nations*, Princeton 1962.
Hassan, P., "The Word 'Arbitrary' as Used in the Universal Declaration of Human Rights: 'Illegal' or 'Unjust'?," *Harvard International Law Journal*, Vol. 10, 1969, p. 225 ff.
Heimsoeth, H., *Die Sechs Grossen Themen der Abendländischen Metaphysik und der Ausgang des Mittelalters*, 4th ed., Stuttgart 1958.
Henkel, H., *Einführung in die Rechtsphilosophie*, München und Berlin 1964.
Hirsch, E. E., "Diskriminierung," in *Wörterbuch der Soziologie*, ed. by W. Bernsdorf, 2nd. ed., Stuttgart 1969, p. 190 ff.
Hiscocks, R., "The Work of the United Nations for the Prevention of Discrimination" in *Die Moderne Demokratie und ihr Recht* (Festschrift G. Leibholz), Tübingen 1966, Vol. I, p. 713 ff.
Hoeven, J. van der, *De plaats van de grondwet in het constitutionele recht*, Zwolle 1958.
Hoffmann, S., "International Systems and International Law," in *The International System*, ed. by K. Knorr and S. Verba, Princeton 1961.
Hudson, M. O., *International Legislation*, 9 Vols., Washington 1931–1950.
Humphrey, J. P., "The United Nations Sub-Commision on Prevention of Discrimination and the Protection of Minorities," *American Journal of International Law*, Vol. 62, 1968, p. 869 ff.
Hunter-Miller, D., *The Drafting of the Covenant*, 2 Vols., New York 1928.
Hyder (Hasan), K., *Equality of Treatment and Trade Discrimination in International Law*, The Hague 1968.
International Organization and Integration, ed. by L. J. Brinkhorst, H. H. Maas and H. F. van Panhuys, Deventer and Leiden 1968.
Jackson, J. H., *World Trade and the Law of GATT. A Legal Analysis of the GATT*, Indianapolis 1969.
Jaenicke, G., *Der Begriff der Diskriminierung im modernen Völkerrecht*, Berlin 1940.
– "Diskriminierung," *Wörterbuch des Völkerrechts*, 2nd ed. by W. Schlochauer, Vol. I, Berlin 1960, p. 387 ff.
– "Gleichbehandlung," *ibidem*, p. 690 ff.
Janowsky, O. I., *Nationalities and National Minorities*, New York 1945.
Jellinek, G., *System der Subjektiven Öffentlichen Rechte*, 3rd ed., Tübingen 1919.
Jenks, C. W., "The International Protection of Freedom of Association for Trade Union Purposes," *Receuil des Cours* Vol. 87 (1955, I), p. 7 ff.
Kant, I., *Kritik der Reinen Vernunft*, ed. by R. Schmidt, Leipzig 1926.
Kaeckenbeeck, G., *The international Experiment of Upper Silesia*, London 1942.

Kelsen, H., *General Theory of Law and State*, Cambridge, Mass. 1946.
– *The Law of the United Nations*, 2nd ed., London 1951.
– *Principles of International Law*, 2nd ed., rev. by R. W. Tucker, New York 1966.
– *Reine Rechtslehre*, 2nd ed., Wien 1960. Abridged English translation by M. Knight: *Pure Theory of Law*, Berkeley 1967.
Kipp, H., "Das Verbot der Diskriminierung im modernen Friedensvölkerrecht," *Archiv des Völkerrechts*, Vol. IX, 1961-62, p. 137 ff.
Kooymans, P. H., *The Doctrine of the Legal Equality of States*, Leiden 1964.
Lannung, H., "The Rights of Minorities," *Mélanges offerts à Polys Modinos*, Paris 1968, p. 181 ff.
Lauterpacht, H., *The Development of International Law by the International Court*, London 1958.
Leibholz, G., *Die Gleichheit vor dem Gesetz*, 2nd ed., München and Berlin 1959.
Lerner, N., *The International Convention on the Elimination of All Forms of Racial Discrimination*, Leiden 1970.
Lipsey, R. G. and P. O. Steiner, *Economics*, New York and Tokyo, 1966.
Macartney, C. A., *National States and National Minorities*, London 1934.
Mandelstam, A. N., "La protection internationale des minorités," *Receuil des Cours*, Vol. I (1923), p. 369 ff.
Mangoldt, H. von, and F. Klein, *Das Bonner Grundgesetz*, 2 Vols., 2nd ed., Berlin and Frankfurt a.M., 1957.
Marshall, G., "Notes on the Rule of Equal Law," in *Nomos IX, Equality*, New York 1965.
McKean, W. A., "The Meaning of Discrimination in International and Municipal Law," *British Yearbook of International Law 1970*, p. 177 ff.
Meyrowitz, H., *Le principe d'égalité des belligérants devant le droit de la guerre*, Paris 1970.
Modeen, T., *The International Protection of National Minorities in Europe*, Abo 1969.
Münch, F., "Volksgruppenrecht und Menschenrechte," *System eines internationalen Volksgruppenrechts*, ed. by Th. Veiter, Wien and Stuttgart, 1970, p. 95 ff.
Murray, A. H., *A New English Dictionary on Historical Principles*, Vol. III, Oxford 1897.
Myrdal, G., *The Challenge of World Poverty*, New York 1970.
Nef, H., *Gleichheit und Gerechtigkeit*, Zürich 1941.
O'Connell, D. P., *International Law*, 2 Vols., 2nd ed., London 1970.
Oda, S., "The Individual in International Law", in *Manual of Public International Law*, ed. by M. Sørensen, London and New York 1968.
Partsch, K. J., "Die Rechte und Freiheiten der Europäischen Menschenrechtskonvention," *Die Grundrechte* Vol. I/1, ed. by K. A. Bettermann, F. L. Neumann and H. C. Nipperdey, Berlin 1966, p. 335 ff.
Peaslee, A., *Constitutions of Nations*, 4 Vols., rev. 3rd ed., The Hague 1965–1970.
Pernthaler, P., *Der Schutz der ethnischen Minderheiten durch individuelle Rechte*, Wien and Stuttgart 1964.
Pescatore, P., "Fundamental Rights and Freedoms in the System of the European Communities," *American Journal of Comparative Law*, Vol. 18, 1970, p. 343 ff.
Pictet, J., *Principes du droit international humanitaire*, Genève 1966.
Podlech, A., *Gehalt und Funktionen des allgemeinen verfassungsrechtlichen Gleichheitssatzes*, Berlin 1971.
Radbruch, G., *Der Mensch im Recht*, 2nd ed., Göttingen 1961.
– *Rechtsphilosophie*, 6th ed., Stuttgart 1963.
Rehbinder, M., "Die Diskriminierung: ihre Ursachen und Bekämpfung,"

Kölner Zeitschrift für Soziologie und Sozialpsychologie, Vol. 15, 1963, p. 6 ff.
Ross, A. *Towards a Realistic Jurisprudence*, Copenhagen 1946.
Russell, R. B. and J. E. Muther, *A History of the United Nations Charter; the Role of the United States 1940–1945*, Washington 1958.
Salomon, M., *Der Begriff der Gerechtigkeit bei Aristoteles*, Leiden 1937.
Schambeck, H., *Grundrechte und Sozialordnung. Gedanken zur Europäischen Sozialcharta*, Berlin 1969.
Schaumann, W., "Gegenseitigkeit," *Wörterbuch des Völkerrechts*, 2nd ed. by W. Schlochauer, Vol. I, Berlin 1960, p. 630 ff.
Scheuner, U., "Comparison of the Jurisprudence of National Courts with that of the Organs of the Convention," in *Human Rights in National and International Law*, ed. by A. H. Robertson, Manchester 1968, p. 214 ff.
Schindler, D., *Die Gleichberechtigung von Individuen als Problem des Völkerrechts*, Zürich 1957.
Schneider, P., "Social Rights and the Concept of Human Rights," in *Political Theory and the Rights of Man*, ed. by D. P. Raphael, London 1967.
Schwarzenberger, G., "Equality and Discrimination in International Economic Law," *Yearbook of World Affairs 1971*, London 1971, p. 163 ff.
– *Power Politics*, 2nd ed., London 1951.
Schwelb, E., *Human Rights and the International Community*, Chicago 1964.
– "The International Convention on the Elimination of All Forms of Racial Discrimination," *International and Comparative Law Quarterly*, Vol. 15, 1966, p. 996 ff.
– "The International Court of Justice and the Human Rights Clauses of the Charter," *American Journal of International Law*, Vol. 66, 1972, p. 337 ff.
Seyersted, F., *United Nations Forces*, Leiden 1966.
Simson, G. E. and J. M. Yinger, *Racial and Cultural Minorities: an Analysis of Prejudice and Discrimination*, 3rd ed., New York 1965.
Sørensen, M., "The Quest for Equality," *International Conciliation* No. 507, 1956.
Sovern, M. I., *Legal Restraints on Racial Discrimination in Employment*, New York 1966.
Stone, J., *Human Law and Human Justice*, London 1965.
– *International Guarantees of Minority Rights*, London 1932.
Tammes, A. J. P., "De gerechtigheid in de internationale verhoudingen en de weerstand die zij daar ondervindt," in *Handelingen van de Nederlandse Vereniging voor de Wijsbegeerte des Rechts*, XXXIX, 1e deel, (1954). p. 29 ff.
Tawney, R. H., *Equality*, 5th ed., London 1964.
Tomandl, Th., *Die Einbau sozialer Grundrechte in das positive Recht*, Tübingen 1967.
Unger, R. M., "Isonomy and Justice," *Archiv für Rechts- und Sozialphilosophie*, Vol. LVI, 1970, p. 181 ff.
Valentine, D. G., *The Court of Justice of the European Communities*, Vol. II, *Judgments and Documents*, London 1965.
G. del Vecchio, *Die Gerechtigkeit*, (German translation), Basel 1950.
Verdoodt, A., *Naissance et signification de la Déclaration universelle des droits de l'Homme*, Louvain and Paris 1964.
Verzijl, J. H. W., *The Jurisprudence of the World Court*, Vol. I, Leiden 1965.
Viefhaus, E., *Die Minderheitenfrage und die Entstehung der Minderheitenschutzverträge auf der Pariser Friedenskonferenz 1919*, Würzburg 1960.
Vierdag, E. W., "Non-discrimination and Justice," *Archiv für Rechts- und Sozialphilosophie*, Vol. LVII (1971) p. 187 ff.
Virally, M., "Le principe de réciprocité dans le droit international contemporain," *Receuil des Cours*, Vol. 122 (1967, III), p. 1 ff.

Vygotsky, L. S., *Thought and Language*, English ed., Cambridge, Mass. 1962.
Weber, M., *Wirtschaft und Gesellschaft*, 2 Vols., Köln and Berlin 1964.
Weinschel, H., "The Doctrine of the Equality of States and its Recent Modifications," *American Journal of International Law*, Vol. 45, 1951, p. 417 ff.
Wengler, W., "The Significance of the Principle of Equality in the Conflict of Laws," in *Law and Contemporary Problems*, Vol. 28, 1963, p. 822 ff.
– *Völkerrecht*, 2 Vols., Berlin, Göttingen, Heidelberg, 1964.
Wintgens, H., *Der Völkerrechtliche Schutz der Nationalen, Sprachlichen und Religiösen Minderheiten*, Stuttgart 1930.
Zacher, H. F., "Soziale Gleichheit," *Archiv des Öffentlichen Rechts*, Vol. 93, 1968, p. 341 ff.
Ziegler, G., *Das Grundrechtsproblem in den Europäischen Gemeinschaften*, Tübingen 1970.

INDEX